UNCOMMON SENSE

UNCOMMON SENSE

Jeremy Bentham, Queer Aesthetics,
and the Politics of Taste

Carrie D. Shanafelt

University of Virginia Press • *Charlottesville and London*

University of Virginia Press
© 2022 by the Rector and Visitors of the University of Virginia
All rights reserved
Printed in the United States of America on acid-free paper

First published 2022

9 8 7 6 5 4 3 2 1

Library of Congress Cataloging-in-Publication Data

Names: Shanafelt, Carrie D., author.
Title: Uncommon sense : Jeremy Bentham, queer aesthetics, and the politics of taste /
  Carrie D. Shanafelt.
Description: Charlottesville : University of Virginia Press, [2021] | Includes
  bibliographical references and index.
Identifiers: LCCN 2021030607 (print) | LCCN 2021030608 (ebook) |
  ISBN 9780813946863 (hardcover) | ISBN 9780813946870 (paperback) |
  ISBN 9780813946887 (ebook)
Subjects: LCSH: Bentham, Jeremy, 1748–1832. | Pleasure—Political aspects. |
  Aesthetics—Political aspects. | Liberty. | Common sense. | Law and aesthetics. |
  Philosophers—Great Britain—Biography.
Classification: LCC B1574.B34 S53 2021 (print) | LCC B1574.B34 (ebook) |
  DDC 152.4/2—dc23
LC record available at https://lccn.loc.gov/2021030607
LC ebook record available at https://lccn.loc.gov/2021030608

CONTENTS

ACKNOWLEDGMENTS

Interdisciplinary research depends on an accumulation of intimacies and arguments with friends, colleagues, and strangers (who often become friends or colleagues), who make up a world one can inhabit, interrogate, and address with the hope of being understood. This book is the culmination of twenty years of world-building intimacies and arguments, beginning in the earliest years of my graduate study, long before I read aesthetic theory or anything substantial by Jeremy Bentham. I am grateful that, wherever I have studied and taught, I have been part of communities in which the pleasure of sharing and debating ideas, learning from one another, and promoting one another's successes has created a shared (but uncommon) sense of what academic work can and should look like. I am grateful to my friends and colleagues at Case Western Reserve University, the City University of New York Graduate Center, Queens College, Franklin & Marshall College, Grinnell College, and Fairleigh Dickinson University (whose generous Grant-in-Aid program partially funded research toward this book), as well as the Universität Osnabrück Summer School on the Cultural Study of the Law, the American Society for Eighteenth-Century Studies, the North American Society for the Study of Romanticism, and the Johnsonians for supporting, including, amplifying, criticizing, and responding to the ideas that follow.

It would have been impossible to write this book without the generosity and patience of the librarians and archivists at University College London Special Collections, where I spent long, emotional days in the summer of 2018 trying not to cry on everything I handled. It was a joy to read there. And due to the extraordinary efforts of the UCL Bentham Project to make Bentham's manuscripts as accessible as possible, I was able to continue reading and verifying my notes from my home in New York. If this work inspires any interest in Bentham among its readers, I encourage them to check out the Bentham Project's unprecedented archival generosity at www.ucl.ac.uk/bentham-project/. There is still so much to be done. Thirty-four of a projected eighty volumes of *The Collected Works of Jeremy Bentham* are in print, led by General Editor Philip Schofield, without whose scholarship this project would never have been imagined.

So many individual people have mentored, collaborated, commiserated, and shared with me during this long process that I struggle to name them all: David Richter, Carrie Hintz, Blanford Parker, Jack Lynch, Jenny Davidson, Mario DiGangi, Rebekah Sheldon, Brooks Hefner, Helena Ribeiro, Chris Leslie, Nola Semczyszyn, Rivka Swenson, Dwight Codr, Tita Chico, William Flesch, Emily Friedman, Paul Kelleher, Laura Miller, Kathleen Elizabeth Urda, Sarah Purcell, Loren Ludwig, Ed Kazarian, Courtney Wennerstrom, Erica Richardson, Kevin Bourque, Laurence Williams, Andrew Benjamin Bricker, Shelby Johnson, Kathryn Temple, Brian Goldberg, Anne McCarthy, Declan Gilmore-Kavanagh, Jennifer Mitchell, and many others have contributed in some form to this project. Thank you to my many writing groups and reading groups, past and present. Infinite thanks goes to Angie Hogan at the University of Virginia Press, who believed in this project and helped bring it to fruition in a season of constant crisis at every scale, as well as Ellen Satrom, Ruth Melville, Scott Sheldon, and the anonymous peer reviewers, whose diligence, attention to detail, and thoughtful suggestions improved this book at every step.

Thank you to my parents, who have always believed in me more than I have. And I am overwhelmed with gratitude for my spouse, Cliff, whose humor, patience, integrity, brilliance, kindness, and love make everything possible.

Part of chapter 3 appears in *Lit: Literature Interpretation Theory* as "Against Rights: Jeremy Bentham on Sexual Liberty and Legal Reform"; and parts of chapters 2 and 5 appear in *The Eighteenth Century: Theory and Interpretation* as "Jeremy Bentham and the Aesthetics of Sexual Difference."

UNCOMMON SENSE

Introduction

Almost twenty years ago, I fell in love with a book that changed me—
Henry Fielding's novel *The History of Tom Jones, a Foundling*, first published in 1749 in London. The characters and their lives were far from
my own experience, but I felt confronted by the narrator, whose aggressive, teasing rhetoric challenged me to reconsider many of my cynical
pet theories about love and human nature. Fielding's narrator appealed
to "common observation," rather than his or my own observations, for
verification of what he asserted was plainly true for others, if not for me.
As Wayne Booth argues in *The Rhetoric of Fiction,* the narrator of *Tom
Jones* offers the reader an imaginary center of moral objectivity that is
not possible for any of the characters—nor even for Fielding himself as a
real person who served as a magistrate.[1] Throughout the novel, Fielding
chides the reader not only to think of our own experiences but to balance
our perception with that of other imaginable readers and lives; he invites
us to be humble about the limitations of our perspective on reality. In
September of 2001, Fielding was my first intoxicating taste of the rhetoric
of common sense, which Immanuel Kant would later define as "putting
ourselves in the position of everyone else"—imagining what "normal"
people think as a check to our unique experiences of the world.[2]

I became obsessed with eighteenth-century British rhetoric in literature and philosophy because I wanted to understand the power of that
appeal to imagine the minds of others. As someone who had always
relied on my own idiosyncratic judgment, I was learning that I was
wrong to trust my observations, not only about love and morality, but
about almost everything. If I wanted to live in peace with humankind,
I needed to learn humility toward a normative understanding. During
this process of pathologizing individual judgment, my country went to
war on the basis of obvious lies intended to foment Islamophobia and
racism, enriching private corporations at the cost of perhaps a million
uncounted civilian lives as well as thousands of working-class soldiers.
At a time when my studies demanded humility toward some conception
of popular opinion, I saw how that same rhetoric of the British Enlightenment had been revived to cloak genocidal nihilism in the socially

enforced pseudohumility of common sense. In US political discourse of the mid-2000s, "common sense" became synonymous with the fearfulness, prejudice, and cruelty that enriched and empowered the same men who profit from every crisis.

As I began to interrogate the history of common sense, I found a strange rhetorical legacy. Before the eighteenth century, following Aristotle, common sense was the term for a mental faculty that collates and organizes information from the five senses into a perception or cognition of experience. It had nothing to do with conceiving of a public opinion or the ideas of common people. John Locke introduces the idea of a consensus-based epistemology, but still uses "common sense" to refer to a faculty of the mind that organizes sensory information into ideas.[3] George Berkeley is the first philosopher I find who refers to "men of plain common sense" with the implication that an educated person loses his common sense and can no longer derive rational knowledge from empirical experience in the manner of an uneducated person. Thus, the philosopher cannot be among "men of plain common sense," but a gardener is. In Berkeley's fictional dialogue *Three Dialogues between Hylas and Philonous,* the two philosophers agree that the goal of their debate about epistemology should be to arrive at a conclusion about epistemology to which the gardener would assent. "I am content, Hylas, to appeal to the common sense of the world for the truth of my notion. Ask the gardener, why he thinks yonder cherry-tree exists in the garden, and he shall tell you, because he sees and feels it; in a word, because he perceives it by his senses." And a few pages later, "I wish both our opinions were fairly stated and submitted to the judgment of men who had plain common sense, without the prejudices of a learned education."[4] Philonous implies that the mind of the philosopher has been somehow damaged by education, so he must subject his views to the presumably objective consensus of uneducated persons to discover if he is correct.

Of course, Hylas and Philonous never speak to the gardener to whom they refer; rather, they use the idea of him to imagine a mind with no formal education, only sensory experience of the world, and hold that standard as the goal toward which the philosopher must aspire. Following Berkeley, "common sense" consistently plays this rhetorically duplicitous role, relegating the arbitration of judgment to the consensus of the minds of these totally imaginary regular folks, while never consulting any individual persons. In the eighteenth century, the philosopher, the art critic, the specialist, the lawyer, and the political theorist begin to make a trade of imagining "everyone" as a homogenous, normative, objective perspective that does not tolerate eccentricity, individuality, or subjectivity. Common sense, as imagined by most philosophers in the eighteenth century, flatters the interests of powerful and educated men by imagining the validation of their ideas by fictional working-class men.

This figure of "common sense" must remain imaginary in order to function as a rhetorical wedge for philosophical debate. If one were to ask a real gardener how he knows the cherry tree exists, perhaps he would tell us that his father told him he planted it, that God put it there to provide food, or that he read a book about cherries, rather than the conveniently empiricist response Philonous imagines for him. When we speak now of a person who has "common sense," it still refers, as Aristotle and Locke did, to an internal faculty of mind that organizes sensory experience into coherent ideas, in the absence of any a priori perspective or prejudice. For this reason, the imagined person of common sense is typically a heterosexual man of European descent, while a woman, a person of color, a child, or a sexual nonconformist could, presumably, only speak from their own marginalized position. The presumed universality of the white male heterosexual perspective created an epistemic feedback loop in eighteenth-century discourse in which every person with academic, legislative, or religious authority shares the same demographic experiential bias as anyone who could plausibly challenge or test that authority.

Whose Happiness Matters?

Jeremy Bentham was one of the few philosophers of the British Enlightenment to note not only that the imagined figure of common sense, the heterosexual European man, was representative of a small demographic minority of the population but also that the invocation of a normative conception of human motivation was being used to deny pleasure and liberty to anyone outside that small minority. In his commentaries on British law, Bentham insisted that the only way to legislate in the interests of most people would be to reform the penal code (along with everything else) on the principle that laws must, without demographic discrimination, secure the liberty of each individual person to seek pleasure or avoid pain, as long as others are unharmed. From the law, he extrapolated that, if marginalized people lack the social, religious, and economic means necessary for self-custodianship, any further considerations of communal utility are irrelevant. As I discuss in chapter 3, Bentham's "felicific calculus"—"*it is the greatest happiness of the greatest number that is the measure of right and wrong*"—should be self-evident; if *most* of the people are dependent on the will of the patriarchs who govern them to allow or forbid them pleasure, then the law is failing to facilitate "the greatest happiness for the greatest number."[5] Bentham rejected the idea that an imaginary consultation with common sense could replace an analysis of real human behavior, or a consultation with people whose desires and pleasures are unimaginable to us, because our ability to imagine minds unlike our own has been degraded by an unrelenting education in prejudice and self-interest.

From his earliest published writing, mostly commentaries on William Blackstone, Bentham was disturbed to realize that the same legislators and lawyers who advocated for common sense, democracy, and "natural law" wrote as if women, children, and slaves have no existence except as the wards of legally enfranchised men. Bentham feared that, because political history focused entirely on the perspectives of property-owning men, expositors and practitioners of the law had become unable to see women, children, and enslaved laborers as persons at all.

> What is curious is, that the same persons who tell you (having read as much) that Democracy is a form of Government under which the supreme power is vested in all the members of a state, will also tell you (having also read as much) that the Athenian Commonwealth was a Democracy. Now the truth is, that in the Athenian Commonwealth, upon the most moderate computation, it is not one tenth part of the Athenian state that ever at a time partook of the supreme power: women, children, and slaves being taken into account. Civil Lawyers, indeed, will tell you, with a grave face, that a slave is *nobody*; as Common Law will, that a bastard is the *son* of *nobody*. But, to an unprejudiced eye, the condition of a state is the condition of all the individuals, without distinction, that compose it.[6]

Bentham's assertion of the humanity of women, children, and enslaved laborers should not have been radical in an era of revolutionary fervor for equality and liberty. Without panegyric or sentiment, Bentham simply asserts that, mathematically, not only patriarchal men should be counted as members of the population in any discussion of democratic representation. The happiness of all persons—not only the happiness of their husbands, fathers, and masters—is the happiness of the state. Injustice toward any demographic group is the state committing violence against itself. If philosophers, legislators, and religious leaders cannot imagine the independent thoughts, pleasures, and desires of any groups of disenfranchised persons, then, Bentham argues, they cannot educate, legislate, or moralize without tyranny, and their egalitarian rhetoric of human rights and common sense must be read as disingenuous, and even dangerous.

Bentham clarified in *An Introduction to the Principles of Morals and Legislation* that the imaginary idea of a "community" had somehow come to mean the interests of the powerful people in that community rather than the members of that community, including the less powerful people who make up most of it. "The interest of the community is one of the most general expressions that can occur in the phraseology of morals: no wonder that the meaning of it is often lost. When it has a meaning, it is this. The community is a fictitious *body,* composed of the individual persons who are considered as constituting as it were its *members.* The interest of the community then is, what?—the sum of the interests of the several members who compose it."[7] Bentham borrows the image from Thomas Hobbes's *Leviathan,* of a state as a being made up of individual subjects, in order to remind readers that the well-being of a community is only as good as that of all the members of its body. In his advocacy for disenfranchised persons, Bentham asks how community leaders could tolerate, much less promote, the misery of large groups of its members, which constitutes the misery of the entire community in the aggregate.

Rights and Happiness

In the twenty-first century, we find ourselves living out the legacy of the British Enlightenment, not only in the United States, a country explicitly founded on Enlightenment principles, but in any part of the world where appeals to human rights, equality, and justice inspire common citizens to become agents in political action. The United Nations' Universal Declaration of Human Rights from 1948 echoes the words of Thomas Jefferson in the 1776 Declaration of Independence, defining these rights as "inalienable"—that "All human beings are born free and equal in dignity and rights,"[8] and that no one shall be tortured, exiled, enslaved, arbitrarily detained, denied a fair trial, robbed of their property, prevented from earning a livable wage, and so forth. Of course, the UDHR was as untrue in the twentieth century as the Declaration of Independence was in the eighteenth; discrimination and persecution of individual persons on the basis of race, gender, religion, sexual orientation, and disability are shockingly frequent in UN member nations, including the United States. At the same time that police brutality against Black, Latinx, and indigenous Americans has inspired widespread public protests resulting in woefully few substantive legal and policy changes, the mere threat of protest from white libertarian extremists successfully prevented any enforceable pandemic restrictions. While some Americans struggle for the right to survive an encounter with the state, others have claimed the right to put others in mortal danger without constraint.

Torture, exile, slavery, detention, plunder, and dearth are regularly inflicted by those whose status and property empower them to revoke so-called human rights at will, and there is little (if any) recourse available to victims of rights violations. Members of disenfranchised populations only rarely have the economic means to demand legal redress, and the adjudication of civil rights violations in a state ruled by common law is especially fickle; even if the injured person has excellent legal representation, a judge appointed by election or selection may interpret the material evidence seemingly at his or her whim. In the case of noncitizens such as displaced children, refugees, and civilian victims of international conflict, or in the case of citizens from disenfranchised populations, what recourse does a person have, other than petition or, if possible, rebellion? When we invoke libertarian rights discourse, it is usually in the midst of atrocities that render those rights absurd: inescapable pain endured by persons who have been denied custodianship of their own will, and who have insufficient economic or social power as individual subjects to demand redress for the wrongs committed against them.

At a time when we are able to be nearly constantly aware of ongoing human rights violations, the juxtaposition of violence and pleasure in eighteenth-century British liberal rights discourse can be startling—enjoyment, happiness, and pleasure serve as counterpoints to torture, exile, and indefinite detention. In Jefferson's phrasing, any infringement of the "unalienable rights" to "life, liberty, and the pursuit of happiness" must result in rebellion when formal petition has failed. But what happiness is, and who has the means and liberty to pursue it—not just the "right" to pursue it—remains a matter for daily legal and political debate. As happiness gradually became synonymous with bourgeois economic stability, the language of pleasure and enjoyment as a means to happiness has largely disappeared from public discourse, having been replaced by the terms of comfort and security. The simultaneous spread of Enlightenment values and globalized capitalism has resulted in a political era in which military supremacy is merely a subsidiary of economic supremacy, and the legal right for an individual subject to pursue happiness extends, at most, to the limit of that subject's economic power. Pleasure that exists outside of commodity or service exchange (such as enjoying an odor or consensual sex) is not subject to relative conditions of economic power, and so it has no grounds for protection in a legal discourse based on property.

In a secular capitalist democracy, the conflation of happiness and wealth is so common as to be effectively true; the pursuit of wealth is protected as an uncontested human right for politically enfranchised persons, while for disenfranchised persons, not even the avoidance of physical pain or death is protected as a legally secure liberty. Philip Goodchild argues in *Theology of Money* that, in the modern era, the absence of a common ethical or religious framework by which various sources of happiness could be assessed creates a vacuum that must, it seems, be filled by economic value. In his introduction to the US edition, he writes, "Enlightenment would appear to be the liberation of human activity from superstitious observances and regulations. There is only work, enjoyment, and recuperation, all in the service of flourishing. What most concerns humanity are the conditions under which flourishing may take place, and if there is any postponement of pleasure, this is merely to ensure that these conditions can be preserved and enhanced. The religious detour is replaced by an economic detour."[9] Pleasure, once deferred to the afterlife as a matter of religious observance or philosophical principle, remains deferred under capitalism as a faithful observance of economic principle. One must not enjoy if, by deferring enjoyment, one might look forward to greater enjoyment in the distant future, and reap rewards only at an ever-receding point of perfect security. Adam Smith describes the secular virtue of deferral in *The Theory of Moral Sentiments* as "self-command, by which we are enabled to abstain from present pleasure or to endure present pain, in order to obtain a greater pleasure or to avoid a greater pain in some future time."[10] Virtue itself, whether stoic, religious, or capitalist, is a performance of one's willingness to put off mere sensory enjoyment—with or without the hope of later reward. As Goodchild argues, the Enlightenment should be understood, not as a revolution from religious to secular values, but as a translation of religious virtue into economic virtue.

Enjoyment and Deferral

Much of this translation took place during the century between the publication of John Locke's *Two Treatises of Government* and the French Revolution, and the political consequences of this translation included the redefinition of political power in Europe, its colonies, and its trading partners. Locke's refutation of Robert Filmer's defense of divine authority in *Patriarcha* provided the foundation for a politics of power dependent on the tacit consent of the governed, rather than on superstitious fealty to patrilineal authority. Locke reimagines God as the creator of human enjoyment, rather than its prohibitor. By the will of God, each individual person is entitled to as much property as one can *enjoy* without decreasing the potential enjoyment of another person.

> The same Law of Nature, that does by this means give us Property, does also *bound* that *Property* too. *God has given us all things richly,* I Tim. vi. 17. is the Voice of Reason confirmed by Inspiration. But how far has he given it us? *To enjoy.* As much as any one can make use of to any advantage of life before it spoils; so much he may by his labour fix a Property in. Whatever is beyond this, is more than his share, and belongs to others. Nothing was made by God for Man to spoil or destroy.[11]

The law of enjoyment extends to liberty as well as property; as far as one's enjoyment extends without violating the enjoyment of another is the natural boundary of liberty. "To understand Political Power right, and derive it from its Original, we must consider what State all Men are naturally in, and that is, a *State of perfect Freedom* to order their Actions, and dispose of their Possessions, and persons as they think fit, within the bounds of the Law of Nature, without asking leave, or depending upon the Will of any other Man."[12] The "Law of Nature," Locke clarifies, is the injunction against suicide, which is the limit of human authority over our own bodies. (Bentham vehemently disagrees with Locke on this point, as it seems especially cruel to force someone made miserable by the powerful to remain alive simply to provide satisfaction to their oppressors.) Locke writes nothing of a duty to defer enjoyment; rather, enjoyment becomes the duty of one who would claim property for private use, as well as the duty of one who would enjoy liberty from legal prohibition. The deferral of enjoyment is a kind of crime against one's community; to hoard potential pleasure indefinitely is theft of the commons, and to use power to prevent a pleasure that does not diminish the commons is a form of tyranny.

Throughout the first treatise, Locke is careful to specify that the laws of nature are universal and extend to women, children, and laborers, not just to patriarchs or rulers. Despite the interdependence that may arise within a household, power within the household must only exist for the benefit of the governed and with their consent. However, despite the vast changes to political power that would emerge as a response to Locke over the following century, none of them resulted in the political enfranchisement of women, children, or laborers, who by the end of the century had, arguably, lost even the modest political clout they had held at the end of the seventeenth century. And as for the freedom to enjoy one's own body—"being Master of himself, and *Proprietor of his own Person*"[13]—not even Locke can imagine granting license to "Adultery, Incest, and Sodomy," as they are "Sins, which I suppose, have their Principal Aggravation from this, that they cross the main intention of Nature, which willeth the increase of Mankind, and the continuation of the Species in the highest perfection, and the distinction of Families, with the Security of the Marriage Bed, as necessary thereunto."[14] Locke suggests a startling moral equivalence between same-sex intimacy and suicide or murder, as it constitutes a refusal to procreate; one might note that Locke applies no such judgment to nonprocreative heterosexual intimacy. As I demonstrate in chapter 3, this is not the only instance where Locke struggles to justify limitations on sexual liberty as a matter of "natural" law, rather than a local prejudice. If one is the proprietor, first and most importantly, of one's own body, and if the enjoyment of one's property is the only true boundary on property rights, then it would seem that a consensual experience of sexual pleasure would be the most basic form of enjoyment available to the common person.

The problem of noneconomic forms of pleasure—especially the pleasures of women and sexual nonconformists—became a consistent sticking point for philosophers and moralists of the British Enlightenment. Locke notes in *An Essay Concerning Human Understanding* that sexual norms differ around the world as evidence against the innateness of moral feeling, though he simultaneously assures the reader that same-sex intercourse is universally abhorred in his own country. David Hume acknowledges that same-sex intercourse was common, and even considered laudable, in ancient Greece, but assures the reader that it is universally abhorred in the present day. I analyze these and other examples in chapter 2 in order to demonstrate the rhetorical absurdities Locke and Hume each commit in attempting to justify their own clearly aesthetic disgust for sexual nonconformity.

In *The Theory of Moral Sentiments,* Adam Smith acknowledges that, as recently as the Restoration, "licentiousness" was deemed evidence of a good character and linked "with generosity, sincerity, magnanimity, loyalty, and proved that the person who acted in this manner, was a gentleman, and not a puritan,"[15] and yet Smith agrees with his predecessors that moral sentiment, such as it is, must be the product of some tacit communal agreement, and that it differs on the basis of gender, age, economic class, and national origin. He concludes that, among any people whose resources are insecure, virtuous self-denial and self-sacrificing generosity must be more highly valued. Yet he consistently imagines a position of supposed objectivity from which the moral contest between persons or cultures may be properly judged. In one instance, he depicts the European colonization and enslavement of Africans from this perspective: "Fortune never exerted more cruelly her empire over mankind, than when she subjected those nations of heroes to the refuse of the jails of Europe, to wretches who possess the virtues neither of the countries which they come from, nor of those which they go to, and whose levity, brutality, and baseness, so justly expose them to the contempt of the vanquished."[16] Smith generously imagines a benevolent objective perspective from which the relative virtues of enslaved Africans and European slave traders can be compared. But of course this objective perspective does not exist, and only the reigning common sense of inherent European superiority and economic domination guided the progression of human trafficking. The authority of economic violence and the "natural" right of oppressive force had long since replaced any useful threat of divine justice.

The Imaginary Man of Common Sense

For Locke, Hume, and Smith, the longing remains for some means of creating an equivalence between an objective and a common sense of what is right or good, even if it is provisional, culturally specific, or merely a rhetorical flourish. Indeed, the ability to imagine a perspective outside of any individual person from which a judgment may be fairly determined would come to form Kant's definition of *sensus communis* in *The Critique of Judgement:*

> By the name *sensus communis* is to be understood the idea of a *public sense,* i.e., a faculty which in its reflective act takes account (*a priori*) of the mode of representation of everyone else, in order, *as it were,* to weigh its judgement with the collective reason of mankind, and thereby avoid the illusion arising from subjective and personal conditions which could readily be taken for objective, an illusion that would exert a prejudicial influence upon its judgement. This is accomplished by weighing the judgement, not so much with actual, as rather with the merely possible, judgements of others, and by putting ourselves in the position of everyone else, as the result of a mere abstraction from the limitations which contingently affect our own judging.[17]

Kant solves the problem of common sense by interpreting the Enlightenment's mourning for a lost objective authority as the actual identity of that authority, such as it is. Rather than consulting one's own mind, or soliciting the judgments of other real people, one must imagine the judgment of others in order to arrive at the *common* sense of what is correct. The process he describes is identical to Hume's in *An Enquiry Concerning the Principles of Morals,* but Hume describes a "common observation" of public opinion as indicative of real utility within a community. For Kant, the common sense begins and ends within the mind of the person attempting to produce an accurate judgment, and it is merely a self-effacing mental exercise.

In his celebrated response to the question "What is Enlightenment?" posed by the Reverend Johann Friedrich Zöllner, Kant celebrated the triumph of the Enlightenment as the ability to make public use of private judgment: "*Sapere aude!* Have the courage to use your *own* understanding! is thus the motto of enlightenment."[18] Yet the private judgment he would have the philosopher employ is subjected to and predicated upon the imagined judgment of others, which may be just as deforming as the real judgment of intellectual and cultural authorities using their own subjective responses as the basis for judgment. Jürgen Habermas writes that Kant "ascribed the function of a pragmatic test of truth to the public consensus arrived at by those engaged in rational-critical debate with one another."[19] Habermas's reading of Kant suggests that as one reads and interacts with other minds in the public sphere, the individual learns to suppress subjective pleasures or pains in favor of mutually asserted opinions taken as common sense, though perhaps actually shared by no one. But in being limited to those with access to the public sphere, one's judgment must be prejudiced by the norms of social decorum as well as the de facto exclusion of disenfranchised populations.

Common sense does not refer to a mean, median, or sum of real human experience. It is limited by what is and can be uttered in public by those who have access to the public sphere. It is also limited by the imagination and social experience of the person who is in the position of imagining the minds of others for the purpose of judgment. Were we to ask a real gardener "why he thinks yonder cherry-tree exists in the garden," would he really say, "because he sees and feels it," as Berkeley's Philonous would have it? The irony of Kant's position is that while seeming to empower the individual to express his own judgment in public, he first demands that he subjugate that judgment to the imagined judgment of others, as they might express themselves in public, but then grants himself a new basis for authority predicated upon the presumed consensus of people who have not spoken.

In the case of physical pleasure, however, the philosopher must arrive at an impasse. I know what my body enjoys, and I know that the bodies of others seem to enjoy different experiences and that we cannot reconcile our tastes. With respect to art, perhaps we can, and our judgment can reflect our sense of the market, of critics, and of crowds. But an odor that is pleasant to me is vile to another, and something exhilarating and joyful to me may horrify someone else. There is no common sense of what is private to one's own body, and no common sense of private physical pleasure. Among eighteenth-century British philosophers, only Jeremy Bentham considers the apparent variety of experiences of physical sensation in the context of Enlightenment political and moral philosophy, and the consequences of that variety for the law, especially

as it applies to those with no access to the public sphere or political participation. In a manuscript from 1800, he writes:

> No one man in short has any accurate and minute measure of the inten-
> sity of the sensations of any other: much less is there any such thing as
> an instrument that is to all persons of man a common measure for the
> intensity of the sensations of all.
>
> I cannot be content just to deliver my judgment and take my chance
> for its concurring with his. I judge in the first place that the sensation
> is a pain: that as a pain its intensity is something. This I must be right
> in: this I must bring him to agree in: otherwise all my speculations con-
> cerning the true dimensions of the value of the sensations fall to the
> ground.[20]

If pleasure is not empirically verifiable—if there can be no common
sense of what is enjoyable to another person—then legally prohibiting
pleasure on a discriminatory basis is effectively denying entire groups
of people the ability to pursue their own kind of happiness. Forcing a
"pleasure" on someone against their will is the same kind of tyrannical
injustice as rendering it impossible for people to defend themselves from
pain or death.

In his private and published work, written over the course of almost
sixty years (roughly 1772–1832), Bentham repeatedly returned to the
problem that physical pleasure posed for Enlightenment discourse.
Unlike Kant, Bentham did not take the subjective turn, differentiating
between the minds of subjects and the experience of objects, but instead
worked to excise subjectivity from every part of the observation. Bentham attempted to understand the experience of other people not by
extrapolating from his own, or even by soliciting accounts of others'
experience, but by observing the actions that people actually perform as
evidence of their desire or pleasure.

Rather than finding that people conform to stereotypes based on
class, gender, race, and so forth, or that they obey recognizable rational
impulses, Bentham found that people behave *strangely*. Whatever they
might say about their own motivations, they seemed to pursue physical pleasures in ways that run directly counter to Enlightenment-era
principles of virtue ethics, and in opposition even to normative ideas
about what is supposed to be pleasurable. It was not only the rich who

sought pleasure but also the poor, not just men but also women, not just adults but also children and the elderly, not just descendants of Europe but everyone. In nearly every walk of life, Bentham found that people pursue their own physical pleasure regardless of social norms, religious injunction, or penal law. He discovered that the variety of human sensation contradicts the pretended common-sense aesthetics and values of political and intellectual elites. Bentham found that Locke was ultimately correct that each human being is, first of all, "*Proprietor of his own Person,*"[21] but he seemed to have drastically underestimated the effects of social, religious, and legal oppression on politically disenfranchised groups like women, children, colonized and enslaved persons, and sexual nonconformists—people whose pleasures were declared immoral, illegal, bizarre, or counterproductive to the production and maintenance of property.

Bentham's lifelong public advocacy against discriminatory laws targeting politically disenfranchised groups has been woefully underexamined, except as a precursor to the far less radical John Stuart Mill, with a few crucial exceptions, beginning with Lea Campos Boralevi's 1984 book *Bentham and the Oppressed* and Louis Crompton's 1985 *Byron and Greek Love.* Boralevi's *Bentham and the Oppressed* analyzes Bentham's private and public writing on discriminatory laws, showing that Bentham's opposition to legal discrimination extended not only to women and laborers but also to sexual nonconformists and even to animals, on the basis that all of these groups are subjected to unnecessary pain and limits on their liberty to pursue physical pleasure, violating the Lockean principle that a just government is one that provides for the self-determination of each individual subject. Bentham includes animals by demonstrating that rationality, body appearance, aesthetic taste, and moral virtue (each commonly used to distinguish between human and animal in secular discourse) are inadequate criteria for forcing anyone to suffer pain.

Although Louis Crompton's *Byron and Greek Love* is mostly focused on sexual nonconformity in the context of Lord Byron's life and writing, it is also the first extended analysis of Bentham's extraordinary manuscripts on same-sex intimacy and other nonnormative practices. More than any other single author of the late eighteenth and early nineteenth centuries, Bentham analyzed the legal, moral, theological, philosophical, and aesthetic problem of sexual nonconformity in the minutest details, comparing forbidden sexual pleasures with the violence exerted to prohibit these pleasures. Crompton notes that in the context of a legal discourse in which even naming same-sex intimacy was considered unseemly, and any justification of punishments for sodomy was deemed unnecessary, the voluminousness of Bentham's writing on sexuality is astounding.

> Bentham first jotted down about fifty pages of notes in 1774 when he was twenty-six. In 1785 he completed a somewhat longer formal essay. In 1814 and 1816 he filled almost two hundred pages with another impassioned indictment of British attitudes. Two years later he produced several hundred more pages of notes on homosexuality and the Bible, and in 1824, eight years before his death at the age of eighty-four, he wrote a final short synopsis of his ideas on sodomy law reform. All in all, this adds up to a sizable book on a subject that British jurists usually dismissed in a paragraph or page.[22]

Crompton quotes extensively from these manuscripts in a chapter contextualizing the homophobic context of this period, putting a few of them into print for the first time. Since 1985, these manuscripts have received some critical attention and praise, but have not formed the basis of a thorough examination of Bentham's legacy in the context of his radical advocacy for bodily pleasure, rather than ability or status, as a foundation for political and social enfranchisement.

Whose Suffering Matters?

In a lengthy footnote in *An Introduction to the Principles of Morals and Legislation,* about half of which I quote below, Bentham explicitly links the suffering of enslaved persons to that of animals. In both cases, he argues, the justification for cruelty is often made on some normative description of perceived appearance, communication, virtue, or ability, rather than on the aspect of the being which is most relevant—the capacity for suffering.

> The day has been, I grieve to say in many places it is not yet past, in which the greater part of the species, under the denomination of slaves, have been treated by the law exactly upon the same footing, as, in

England for example, the inferior races of animals are still. The day *may* come, when the rest of the animal creation may acquire those rights which never could have been withholden from them but by the hand of tyranny. The French have already discovered that the blackness of the skin is no reason why a human being should be abandoned without redress to the caprice of a tormentor. It may come one day to be recognized, that the number of the legs, the villosity of the skin, or the termination of the *os sacrum,* are reasons equally insufficient for abandoning a sensitive being to the same fate? What else is it that should trace the insuperable line? Is it the faculty of reason, or, perhaps, the faculty of discourse? But a full-grown horse or dog, is beyond comparison a more rational, as well as a more conversible animal, than an infant of a day, or a week, or even a month, old. But suppose the case were otherwise, what would it avail? the question is not, Can they *reason?* nor, Can they *talk?* but, Can they *suffer?*[23]

Bentham consistently demonstrates that the tests for humanity applied to women, disabled persons, people of color, children, and sexual minorities would be obviously absurd if the same tests were applied to powerful men. Whatever normative definition of humanity may be chosen as the boundary for self-determination and full political and social enfranchisement—male, white, heterosexual, able-bodied, adult, rational, articulate, human, etc.—one finds that the resulting category of beings who may *not* be forced to suffer pain against their will is a vanishingly small group of men who were represented in literally all positions of political and legal authority in England in Bentham's time, as well as most positions of authority in the Anglophonic world today. The bulk of the populace is under the rule of a tiny minority of the population who claim the exclusive use of "common sense," while the rest of us apparently lack the ability to make sense of what is right and wrong to do, even with our own bodies. When we are asked to use "common sense," we are being asked to participate in a kind of virtue ethics in which we deny our empirical experience, desire, and judgment in favor of some imagined consensus of people who lack the "bias" of our experiences of oppression.

The stakes of this debate could not be higher for disabled persons, especially those who are nonspeaking. The status of people with intellectual disabilities in eighteenth-century England was a matter of continual debate, and in that post-Lockean age of reason, a perceived incapacity for abstract thought or verbal communication was often deemed justification for dehumanizing abuse. D. Christopher Gabbard notes that one of the few exceptions to the literal dehumanization of nonspeaking disabled persons in eighteenth-century British discourse is found in John Cleland's *Memoirs of a Woman of Pleasure,* in which the "idiot" Good-natured Dick is represented as experiencing sublimely powerful sexual pleasure with Fanny and Louisa. Gabbard argues that Cleland uses Dick to challenge Locke's description of "human" understanding as the ability to construct abstract thought from sensory experience. "By celebrating human mental imperfection, the Good-natured Dick passage unfolds not just a dissenting Enlightenment vision with regard to John Locke's theory of mind but also a locus classicus of anti-Lockean epistemology."[24] Gabbard describes an emerging anti-Lockean discourse of French and English natural philosophy influenced by Pierre Gassendi that Cleland may have drawn from, arguing that humanity is not inherently rational but sensory, and that one's ability to distinguish between the sensations of pleasure and pain, enjoyment and disgust—an individual *aesthetic* sense—is a proper basis for demanding human dignity.

For many post-Lockean philosophers, the full humanity of women and non-Europeans was also a matter for both explicit and implicit debate. Though Locke himself repeatedly asserts that evidence of human understanding from women and non-Europeans must, of course, be taken into account when describing human nature, it is always that they are human, with the apparent difference that they will tolerate servitude. If "Slavery is so vile and miserable an Estate of Man,"[25] as he begins the first *Treatise,* not to be endured by a rational person, then, as many later figures of the British Enlightenment would conclude, the continuous political and economic oppression of women and enslaved Africans serves self-evidently to prove that they are not fully rational beings because of their continued oppression. The humanity and rationality of rapists and slaveholders, if they were wealthy European men, remained beyond question.

David Hume very clearly excludes women from most of his conceptions of so-called human nature, and when he discusses them at all, it is to show that their lives are usefully restricted by discriminatory moral and legal injunctions that protect the property rights of men. In *An*

Enquiry Concerning the Principles of Morals, he demonstrates the utility of marital fidelity for promoting the economic security of the family, but also justifies the discriminatory burden of chastity that falls on women. "The long and helpless infancy of man requires the combination of parents for the subsistence of their young; and that combination requires the virtue of CHASTITY of fidelity to the marriage bed. Without such a *utility,* it will be readily owned, that such a virtue would never have been thought of. / An infidelity of this nature is much more *pernicious* in *women* than in *men.* Hence the laws of chastity are much stricter over the one sex than over the other."[26] Because Hume makes no distinction between the common sense of morality in the masculinist public discourse of his own culture and some objective sense of morality or fairness, the fact of the oppression of women by the concept of chastity is evidence that the oppression of women is of great utility. Unlike Smith, who longs for an objective authority outside of common sense to judge the relative virtue of human action on a global scale, Hume does not allow for any such sublime longing to complicate the epistemic loop of empiricism, in which any group of persons oppressed by their gender or national origin must be oppressed for the purpose of utility.

In a more notorious and acute example, Hume's justification of the common sense of prejudice extends to the oppression of colonized and enslaved Africans. In his essay "Of National Characters," Hume only deigns to address Africans in a disturbing and dehumanizing footnote: "I am apt to suspect the negroes and in general all other species of men (for there are four or five different kinds) to be naturally inferior to the whites. There never was a civilized nation of any other complexion than white, nor even any individual eminent either in action or speculation."[27] In the face of legions of public examples of contemporaneous women and Africans who were obviously capable of abstract thought in any field of study, Hume's principle of utility—of usefulness to the white men whose interest defines "common sense"—employs the self-evident fact of ongoing oppression to prove the lesser humanity of female and African persons.

In the mid-1990s there was a brief flurry of debate following the publication of Richard Popkin's recantation of earlier claims that Hume was virulently racist, now asserting that Hume's stated views on Africans are inconsistent with his general advocacy of "tolerance," and so they may be forgiven.[28] John Immerwahr responded to suggest that it does not matter what follows logically from Hume's principles; the racist statement must still be considered to be a part of Hume's worldview.[29] Robert Palter then retorted that holding historical thinkers to current ethical standards is unfair to them and asserted that Hume later changed his mind anyway.[30] Similar debates about Enlightenment figures such as Locke, Hume, Adam Smith, Benjamin Franklin, and Thomas Jefferson as racist or sexist are restaged periodically, in conference panels and journals made up almost entirely of white male philosophers and historians, without any citations of historical or current advocates for the enfranchisement of women or nonwhite people. The problem, as they see it, is one of presentism: ought we hold historical thinkers to "our" current cultural standards? (The question assumes that we all do, in fact, share antiracist and antisexist cultural standards.) To anyone familiar with eighteenth-century discourses of gender and race, the question need not be a presentist one at all. In addition to eighteenth-century African and female writers, antiracist and antisexist white men were also publishing critical work alongside and in response to each of these figures, and any of them could be consulted for a sense of the range of contemporary reactions to racist and sexist justifications of the ongoing oppression of women and colonized and enslaved persons.

For heterosexual cisgender able-bodied bourgeois male philosophers descended from light-skinned Europeans (that is, a small minority among the general populace that nevertheless holds most university positions in philosophy today),[31] the solution to the problem of racism, sexism, and ableism in the legacy of the British Enlightenment has been to insist that *had they known what we know now,* the promises of a Lockean civil government—the consent of the governed, equal opportunity, rational secular legislators, liberty and justice for all—would have been fulfilled, and still could be, if only we could teach oppressed persons how to participate fully in a public sphere using the discourse of common sense. Like many would-be philosophers from populations deemed incapable of common sense—i.e., adopting the imagined perspective of the powerful at the expense of the oppressed—I came to realize that these promises could be fulfilled only at the cost of genuine diversity in empirical experience and aesthetic taste, in addition to the complications of epistemic and rhetorical diversity. As long as the "utility" of every moral and political concern is the uncontested majoritization of a small minority of white heterosexual male elites, then the common sense we must manifest in order to participate in post-Enlightenment philosophical discourse is, for most of us, a performance of epistemic self-annihilation.

In the case of sexual nonconformity, annihilation has long been the explicit end of attempts to regulate sexual behavior or expressions of sexual desire in the public sphere. Unlike other crimes like theft or vandalism, the sexual nonconformist has historically been subjected to total eradication, in the form of both physical destruction and erasure from the public record. Eve Kosofsky Sedgwick analyzes the history of these erasures in *Epistemology of the Closet:*

> From at least the biblical story of Sodom and Gomorrah, scenarios of same-sex desire would seem to have a privileged, though by no means an exclusive, relation in Western culture to scenarios of both genocide and omnicide. That sodomy, the name by which homosexual acts are known even today to the law of half of the United States and to the Supreme Court of all of them, should already be inscribed with the name of a site of mass extermination is the appropriate trace of a double history. In the first place there is a history of the moral suppression, legal or subjudicial, of gay acts and people, through burning, hounding, physical and chemical castration, concentration camps, bashing—the array of sanctioned fatalities that Louis Crompton records under the name of gay genocide.[32]

The mass murder, torture, and *disappearance* of sexual nonconformists in Western culture is, as Sedgwick shows, both very literal and a manipulation of public discourse, in which the supposed crimes of nonconforming sexual practices are so vaguely indicated, even by the laws that forbid them, that, in a strange sense, all erotic desire, or even physical enjoyment, takes on the moral taint of queerness. It is especially noteworthy to this book that Sedgwick cites Louis Crompton as the source of the term "gay genocide," as he was also the first scholar of Jeremy Bentham to bring some of his manuscripts on sexual nonconformity to print. Long suppressed, mislabeled, or ignored as a curiosity, these manuscripts offer a coherent, stunningly radical argument for the full enfranchisement of sexual minorities, not as an end in itself, but as a step toward truly egalitarian reform of the law that could facilitate an unprecedented diversity of aesthetic, intellectual, and moral perspectives to participate as equals in the public sphere.

Common Sense and Revolution

The tension created by this legacy is perhaps keenest for those of us raised outside the ruling class in the United States, indoctrinated from birth in the post-Lockean revolutionary rhetoric of "unalienable rights" and a Constitution written in the voice of "We, the People." As Michael Warner masterfully argues in *Letters of the Republic,* the Constitution enacts a uniquely coercive rhetorical effect; it is a body of laws written *as if* in the voice of the populace speaking to itself. Referring to the rhetorical coercion of the populace, Warner writes, "I say 'their' own coercion, but of course this is what the Constitution will not allow me to say. There is no legitimate representational space outside the constitutive we. When someone calls out to the people, you will answer."[33] The Constitution of the United States could perhaps be described as the full political legitimation of the common-sense rhetoric of the Enlightenment; the powerful speak with the tacit consent of the oppressed, who have been preemptively silenced by having been spoken for, in the interest of their oppressors. To protest "We, the People"—or common sense—is to take up arms against the only legitimated representation of ourselves as political agents.

Samuel Johnson, whose resistance to nearly all the major figures of the British Enlightenment was a matter of some intellectual scandal, was among the first to note the irony of colonial slaveholders crying oppression because they had to pay taxes in 1775. He mockingly writes, "We are told, that the subjection of Americans may tend to the diminution of our own liberties; an event, which none but very perspicacious politicians are able to foresee. If slavery be thus fatally contagious, how is it that we hear the loudest yelps for liberty among the drivers of negroes?"[34] But of course, the Revolutionaries were merely echoing the opening lines of John Locke's first treatise, in which he sets the precedent for the quintessential rhetorical trope of Enlightenment political theory: categorically denouncing oppression while personally profiting from the oppression of others. In 1776 Johnson was joined by an anonymous English pamphleteer—Jeremy Bentham—whose response to the Declaration of Independence offered a somewhat subtler critique of the Americans' political legitimation of liberal rights discourse.

Bentham's response to the Declaration urged American revolutionaries to see that, rather than promise to liberate those among them who were actually impoverished, enslaved, and disenfranchised, they had instead declared anarchy, in which the powerful have as much control of the powerless as they can maintain by force and cruelty. The Declaration clearly states that oppressed people *will* "in the course of human events" reject tyranny, with violence if necessary. But the ill-defined nature of the supposed abuses against the obviously powerful signatories of the document sets a precedent, Bentham argues, that any citizen may revoke consent to be governed at any moment as long as he can amass the power to kill his oppressor. Bentham wonders if the disenfranchised native inhabitants, kidnapped Africans, indentured servants, and women who together make up most of the population also have a "right" to pursue happiness. "If the right of pursuing happiness be unalienable, how is it that so many others of their fellow-citizens are by the same injustice and violence made miserable, their fortunes ruined, their persons banished and driven from their friends and families?"[35] Bentham predicted that the postrevolutionary United States would endure constant threats to national sovereignty by armed mobs of people who feel oppressed by the existence of a government at all. If the will of the people were to be the rule of law, one must notice that most people in the new republic had no means *but* violence to express that will.

In this early period of his career, Bentham seems to have believed that the agents of power were earnest in their desire to create an equal and participatory republic, but simply lacked the ability to imagine disenfranchised persons as members of the state. His open letter to the French Republic (better known as "Emancipate Your Colonies!") in 1793 takes this tone of concern, warning that the Republic would be exposing itself to perpetual violence and terror if they promised "Liberté egalité fraternité ou le mort" without offering full political and economic enfranchisement to colonized people abroad.[36] In a similar series of letters addressed to the King of Spain (known as *Rid Yourselves of Ultramaria*), Bentham offered the same advice, with clarifications about the obvious economic and political benefit of becoming equal trading partners with nations of free people, rather than sending viceroys to govern them into a state of humiliation and steal the products of their labor.[37] And in 1811, after the new US government had a chance to settle in, Bentham wrote to President James Madison to offer his services in recodifying the laws of the United States in order to help rid them of the corrupt influences of discriminatory, incoherent English common law.[38]

This early period is also when Bentham took on the project for which he is best known today: his ill-fated plan for the Panopticon, which I discuss at greater length in chapter 1. Like his letters to various heads of state, the Panopticon was a project born of Bentham's naive assumption that lawmakers and enforcers have no motivation to cause unnecessary suffering to the bulk of the populace and expose them to life-threatening cruelty, but the paucity of resources available to be allocated to the care of prisoners, laborers, and so forth, makes it impossible to provide them with any comfort or hope. In *An Introduction to the Principles of Morals and Legislation,* Bentham convincingly argues that punishment itself is evil because it causes pain and "ought only to be admitted in as far as it promises to exclude some greater evil."[39] During the first half of his career, Bentham believed that the state could be moved by economic self-interest to alleviate human suffering if the public could be convinced that social order would be maintained. (Bentham proposed that he would serve as the architect and guard of the Panopticon at no cost, just as he offered his services to the United States at no cost.) When the plan to build the Panopticon fell through for the final time, Bentham began to develop a far more radical vision of Enlightenment liberal political philosophy—that it is not an earnest attempt to liberate anyone from servitude, dependency, and suffering but a rhetorical gambit to make oppressed people feel their suffering more bitterly. Bentham began to refer to this sadistic impulse as the "sinister interest" behind political and legal discourse.

If Bentham is celebrated at all, it is usually for the extraordinary projects of political and philosophical radicalism that dominated the latter half of his career. No longer solely framing his arguments as a potential benefit to the economic condition or security of the state, he more fully and publicly explored his theories of human motivation, aesthetics, and theology, publishing under pseudonyms material that he had been working on in private notes. One of his later projects was a *Table of the Springs of Action,* which would ultimately form the basis for his posthumously published *Deontology,* which provided a system for reimagining moral and ethical judgment by comparing the eulogistic and dyslogistic language for each motivation with its relative potential consequences for the pain or pleasure of oneself and others.[40] That is, rather than taking for granted that the way we talk about the virtue or vice of an action is evidence of its real social utility, as Hume does, we must first compare the way we talk about virtue or vice with an action's observed effects on the happiness of real, diverse, non-imaginary people.

Bentham on Sexual Nonconformity

Over the course of over fifty years of analysis, Bentham found that the most intense social disapprobation seemed to be reserved for pleasures that are literally harmless—especially those of consensual same-sex intimacy between social equals. One could not say that same-sex partners would be *more* in danger of coercion than male-female couples—and all without the threat of unwanted pregnancy—nor that their intercourse would, in itself, waste resources, damage health, engender enmity, or any of the consequences that attend celebrated pleasures such as drinking wine or playing cards. Rather, Bentham notes, the liberty to enjoy consensual same-sex intercourse could offer a well of relief to many people living in terror of draconian English laws and the violence of the mob, while providing a source of pleasure that could vastly increase the general well-being of the populace. Same-sex intimacy obviously goes on in spite of any threatened punishment, so putting an end to it is not only counterproductive to happiness, it is also impossible. In a favorite comparison, Bentham finds that a person could no more be coerced out of a strong sexual preference than to be told they must dislike the smell of tobacco.

The 2014 publication of a selection of Bentham's writings on sexual nonconformity from the 1810s has drawn some attention to what was formerly only known to those like Crompton and Boralevi who have read widely in his personal papers, most of which are held in special collections at University College London. The volume *Of Sexual Irregularities* contains three sets of these notes from the period when Bentham's analysis of sexuality was most concentrated, and can be categorized into discrete applications for law and ethics, epistemology and aesthetics, and theology. However, the philosophical problem of sexual nonconformity appears in his papers from his earliest philosophical inquiries to his last, often as marginal notes alongside broader questions of political theory, especially with respect to personal liberty. In these earlier papers, Bentham expresses tremendous anxiety about even addressing such a fearsome topic, one that could result in fatal legal or social persecution. By the time of the 1810s manuscripts, however, it is clear that Bentham is no longer self-censoring or hesitant to write explicitly about sexual variety in all of its licit and illicit forms.

Frances Ferguson argues that the publication of these notes on sexual pleasure offers the basis for a reconsideration of Bentham as an indispensable aesthetic theorist in his own right.[41] For too long, modern aesthetic theory based on the tradition of Kant and Mill has assumed the superiority of a purportedly disinterested common sense of aesthetic value over the aesthetic pleasure of the individual. Though both Kant and Mill conceive of aesthetic judgment as subjective, they also insist that socially constructed aesthetic hierarchies must inform and mitigate immediate subjective responses for proper judgment. For Bentham, the pretense of disinterested judgment is simply yet another way in which the powerful oppress others, by convincing them that they do not even really enjoy what they enjoy, or that their pleasure itself is inferior to the pleasures of educated people, who claim even their *tastes* are more useful to the moral health of society. Bentham was suspicious of aesthetic hierarchies that serve as a proxy for denying innocent pleasures to people who can ill afford more expensive entertainment or the education to appreciate it. By focusing on sexual pleasure as a particularly individual aesthetic sense, Bentham demonstrates that even secular discourses of aesthetics are merely translations of the same old religious asceticism into the new economic terms of comfortable wealth and the heterosexual family.

As Ferguson shows, Mill's accusation that Bentham had no sensitivity to art or beauty is an attempt to dismiss the legal and political questions that Bentham understood as fundamentally aesthetic problems. From some of his earliest notes on the law, it is clear that Bentham understood that the penal code was not really legislation with the purpose of promoting "moral" behavior, but rather a representation of the aesthetic disgust that wealthy and powerful men have for the pleasures of politically and socially disenfranchised persons. Ferguson writes, "And while Kant suggests that aesthetic pleasure provides something like training in individual autonomous judgment that is an intimation of morality, Bentham argues that the laws governing sexuality provide a basis for challenging the morality of the law itself."[42] Likewise, in his analysis of nonprocreative sexual pleasure in scripture, Bentham argues that the variety of sexual feeling and desire represented as positive or neutral in the Bible is evidence that it might even be anti-Christian to base church doctrine and ecclesiastical law on the epistles of the ascetic antisexual Paul.

But of course, Bentham could not and did not publish any of his explicit work on sexual nonconformity in his own lifetime, and these papers were largely suppressed, some even mislabeled and mishandled from his death until quite recently. Throughout his notes, he speculates about some future time when it will be possible to engage in public discourse about sexual oppression as a form of injustice, alongside gender oppression, racial oppression, labor oppression, and the rampant abuse of children, people with disabilities and mental illness, and animals. Bentham explicitly links these categories of disenfranchisement, not in an attempt to paint them with a broad brush, but to make apparent just how few people remain who are *not* humiliated, exposed to derision and violence, and living with extremely reduced expectations for pleasure, liberty, and self-determination. His point is never to suggest that all of these groups are suffering the same way or to the same degree, but rather that they are suffering at the same few hands—those of the men who are legislators, philosophers, and religious authorities.

In the twenty-first century, these same oppressed groups are still struggling toward a kind of big-tent politics of anti-oppression that does not ultimately replicate the marginalization we have experienced at the hands of the pro-oppression advocates who still dominate law and its enforcement in most global political systems. Each of us has been carefully disciplined to identify with power whenever possible, and to look at others with the borrowed perspective of the powerful—"common sense" only because we share this delusion in common—even as we demand greater liberty for ourselves and our communities. Bentham's "felicific calculus"—"the greatest happiness for the greatest number"— has the potential to remind us that, together, so-called minorities far outnumber our oppressors, as long as we recognize that we must not empower those oppressors by doing the work of oppression for them.

This book, *Uncommon Sense,* is inspired by Bentham's resistance to the philosophy and politics of common sense in the eighteenth century, as well as by his disillusionment with the revolutionary era, in which power did not demographically change hands, it merely wrote a new myth to justify itself. I am awed by Bentham's consistent attention to bodies in his work, asking who has the liberty to move, speak, learn, fight, play, love, work, eat, and grow, and who has the power to take away that liberty. Queer pleasure is only one aspect of bodily liberty in which Bentham sought to establish a philosophical basis, rooted in epistemology and applied to theology and economics, for a politics of maximal individual happiness. As one of the vanishingly few educated, wealthy English men in the eighteenth century who consistently learned from and advocated for politically disenfranchised persons, Bentham offers a striking counterargument to the too-common justification in histories of philosophy today that it was impossible for a man of status at that time to recognize and oppose systemic discriminatory violence committed or permitted by the state.

I began this introduction with an account of how I fell in love with common sense through the fiction of Henry Fielding, whom Bentham excoriates as one of the writers most consistently hostile to sexual and gender nonconformity in all of British literature. I have struggled since 2001 to reconcile my admiration of Fielding as a brilliant and hilarious writer with his apparent disdain for marginalized people and victims of sexual and economic violence. For most of that time, I chastised myself (and my students) for unfairly projecting anachronistic politics onto someone who could not have understood the violence of his own rhetoric, until I read Bentham's sensitive near-contemporary assessment of Fielding's especially aggressive normativity.[43] For his own pleasure reading, Bentham far preferred gothic novels by politically radical women such as Charlotte Smith and sexual nonconformists like William Beckford, since they represented not what was supposed to be a common understanding of a normative life but an indulgence of desire for strange, illicit, vicarious, and excessive pleasures—or, what I called in a 2014 *CEA Forum* article "non-empiricist aesthetics."[44] From Bentham, I am learning how to resist the urge to sell my own liberty for the momentary pleasure of misidentification with my oppressors. For many of us, rejecting the common-sense ideology of post-Enlightenment political life is not merely a matter of joining a particular party or protesting a certain policy; it is a lifelong process of remembering how we have betrayed ourselves and our would-be allies to get along with those who have tirelessly fought to make us miserable and dependent. Bentham reminds us that if general happiness is a political goal worth pursuing, it must be the happiness not of the most elite or of the wealthiest, nor even of the most common kind of person already in the public sphere, but of *the greatest number,* a phrase that is perhaps most rhetorically precise as a threat.

THIS BOOK begins with a chapter on the legacy of criticisms of Bentham ("The Trouble with Bentham"), including his own, as well as my attempts to reconcile these criticisms with the largely unknown manuscript writing that may help reluctant readers of Bentham to find in him a voice worth hearing out, at least. The second chapter ("Aesthetics of Pleasure, Ethics of Happiness") analyzes Bentham's revision of empiricist theories of pleasure, and the ways that sexual nonconformity complicates Enlightenment ideas of what enjoyment is and is for. In the third chapter ("Against Rights"), I focus on the relevance of the sexual nonconformity papers to Bentham's larger goal of legal and constitutional reform, in the context of the era of revolutions and the rise of libertarian rights discourse. The fourth chapter ("Bentham's Queer Christ") engages with queer theory and theology, examining Bentham's manuscripts on Jesus and natural religion in the context of sexual nonconformity. And finally in the fifth chapter ("Politics and Poetics of Liberty"), I consider Bentham's relationship to contemporary literary authors, both in prose and in poetry; long considered a sort of philistine for his skepticism about the supposedly radical Romantic poets, Bentham seemed rather to prefer the works of women and sexual nonconformist novelists who challenged a naturalized patriarchal social order.

This book does not use Bentham to propose an anachronistic scheme for the future, nor does it attempt to settle scores with long-dead philosophers, but to perform an excavation of Bentham's private writings on nonconformity as an act of philosophical mourning for the Enlightenment and the promises it has never kept except to men who look like those who made them. With Bentham, we can imagine an empiricism based in accounts of experience rather than prejudiced imagination, and ethics without virtue, maximizing happiness in the present rather than gambling on security for a few. Perhaps, like Bentham, we can practice seeing unnecessary cruelty as a crime against all, rather than evidence that we have been spared, and we can choose to listen to the voices of the marginalized, and hear with suspicion those who have been amplified by power. For sexual and gender nonconforming people, Bentham may offer a queer intellectual history, a genuine historical ally, and the best legal advocate who never practiced law. When we read Bentham, we can know that, for once, someone meant to include us when he wrote "the greatest number."

1

The Trouble with Bentham

Like most students of eighteenth-century British philosophy working in American universities, I skipped Jeremy Bentham. From what I gathered secondhand, Bentham's best ideas had been rearticulated by the evidently saner John Stuart Mill, and his worst ideas had been adopted by oppressive institutions to terrorize the laboring class. At the root of Bentham's work is a strange proposal to quantify human happiness in measurable units so that it could be compared and prioritized by the state. What he called "felicific calculus" was a calculation he proposed in his first major work, *A Fragment on Government,* based on the principle that "it is the greatest happiness of the greatest number that is the measure of right and wrong."[1] Potentially reducing human liberty to a matter of majoritarian rule, the felicific calculus suggests a justification for the dehumanization of cultural, sexual, religious, racial, and gender minorities. In eschewing a moral justification for the assertion of human rights, Bentham seemed to undermine the political progress made in the spirit of secular liberal Enlightenment philosophy. In a nation founded on the principles of secular liberalism in the same year as his first attacks on the discourse of natural rights, I learned that Bentham's philosophy was mocked far more often than it was read, and seemingly for good reason.

As an undergraduate student of political theory, I was assigned Charles Dickens's satirical 1854 novel *Hard Times* instead of anything written by Bentham in order to understand the disturbing legacy of Benthamite utilitarianism. In the novel, the utilitarian teacher Thomas Gradgrind disciplines his students to hate "fancy" and imagination, and to think only in terms of facts and data. Rather than conceiving of their own lives as valuable, Gradgrind's students are catechized in their own insignificance compared to national progress and economic security. Dickens describes Gradgrind as a moral monster, devoid of sentiment or sympathy: "With a rule and a pair of scales, and the multiplication table always in his pocket, sir, ready to weigh and measure any parcel of human nature, and tell you exactly what it comes to. It is a mere question of figures, a case of simple arithmetic."[2] In this parody of the felicific calculus, Mr. Gradgrind uses that arithmetic to prove to his laboring-class students that they are merely cogs in a much larger machine in which the joylessness of their lives is mathematically irrelevant. Whatever Bentham may have intended to promote with his felicific calculus, his ideas became a shorthand for the systematic attack of power on the dignity of the human soul within only a few decades of his death.

Frances Ferguson notes that Dickens also satirizes a kind of evil Benthamite in Bradley Headstone, the murderous monomaniacal schoolmaster from *Our Mutual Friend*, who expounds the basic educational principles outlined by Bentham in his *Chrestomathia*, published in 1817. Bentham advocated for the creation of a system of universal education that, in including orphans and laborers' children, should not depend on nor aim at instilling elitist aesthetics and virtues, but instead make learning as accessible, useful, and enjoyable as possible. In *Our Mutual Friend*, the orphaned Charley Hexam, who aspires to go to school, finds himself surrounded by bored, violent, lazy kids and is quickly able to distinguish himself to his schoolmaster Headstone through flattery, obsequiousness, and cruelty, in a school that rejects virtue ethics and aesthetic training in favor of simplistic recitation exercises in practical knowledge. Ferguson writes, "The chief aim of those educational techniques was to extend opportunities for learning to the masses, and particularly to the children of the laboring poor whose ranks in the city of London had swelled with the growth of urban manufactures."[3] As Ferguson shows, Bentham's plan intended to provide laboring or absent parents with child care, offer practical skills for both pleasure and future employment, and create an alternative social structure for young people whose homes offered little. If nineteenth-century schools for poor children ultimately left much to be desired in comparison with the education of elites, Ferguson argues, they at least provided laboring-class youth with the opportunity to "create an artificial association" among students that could replicate the nonfamily ties that bind elites in interest with one another.[4]

Perhaps Dickens and Bentham had more in common than we—or Dickens—might assume. In *Pleasures of Benthamism*, Kathleen Blake analyzes F. R. Leavis's assumption, now taken for granted, that Dickens's body of fiction constituted a wholesale excoriation of Bentham, extrapolating from the satire of *Hard Times* to account for every character who advocates for political economy or reform of the Poor Laws. Drawing from Bentham's manuscripts on sexual nonconformity, Blake shows that both Dickens and Bentham desire nothing more than to make social and aesthetic room for human eccentricity in individual, nonelite aesthetics of pleasure. "To back the eccentric is to back individuality and the notion, as found in Bentham, that different minds are different. Not only are they different, but their difference is a good thing."[5] Though the satire of utilitarian extremism in *Hard Times* or *Our Mutual Friend* may serve as a warning against civic implementations of utilitarianism that capitalized on the prospect of maximizing efficiencies while further oppressing indigent laborers, children, and other marginalized people, Dickens's novels may have been written with the intent of satirizing the utilitarianism, not of Bentham, but of England. If so many scholars like me formed our earliest understanding of utilitarianism by reading a satire of its cruelest misinterpretation, we may be a generation of readers who were encouraged at a young age to develop a deep-seated intellectual prejudice against Bentham's radical liberationist philosophy.

Foucault on the Panopticon

While my colleagues in literature still cite Dickens to me as the origin of their distaste for Bentham, philosophers most often name Michel Foucault, even before John Stuart Mill or Karl Marx. Foucault's *Discipline and Punish* was how I first learned of Bentham's ill-fated Panopticon project, in which he had planned to solve the prison reform crisis by inventing a penal facility that would increase efficiency, lower costs to the state, and decrease the suffering of prisoners.[6] Although Bentham's intention seems to have been rooted in genuine concern for the well-being of convicted criminals, the principles of efficient discipline he introduced became, after his death, a system of political control through perpetual surveillance. Foucault uses Bentham's Panopticon—a series of letters and plans for a prison that was never built to his specifications—as a metaphor for the means by which the modern state terrifies the populace by insinuating that we might be visible to its agents, even in our most private moments.

The Panopticon, as Bentham proposed it, was intended to replace the older kind of prison exemplified by Newgate—a dungeon in which prisoners, most of them sentenced to death, were chained to a wall over an open sewer and where they often fell victim to brutal violence, disease, and suicidal despair. Bentham's proposal for the Panopticon suggested that many of these prisoners could be reformed and reintroduced to society if they were offered sufficient food, clean clothing, a comfortable bed, warmth, privacy, schooling, payment for their labor, exercise, and encouragement not to return to crime.[7] Bentham offered not only to serve as an unpaid guard in this prison but also to supply payment to workers and life insurance as a personal guarantee for their good care. He proposed that a dark place in the Panopticon could be arranged such that the prisoners would not know whether the guard was watching or not. In Foucault's summary of Bentham's project, he writes, "All that is needed, then, is to place a supervisor in a central tower and to shut up in each cell a madman, a patient, a condemned man, a worker or a schoolboy."[8] Of course Bentham had no intention of shutting up any schoolboys or patients, and the project does seem to depend on he himself serving as a benevolent invisible supervisor rather than some would-be torturer.

Foucault is not really describing Bentham's Panopticon, but ours— the systems of surveillance and isolation that allow the state to monitor and discipline its citizens with low cost and effort, using psychological manipulation rather than spectacular violence. In her analysis of Foucault's reading of Bentham, Frances Ferguson notes, "The superintendent's impersonality, his having no personal views of those he supervises, further diminishes the contractual nature of the interaction, and being visible seems thus to acquire a particular resonance from its opposition to the notion of a potentially verifiable contractual agreement."[9] Foucault asks us to consider the Panopticon as a metaphor for the less spectacular but more insidious role that modern state power plays in exercising its authority over our bodies. For readers of Foucault unfamiliar with Bentham's papers on the Panopticon, it is only as this metaphor that it survives, rather than as a humanitarian project to give hope to miserable people whose convictions had placed them far out of the reach of the liberal Enlightenment's so-called human rights.

In her 2012 book *Utilitarian Biopolitics*, Anne Brunon-Ernst has challenged this reading of both Foucault and Bentham. Many Anglophone scholars of Bentham since 1975 have greatly lamented Foucault's reading of Bentham in *Discipline and Punish* because of its apparent dismissal of Bentham's passionate and consistent advocacy against legal and extralegal oppression. By focusing on this one project, and in a way that seems to downplay the inhumane conditions it was intended to ameliorate, Foucault is often held responsible for turning Bentham into a philosophical punch line. However, Brunon-Ernst points out that, before 1975, Bentham had already faded into obscurity except in the work of a few specialists. Foucault inspired a genuinely rejuvenated interest in Bentham among French philosophers, beginning with Jean-Pierre Cléro and Christian Laval, whose translations and advocacy for Bentham scholarship since the 1990s have produced a wave of Bentham scholarship in the French context, including Emmanuelle de Champs's excellent recent book *Enlightenment and Utility.* Brunon-Ernst goes on to show that truly Benthamite utilitarian concepts and ideas abound in Foucault's oeuvre, even if, as she writes, "Foucault's aim was not to interpret Bentham's thought, but to use his theories, projects and concepts to feed into his own strategic discourse."[10] While Foucault has inspired French philosophers to take up Bentham for serious reconsideration, the effect of Foucault's *Discipline and Punish* on Bentham studies elsewhere has had a less salutary effect. It may be difficult to see that much of what we admire in Foucault's oeuvre is Benthamist; the subtitle of the second volume of *The History of Sexuality* is *The Use of Pleasure,* distinguishable from utilitarianism only in that, for Bentham, there is no use but pleasure.

Soni on *Eudaimonia*

In my own academic field of interdisciplinary eighteenth-century studies, Bentham has not fared well outside of the work of Frances Ferguson. As a counter-Enlightenment philosopher who despised the normative aesthetic, political, ethical, theological, economic, and social values of his contemporaries but never produced any galvanizing works of beauty or genius, he is barely read at all. Unlike the French or British Jacobins of his time, Bentham was cynical about radical political movements, which tended to employ the soaring discourse of egalitarian rights only to weaponize the resentment of disenfranchised persons to whom liberty and representation would never actually be extended. In literary and cultural studies, that Jacobin rhetoric of radicalism is often read as inspiring, rather than disingenuous, and Bentham's critiques of virtue ethics and liberal rights do not offer an equally powerful alternative rhetoric of radical legal and social reform—a failure he felt keenly throughout his life.

In that vein, Vivasvan Soni's *Mourning Happiness,* published in 2010, identifies Jeremy Bentham as the philosopher who effectively killed happiness by reducing it to a mere quantum of individual pleasure. Soni demonstrates that the classical secular definition of *eudaimonia*—flourishing as the result of a satisfying life devoted to excellence—was eroded in eighteenth-century literary and philosophical discourse by sentimentalism, commerce, philosophy, and literature, culminating in Bentham's reduction of happiness to mere enjoyment. Soni argues that Bentham, like most modern political theorists, wants to recover the supreme value of happiness/*eudaimonia* from classical thought, while employing a selfish, consumerist, hedonistic modern meaning of happiness as a simple feeling. "When we attempt to accord the absolute privilege of the classical concept to the modern affective one, we discover that it cannot support this privilege."[11] Of course, happiness is not a matter that Bentham took lightly, nor took for granted in the same sense intended by novelists, politicians, or advertisers, for whom "happiness" may conveniently accord with whatever coercive moral or commercial behavior they are presenting as desirable. The presumptive "we" of Soni's analysis were not a coherent discourse community in Bentham's time any more than we are in the twenty-first century.

It may seem that to recategorize happiness as a matter of pleasure rather than moral satisfaction would be to trivialize it. Soni concludes that Bentham's collapse of happiness into personal enjoyment is responsible, in part, for the destruction of the Enlightenment's neoclassical formulation of happiness as the highest good of moral and political discourse. "At the moment that the word 'happiness' is captured by pleasure, we lose an important way of relating to the narratives of our lives. . . . This will always risk sounding like asceticism but it is our only chance for a concept that will be able to sustain a politics of happiness."[12] In Soni's account, the liberationist potential of happiness as a political end lies in its dependence on a personal narrative of moral fulfillment, and to empty happiness of moral content is to render it politically powerless.

It is important to note that pleasure is never limited in Bentham's work to sensory pleasure, but also includes emotional, moral, social, intellectual, and other pleasures, as outlined in the delightful *Table of the Springs of Action.* The *Table* lists fourteen classes of pleasures and pains in total: Palate, Sexual Appetite, other Senses, Wealth, Power, Curiosity, Amity, Reputation, Religion, Sympathy, Antipathy, Labour, Death, and

Self-Regard.[13] Under each class is a list of corresponding desires, actions, emotions positive and negative, as well as lists of attributes ascribed in common discourse to persons who seek each pleasure, labeled eulogistic, neutral, or dyslogistic. That is, Bentham did not seek to define happiness or pleasure, nor to prescribe a correct means of attaining either, but to study the widest possible variety of human action in the context of the discourse available to describe those actions. The only prescriptive aspect of Bentham's study of pleasure is that he laments the paucity of eulogistic terms available for sensory pleasures, especially when they are enjoyed by members of disenfranchised groups, such as women, laborers, and sexual nonconformists.

These groups, who lacked direct representation in positions of authority in politics, philosophy, and religion, were conveniently expected to comfort themselves with the classical ethos of stoicism and asceticism that would produce "true" happiness, while men of means enjoyed the pleasures of the bottle and the body to any excess they pleased. In a pseudonymous work titled *Analysis of the Influence of Natural Religion on the Temporal Happiness of Mankind,* Bentham skeptically interrogated the claims of philosophers who advocated for a return to the classical ethics of *eudaimonia* from within a vaguely Christianist social system. He writes, "There can be no sympathy either for the enjoyments or the sufferings of others, where the thoughts of an individual are absorbed in averting posthumous torments or in entitling himself to a posthumous happiness—and where this object, important as it is, is involved in such obscurity, as to leave him in a state of perpetual anxiety and apprehension."[14] Without pleasurable experiences of any kind, and under the threat of eternal damnation, all of the positive community-building virtues of generosity, kindness, and sociability become impossible. Bentham's concern in this work is specifically directed at proponents of so-called natural religion, in which doctrine was not primarily based on scripture but on semi-secular classical ethics of goodness and happiness. He feared that "natural religionists" had effectively made misery a disciplinary mechanism of social control by convincing disenfranchised persons that happiness is waiting for them at the end of a life supposedly well lived, without pleasure, safety, or even custodianship of their own bodies.

While much of the secondhand mockery of Bentham by people who have never read him might be waved off, the charges against Bentham by Dickens, Foucault, and Soni are all serious. They describe a recognizably modern form of despair, a sense that the potential for joy has been stolen from our lives by quantification, even as we strive to realize our ambitions for education, work, and family. Anyone who lives and works in the twenty-first-century economy is too familiar with claims that individual happiness must be sacrificed for the sake of efficiency, discipline, surveillance, progress, optimization, austerity, and "the bottom line." When we consider how Bentham's felicific calculus has been used by capitalists and fascists to obfuscate the spiritual essence of humanity behind clouds of easily manipulated data, it seems efficacious to dismiss Bentham's utilitarianism rather than engage with its frustrating and thorny particulars. Bentham was well aware that presenting a new method of conceiving of right and wrong and applying it to penal law was answering a question that no one had asked, in a manner that neither flattered nor entertained his reader. I must admit that my initial attempts to engage with Bentham's work were put off in this way by Bentham himself, who seems to find even his own writing unbearable.

My assessment of Bentham shifted in 2014, when the *Guardian* published a review by the historian Faramerz Dabhoiwala[15] of a new volume containing a series of notes Jeremy Bentham wrote during the 1810s on the topic of what he then called "sexual irregularity." Far from the image I had in my mind of Bentham as an inhumane calculator, I found this work devastating in its compassion, rage, and desire for justice for disenfranchised groups. In one of these essays, Bentham compares same-sex intercourse to abortion and the uprising of enslaved and colonized people, noting that all three are described by politically enfranchised European men as "unnatural" behaviors, only because they can offer no evidence that they are more harmful to society than the evils to which they are reactions (violence against same-sex partners, repudiation of single mothers, or enslavement). And the mere feeling of disgust for the behavior of another does not constitute any real form of harm. Addressing the physical abhorrence for same-sex intimacy in an early manuscript from when he was in his early twenties, Bentham writes:

> I remember once to have affronted a female relation by not killing a Toad which had incurred her indignation by looking ugly: The harmless and persecuted reptile looked up at me as if to supplicate my compassion: I laid hands on him, but it was to remove him to a place of safety.

The unhappy wretches of whom I am speaking, are like this Toad:
they are very ugly, but there is no reason for killing them for all that.

The reason too of the bulk of the people for wanting to see them lose
their lives is precisely the same which endanger'd that of this animal.[16]

A mere difference of aesthetics is all that causes disgust, and, Bentham
makes clear, disgust is often the reaction relatively powerful persons have
to the less powerful when they engage in behavior and experience feelings that are unfamiliar. Like abortion and rebellion, same-sex intimacy is
apparently worth risking death for; Bentham argues that all three must be
seen as resistance to intolerable social servitude, in which the majority of
people have been forced to relinquish custodianship of their own flesh to
those who would use them for their own purposes.

In Bentham's felicific calculus, the numbers should obviously fall out
on the other side: that wealthy and powerful men would be forced by
data, if not by compassion, to realize that women, laborers, colonized
and enslaved persons, and sexual and gender minorities far outnumber them, and that the happiness of society depends on the recognition of each of those persons as a full citizen whose political, social,
and economic enfranchisement was—and is—an emergency. "It is the
greatest happiness of the greatest number that is the measure of right and
wrong."[17] That is, a member of a legally disenfranchised group of people
cannot trust the tiny minority of self-interested property-owning men,
who control the government, the economy, the church, and philosophical
discourse, to decide whose pleasure may be allowed and whose is a crime.

The publication of these excerpts from Bentham's manuscripts on
sexual nonconformity has helped to clarify the ethical purpose behind
some of Bentham's more baffling and circular arguments, where he
seems to have intended to advocate for sexual minorities and other
oppressed groups, but feared that even naming the discriminatory laws
against them could be dangerous. In 2016 Stefan Waldschmidt published "Bentham, Pater, and the Aesthetics of Utilitarian Sex," on the
relationship between Bentham's epicureanism and that of later Victorian Aestheticists. Bart Schultz's chapter on Bentham in his 2017 book
The Happiness Philosophers asks readers to consider him not as a dull
calculator but as a kind of prophet, especially in the light of the papers
on sexual nonconformity. Malcolm Quinn's 2017 article "Jeremy Bentham on Liberty of Taste" reads Bentham's sexual nonconformity papers

as an extended repudiation of David Hume's aesthetic theory. In 2019 Frances Ferguson published her analysis of Bentham's aesthetic theory with respect to sexual nonconformity, "Not Kant, but Bentham: On Taste." And in the spring of 2020 UCL Press published a collection of essays inspired by Bentham's writing on aesthetics, sexual nonconformity, and the penal code, *Bentham and the Arts* (ed. Julius, Quinn, and Schofield). This renewed interest in Bentham suggests that the publication of *Of Sexual Irregularities* facilitated a shift in attitudes toward Bentham's work that was difficult for Anglophone readers of philosophy to make without ready access to this material. In these short excerpts from Bentham's disparate and disorganized manuscripts on sexual nonconformity, an intriguing conception of Bentham emerges as a writer whose most urgent priority was not, as many suspect, developing efficient and effective methods for state and economic power, but to convince the state to make life endurable for people whose knowledge, tastes, and experiences as disenfranchised persons disqualify them from participation in the common-sense rhetoric of liberal post-Enlightenment discourse.

In the light of the excerpts published in *Of Sexual Irregularities,* Bentham's archival manuscripts at UCL become legible in a new way, as nearly every period of Bentham's writing is supported by lengthy annotations regarding the intended political purpose of his published work, narrating his thought process in analyzing the legal and philosophical paradoxes that he found in the extant discourses of power based on sex, gender, and class. Historically, Bentham scholars have attempted to bisect his career into reformist and radical phases, suggesting that he recanted some of his youthful complicity with oppressive power. Anglophone philosophers of the past two hundred years have tended to pit Bentham against himself by seeing in this shift a genuine philosophical rift between his earlier and later ideas.

This rift is less apparent, it seems, for philosophers familiar with his extensive writings in French as well as with his manuscripts. Emmanuelle de Champs writes that she "attempts to avoid two pitfalls into which studies of Bentham are liable to fall. The first is presenting the philosopher's ideas as an isolated system, abstracted from the historical conditions in which they were put to paper. . . . The second pitfall is segmenting the study of his thought chronologically."[18] Like de Champs, I find that these two "pitfalls"—his supposed philosophical isolation, and his supposed rift with himself—all but disappear with examination into

Bentham's manuscript writing and correspondence, in which it is clear that Bentham's intentions were always radical and responsive to historical conditions and events, though his more youthful published works demonstrate a desire to engage rhetorically with the agents of power he would later criticize more openly. His radicalism as an older man must also be considered in the context of criticism he leveled at many self-identified radicals and revolutionaries of his own time, whom he found to be as oppressive to vulnerable groups as the supposed moderates.

Rather than divide Bentham's career into the reformist and the radical phases, I believe it would be more accurate to divide it, roughly, into the eighteenth-century optimist phase and the nineteenth-century pessimist phase. During his rhetorically optimistic period, Bentham believed that he could promote the amelioration of suffering by developing schemes to demonstrate the benefit of liberation for the patriarchal oppressors themselves. If he could only convince them, through reason, that it was in their self-interest to do so, they would change the laws, divest from colonialism, promote women's education, suffrage, and bodily autonomy, and decriminalize consensual nonreproductive sexual intercourse.

Bentham developed his theory of the felicific calculus during this early, optimistic, ameliorationist period. Having qualified for the bar in 1769, he rejected a career in the law, since, as an "expositor" of British law, he could only become an accessory to the oppression of the penal code. As a reformer, however, he would tirelessly advocate for revisions of the penal code, including extensive critical commentaries on the Poor Laws. As they stood, the Poor Laws made it nearly impossible for laborers and people in debt to get the bare necessities of life. For example, Bentham notes that the new government licensure of midwives made it effectively illegal for women who had expertly served impoverished communities all their lives to practice their trade. In every realm of society, the people who needed the most help were the least able to get it, as the laws created incentives to see the poor as a drag on the economy, rather than a source of valuable labor and expertise, and, if they could be kept healthy, the political backbone of the nation.

Likewise, during this period Bentham seems to have believed he could successfully argue that the government ought to protect victims of homophobic mob violence by repealing the Buggery Act 1533 and instead instituting protections against its would-be vigilantes.[19] The bigotry of the penal code was that it criminalized everyone who was already

politically and socially disenfranchised. The case of male same-sex intimacy seemed to Bentham an obvious testing ground for the law to correct itself; if violators were, in many cases, otherwise fully enfranchised
men with access to "rights," then surely legislators could be convinced
to extend the liberty of bodily pleasure to them. That one person might
prefer same-sex partners rather than heterosexual intercourse was a
matter as immutable and morally insignificant as preferring a particular
flavor or smell. And if he could be successful in this argument, he could
also convince legislators that physical liberty must be extended also to
the poor, to laborers, to colonized persons, and to women.

However, despite the rise of secularism, the spread of education, the
increasing inclusiveness of the press, and the movement toward libertarian rights discourse, violence against sexual nonconformity seemed
to grow with each year. Bentham suspected that the problem was normativity itself—that legislators had confused aesthetic disgust for penal
imperative, and that when aesthetic disgust is confused for justice, it
results in performances of excessive, even limitless cruelty. In one of his
1770s manuscripts, as he wrestled with his rage about the injustice of the
penal code, Bentham wrote, "Vain man, that makest thyself the standard of every thing—that can't suffer no passions but what are thy Passions—that makest even a merit of feeling nothing like indulgence for a
fellow-creature who neither injures thee nor any one—Say are there not
miseries enough already upon this Earth without thy heedless cruelty
adding to the Heap?"[20] The biggest obstacle to the liberation of disenfranchised people was that authorities simply had no ability or motive
to imagine with compassion the experiences of people whose pleasures
or conditions of life were significantly different from their own. Bentham feared that although the penal code might mercifully treat a man
of status who commits fraud, the aesthetic disgust legislators felt for the
motivations of sexual nonconformists, women, and laborers inspired
sadistic impulses, wishing to see the perpetrator humiliated, if not anni-
hilated, rather than merely chastised. They could not sympathize with a
craving for same-sex intimacy any more than they could imagine being
a woman impregnated through coercion, a laborer whose livelihood has
been criminalized, or a person kidnapped and enslaved thousands of
miles from home.

The solution to the bigotry of the law was clearly the full political enfranchisement of marginalized persons who could represent themselves.

Bentham watched in dismay as the so-called revolutionary era produced soaring rhetoric about equality and rights, while perpetuating an exclusively patriarchal ruling class, who owned human beings, profited from colonialism, abetted genocide of indigenous peoples, exploited laborers, controlled women's bodies and limited their minds, and persecuted anyone whose sexual pleasure did not contribute to population growth. Bentham wrote a series of open letters and pamphlets to the governments of Great Britain, the new United States, Spain, and revolutionary France, demanding each of these nations live up to the promise of their political rhetoric and grant all of their citizens *bodily* autonomy at least, as a start.

In this early, optimistic phase of Bentham's career, he believed that the suffering of the populace could be ameliorated by convincing legislators that it was in their own economic and political interest to expand and secure liberty from law, with protections for groups without the means to sue or threaten for redress. He warned oppressors that the time would come when all these groups would join together, rise up, and seize power, with violence if necessary, often in language that sounds sympathetic to the plight of discriminatory rulers. Bentham assured each of these governments that if they expanded protections for liberty and security to all citizens, the result could only be economic and political stability.

The most controversial project Bentham embarked on during this time was his plan for the Panopticon prison, which was an attempt to convince the British government to invest in the health and reform of convicted felons, rather than leaving them in a dungeon to die of disease or violence while waiting for the hangman. He knew that the abhorrence of criminals ran so deep that in order to advocate for their survival, he had to develop a way to make their survival profitable. The Panopticon would consist of individual cells arrayed around a central tower, wherein a guard might or might not sit; Bentham proposed that he himself should be the first gaoler, and he would take no pay at all. Additionally, he imagined a device that would allow prisoners to get as much exercise as they wished while helping to turn a watermill, thus earning their keep through their labor and offsetting the costs of building and maintaining the prison.

During Bentham's lifetime, the Panopticon was never built, and he complained bitterly about the project's failure after the resignation in 1801 of Prime Minister William Pitt the Younger, who had entertained Bentham's correspondence. It had been a proposal in which all boats would rise: prisoners would be healthier and more capable of return-ing to society, and the government would spend less on prisons and executions. This disappointment contributed to the more cynical, sec-ond phase of Bentham's philosophy, in which he began to realize that the suffering of oppressed people was not just an unfortunate side effect of limited resources, but the entire motivation for having resources to begin with.

Long after Bentham's death, the Panopticon has become a metaphor-ical and even architectural model for every kind of institution: prisons, factories, public spaces, offices, schools, and shopping malls all repli-cate the appearance of privacy with the fear of invisible surveillance to encourage each individual subject to contribute to maximum produc-tivity, repressing their own will for the sake of the purported collective good. What Bentham failed to predict in the first half of his career was the limitless sadism of powerful men. He believed that if they could be convinced to invest in general happiness with the temptation of greater economic benefit, they would. Instead, he found that they only wanted to employ his schemes for economic benefit while maintaining the dehumanizing fear and demoralizing sorrow they extracted from those they exploited. Creating pain was the goal, not a side effect.

Throughout his earlier writings, Bentham regrets his rhetorical fail-ures, having failed to convince anyone with political power to extend even harmless liberties. After the failure of the Panopticon project, he began to develop a theory of "sinister interest," which is the name he gave to the unaccountable, excessive sadism of powerful men. In some cases, sinister interest seemed to be material—denying liberty and political and economic power is one way for the powerful to maintain control without challenge—but as he would later find, sinister interest even seemed to operate where no material benefit could be identified. His former skepti-cism about particular institutions, like law, religion, or philosophical dis-course, began to bleed into one another as he saw that what they all had in common was a unified desire to humiliate, marginalize, and persecute anyone who might demand custodianship of their own body.

While claiming to promote the happiness and liberty of all people, these institutions have quietly perpetuated premodern patriarchal con-ceptions of social order, in which the bulk of the populace lives in self-denial and privation so that the power of the landowning class can be maintained without challenge. In an 1822 note to a new edition of *An*

Introduction to the Principles of Morals and Legislation, Bentham recalls having heard that in 1776 Alexander Wedderburn, then solicitor general, had expressed fear that the "greatest happiness principle" of utilitarianism was "dangerous." Forty-six years after Wedderburn's original comment, Bentham publicly identifies the motivation for this fear, not in his own lack of clarity or rhetorical skill, which he had often lamented, but in the "sinister interest" that a man of power and wealth like Wedderburn has in holding the bulk of the populace in a state of misery and disenfranchisement. "*Dangerous* it therefore really was, to the interest— the sinister interest—of all those functionaries, himself included, whose interest it was, to maximize delay, vexation, and expense, in judicial and other modes of procedure, for the sake of the profit, extractable out of the expense. In a Government which had for its end in view the greatest happiness of the greatest number, Alexander Wedderburn might have been Attorney General and then Chancellor: but he would not have been Attorney General with £15,000 a year, nor Chancellor, with a peerage, with a veto upon all justice, with £25,000 a year, and with 500 sinecures at his disposal, under the name of Ecclesiastical Benefices, besides *et ceteras.*"[21] In this shocking accusation, Bentham gives Wedderburn's sinister interest a name and numbers; his literal interest is a financial investment in denying enfranchisement to the bulk of the people. But Wedderburn's fear is expressed as fear, not of the political danger of widespread enfranchisement, but of the social chaos of widespread happiness. In the last part of his career, Bentham began to recognize that his detractors only pretended not to understand his argument; rather, they were terrified of ruling over people who could become the rightful custodians of their own bodily pleasure and political power.

In his projected third volume of *Not Paul, but Jesus,* discussed at greater length in chapter 4, Bentham traces this connection between material and social sinister interest back to the Pharisees, who promoted not only a fear of God and of power but also a fear of pleasure and happiness in the present. "Set in array to him at every turn did Jesus find the Pharisees: the Pharisees with their asceticism, their hypocrisy, and their overweening influence. / Every superstition by which human comfort is abridged found his doctrine occupied in undermining it, found them and their sinister interest no less busy in its defence."[22] Here the sinister interest of the Pharisees is pitted against the power of Jesus, whose life Bentham interprets at monumental length as a martyrdom for *true* utility—refusing economic and reproductive imperatives; erasing discrimination on the basis of status, gender, and ethnic identity; and facilitating intimacy, comfort, and the present enjoyment of human life. Bentham came to see that sinister interest was often not a particular amount of money or a titled position; the pleasure of sadism toward less powerful people was a reward in itself for men in positions of authority.

On January 3, 1818, in a haunting series of numbered notes titled "Pleasures of the Bed," Bentham speculated on the urge to use religion and philosophy as justifications for inciting violence against nonreproductive sexual pleasure. He concluded that legislators have restricted the physical pleasure of sexual intercourse to reproduction while prohibiting sexual liberty in order to render the populace joyless, guilty, lonely, and miserable—hopeless enough to be silenced in their demands for political or economic enfranchisement.

> 39. Pleasures
>
> life valueless: being without well-being. Pain remaining its value to be negative.
>
> 40. Philosophic pride, and religious terror have joined in the endeavour to deprive men of all pleasure of which mind is not the seat yet take away impressions you take away ideas take away sensation you take away understanding: take away pleasures of the body you take away those of the mind.
>
> 41. With all this before them men have waged unceasing war against bodily pleasure, wholesale and retail.[23]

In this sense, Bentham is perhaps the most empiricist of all eighteenth-century British philosophers in that he refuses to allow any of what he called "fictions"—what we might term "ideology"—to intervene in the value of sensory experience, which exists for its own sake rather than to elevate our attention elsewhere. As Waldschmidt notes, Bentham's attention to sensory experience is tantamount to that of Walter Pater: "For both Bentham and Pater, the art of life is a matter of maximizing sensations without the reproductive family."[24] While Pater wrote about sensory experience in a lively, literary way that wins him many undergraduate acolytes even today, Bentham never managed to make the case for sense compelling to readers, in part perhaps because, unlike Pater, in whose work queerness remains a tantalizing suggestion, Bentham lacked the subtlety to merely suggest the acts for which he advocated decriminalization.

Bentham goes on in this 1818 manuscript to speculate that legislators, philosophers, and religious leaders have all joined their efforts to stop nonreproductive sexuality for the same reason that they forbid suicide. In denying the masses custodianship of their own bodies, the "sinister interest" of the powerful is made clear: "44. Maximizing life and minimizing pleasure being the object of the [ ]²⁵ he must keep up life as a receptacle for pain, and allow pleasures of the bed adequate for the production of the maximum of those who for the purpose of this pain shd possess life."²⁶ Near the end of his life, and hopeless of success in reform, Bentham instead theorized that power feeds on human misery—on the joyless people who do not even have the liberty to end their own lives, and who are damned to satisfy themselves with exclusively reproductive sex, only so that pain may be perpetuated in the next generation.

Bentham developed his theory of "sinister interest" in the 1810s, alongside his most complete and explicit arguments about sexual persecution, which he came to link with slavery, colonialism, and the oppression of women. Victims of these forms of political violence were expected to recognize, or *to already know,* that the sublime language of rights was never intended for them. Without custodianship of their own bodies, or even the Lockean natural right to protect themselves from harm, these groups became, Bentham suggests, "a receptacle for pain," with neither the right to take their own lives, nor the power to overthrow those who celebrate their misery.

The Totalizing Impulse

Jeremy Bentham has had a particularly troubled legacy in the history of philosophical discourse, for a different set of reasons from those of literary and cultural historians. His work is more often described by philosophers than studied, as he represents a kind of philosophical extremism only invoked for the purpose of demonstrating the evils that would necessarily arise from respecting the desires of the masses over those of the ruling class. In philosophical contexts as a graduate student,

I only heard him invoked as a spokesman for radical libertarianism, or confusingly, bureaucratic totalitarianism, both of which, I would later learn, were ideologies he spent his entire career battling. His contemporaries, including his protégé John Stuart Mill, mocked his eccentric distaste for elite aesthetics; they found something dehumanizing in his rejection of virtue ethics and poetic sentiment in favor of a protosociological deontology of individual human motivation and its observable effects. Bentham's style—methodically organized, obsessively detailed, rhetorically precise—suggested to Karl Marx a mind devoid of beauty or human feeling, without any appeals to the epistemology of consensus that formed the basis for European philosophical discourse of his era. Too Scholastic for the Enlightenment, too egalitarian for Romanticism, and too epicurean for Victorians, Bentham was an outrage to those who read his published work, and a scandal to those who read his private manuscripts.

Reactions to Bentham's political and philosophical work range from flippantly dismissive to deeply enraged. Most, but not all, of these critiques have been made by those whose political, economic, and cultural enfranchisement has never been seriously challenged by systemic legal oppression. Many of these critiques come in the form of aesthetic distaste for Bentham's writing and ideas, but others have been made out of genuine concern for a legally oppressed population that the writer feels has been made *more* vulnerable by the supposedly widespread adoption of utilitarian ideas and methods. I will not claim that implementations of certain Benthamite arguments and efficiencies have been a positive influence; clearly, the common usage of the word "utilitarian" suggests grim asceticism for the greater good—the opposite of Bentham's definition of utility as a personal experience of pleasure. His felicific calculus values the personal pleasure of the masses over the pleasure that elites take in depriving others of pleasure. So how did this come to pass? How did Bentham's ideas—even his name—become synonymous with economic and penal systems in their most oppressive iterations?

The central claim of Bentham's utilitarianism is that the individual subject must have the liberty to do what one enjoys, as long as the action itself does not cause pain to another person, no matter how uncommon the pleasure may be, and not what an authority says will contribute most to the benefit of society. For Bentham, asceticism—self-denial of a desired pleasure—is the internalized voice of sadistic authority, long before there was any conception of a Freudian superego. In a manuscript dated November 14, 1817, he writes:

> By the *ascetic principle,* the *principle of asceticism,* is for shortness *asceticism,* understood that principle which prescribes the rejection of pleasure in any shape or in any quantity, on any other ground than that of the acquisition of pleasure in a greater amount, or the avoidance of pain or uneasiness to an amount more than equivalent: or in regard to pain, the avoidance of pain in any shape or in any quantity on any other ground than that of avoidance of pain in a greater amount or the acquisition of pleasure to an amount more than equivalent.
> This principle is the direct opposite of the principle of utility.[27]

Without maximal liberty for everyone—including women, laborers, and sexual minorities—to seek pleasure and avoid pain as its primary goal, the logic of utilitarianism can only be exercised as a justification for oppression. John Stuart Mill's introduction of ideological hierarchies of aesthetics and virtue has resulted in a philosophy of utilitarianism that is drained of its radical power, because it perpetuates the common-sense rhetoric of the Enlightenment that normative aesthetics and moral sentiment may take over authority from religion to tell the individual subject what and how to desire in the modern state.

This tension between the individual and the collective, between shared experience and differentiation, suggests an epistemic paradox. The purported universality of any normative, common-sense hierarchy of aesthetic and moral value is not based on anyone's individual experience, and serves as a standard against which the interests of *most* people can be marked as irrelevant, or even pathological. The Marxist queer theorists Eric O. Clarke and Kevin Floyd have each wrestled with this problem of totalization, demonstrating that advocates of queer liberation find themselves either replicating the terms of exclusion and differentiation imposed by bourgeois heteronormative oppression, or else asserting a kind of alternate queer totality in which oppressed sexual minorities are presumed to share the same experiences of marginalization and erasure. In *Virtuous Vice,* Clarke writes, "An equality of competitive, atomistic individuals, Marx argued, was an equality contradicted by its retention of a bourgeois standard of the citizen. Bourgeois civil society could only ever effect what might be best termed a managed inequity. It thus stalled, and thereby dissembled, its self-proclaimed project of 'human emanci-pation.'"[28] The logic of mediated representation and public advocacy is inherently universalizing; any attempt to present an individual experience of nonnormative desire is to render it, at worst, a spectacle of perversity or, at best, a meaningless personal choice among legitimated options for desire. Advocates for sexual nonconformists continue to struggle with the same rhetorical problem that Bentham wrestled with throughout his career; how can legal, political, and social toleration of sexual nonconfor-mity come about in the context of the disgust of people with the power to commit violence? They ask queer people not to act on their queerness; we ask disgusted people not to act on their disgust. Bentham suggests that this is a false conflict; we must only convince disgusted people not to participate in the queer sex that disgusts them. In this sense, Bentham's idealism seems naive; Marx insists that in a capitalist system of knowledge production, all representations of value are normative and prescriptive.

Kevin Floyd attempts to reconcile Marx with queer particularization in *The Reification of Desire,* suggesting that emerging forms of queer advo-cacy may begin to challenge the epistemological limitations of bourgeois normativity in the public sphere. "Queer thought in this way operates in the context of a history of competing forms of critical knowledge produc-tion, competing critiques of compulsory heterosexuality, which cannot be separated from practice, which both emerge from and feed back into practice. And the queer critique of sexuality's epistemological particular-ization is again itself as dynamic as it is limited; these limitations are elas-tic rather than given."[29] Although there is no "outside" capitalism within capitalism, there is a potentially destabilizing critique based on individual desire and pleasure that has found voice in the public sphere through emerging media. Floyd argues for a queer Marxism that challenges con-sensus epistemology without erasing or marginalizing the bodily pleasure of the individual subject. Floyd's reading of Marxism is more optimistic than Clarke's, suggesting possible parallels with Jeremy Bentham's politics of individual pleasure and maximal human liberty.

Sadly, Marx himself derided Bentham ("a genius in the way of bour-geois stupidity") as "that soberly pedantic and heavy-footed oracle of the 'common sense' of the nineteenth-century bourgeoisie."[30] In a foot-note, he clarifies that Bentham's greatest fault was that "with the dry-est naïveté he assumes that the modern petty bourgeois, especially the English petty bourgeois, is the normal man. Whatever is useful to this peculiar kind of normal man, and to his world, is useful in and for itself. He applies this yardstick to the past, the present, and the future."[31] It is a challenge to imagine where in Bentham's work Marx found evidence of this normative "yardstick" when, in every aspect of his work, Bentham rigorously foregrounded the experiences and desires of nonnormative, nonconforming, disenfranchised, marginalized, and oppressed groups as deserving of liberty and custodianship of their own bodies—including not only women, enslaved persons, and people who seek same-sex intimacy but also necrophiles, suicidal people, and nonhuman animals. I can only presume that Marx read Bentham through the deforming lens of the normative bourgeois discourse he described as inescapable, which makes every description into a prescription. Marx presumes that Bentham's defense of the pleasures of less-educated people is somehow a declaration that those tastes must in turn be elevated in value above those of the educated, rather than merely permitted to continue. But it is important to note that Marx's distaste for Bentham is posed as aesthetic distaste, when its aim is to discredit Bentham's principled rejection of any normative idea—bourgeois, elite, or otherwise—of "human nature."

Likewise, Friedrich Nietzsche characterized Bentham's influence on moral philosophy to be on the whole pernicious, not because of what he wrote, but because his writing was too boring.

> May I be forgiven the discovery that all moral philosophy so far has been boring and was a soporific and that "virtue" has been impaired more for me by its *boring* advocates than by anything else, though I am not denying their general utility. . . . Consider, for example, the indefatigable, inevitable British utilitarians, how they walk clumsily and honorably in Bentham's footsteps. . . . Not a new idea, no trace of a subtler version or twist of an old idea, not even a real history of what had been thought before: altogether an *impossible* literature, unless one knows how to flavor it with some malice.[32]

That Nietzsche would not see in Bentham a fellow traveler seems almost absurd; like Nietzsche, Bentham also wished to destroy the hold that classical "virtue" maintained over modern life, though with admittedly far more egalitarian aims in mind. Bentham stands in here for the whole range of British moral philosophy, despite not being a moral philosopher and spending his entire life attacking the hypocrisies of moral philosophy. Nietzsche's distaste for Bentham, like Marx's, is entirely on aesthetic grounds. Even if he had something important to say, it simply does not matter because Bentham did not express it in an important-sounding manner.

As I discuss in the next chapter, John Stuart Mill also criticized Bentham's rejection of aesthetic hierarchies, arguing that the pleasures of uneducated people offer no opportunity (unlike poetry) to instill useful moral and cultural values. Like Marx, Mill also assumes that Bentham is not advocating for liberty from elitist indoctrination but is instead advocating for antielitist cultural supremacy—a tyranny of dolts and babies. These totalizing impulses of modern Eurocentric philosophy, whether based in consensus epistemology, categorical imperative, or rational pragmatism, render Bentham's work monstrous, assuming that, for example, his defense of "push-pin," a simple children's game, implies that all poetry and music must cease and everyone must take up push-pin.[33] Rather, in the context of his private work, Bentham demonstrates a consistent concern that aesthetic hierarchies of any kind too easily become an efficient proxy for discrimination and disenfranchisement. As Floyd argues about capitalism, purportedly universal rights and opportunities are ultimately limited on the basis of the subject's complicity in reifying dominant paradigms of desire and pleasure. But in a philosophical discourse prone to totalization, it becomes rhetorically impossible to advocate for oppressed minority groups without being accused of championing an antidemocratic tyranny of one sort or another.

The revolutionary potential of utilitarianism was never realized, in part because later philosophers who might have otherwise admired Bentham's egalitarian impulses balked at his intent to cleanse the law, philosophy, and religion of normative aesthetics. Marx, Mill, and many others have responded with disgust to Bentham's idea that the powerful must allow less powerful people to like or dislike what they please, because taste is immutable. As Bentham himself articulated in a fragment from 1821, "A man can no more cast off regard to his own happiness meaning the happiness of the moment than he can cast off his own skin, or jump out of it."[34] It is perhaps worth noting that these same philosophers have felt that universal suffrage and political representation for disenfranchised groups was premature; borrowing the tactics of utilitarianism but none of its priorities, they insisted that oppressed people must first be educated into a particular set of aesthetic values before they are allowed to obtain and exercise their own political will. For Bentham, forcing someone to want something they do not is not only an act of violence, it is an impossibility. The post-Benthamite strain of practical utilitarianism has been tremendously influential, guiding everything from neoliberal capitalist policy to postrevolutionary cultural genocide and the emergence of the surveillance state—all the aspects of postmodern life that are fundamentally at odds with Bentham's radical advocacy for maximal individual liberty.

Because Bentham's writings on sexual nonconformity and individual pleasure remained suppressed or ignored until quite recently, post-Freudian theory was the only philosophical basis available for the emergence of a twentieth-century politics of queer liberation, which treats sexual variety as a symptom of trauma, at best, if not a pitiable pathology. In Bentham's utilitarianism, the etiology of sexual difference is irrelevant to its political effects; what matters is not why someone desires same-sex intimacy, but that they do, and that they prefer it. I am reminded of Samuel Delany's description of the etiology of sexual nonconformity in *Times Square Red, Times Square Blue,* in the context of the policing of same-sex encounters in modern urban space:

> Consider a large ballroom full of people.
> At various places around the walls there are doors. If one of the doors is open, and the ballroom is crowded enough, after a certain amount of time there will be a certain number of people in the other room on the far side of the open door (assuming the lights are on and nothing is going on in there to keep them out). The third-level theoretical answer to the question "What makes us gay?" troubles the ordinary man or woman on the street for much the same reason it would trouble them if you said, of the ballroom and the room beside it, "The open door is what makes people go into the other room."[35]

Like Delany, Bentham is totally uninterested in what "makes" a person a sexual nonconformist, as if there are not forces that also "make" most people prefer heterosexual partners. The only aspect of same-sex intimacy that matters for the purposes of legal and social enfranchisement is that it happens, rather than why. Sexual choice is, most importantly, a matter of enjoyment and opportunity, rather than a question of normal and abnormal.

Questions about social order, family structures, and moral feeling remain sources of anxiety for many other post-Freudian queer liberationists, who must either assert that "love is love" and disavow difference, or else label themselves as angry, traumatized outcasts. As Kevin Floyd observes, "If gay liberation appropriated the revolutionary erotic implications of universalized desire—directly from Marcuse, indirectly from Freud, and against the assimilationist tendencies of the minoritizing homophile movements—this was necessarily a critical appropriation on the part of a formation that could challenge sexual minoritization and political individuation only by way of a collective, historically situated, insurrectional subjectivity."[36] The consequences of a politics based on a subjective sense of having been *wronged*, either resulting in or as the result of queer desire, has limitations that are beginning to emerge in the twenty-first century. If gay sex, for example, is no longer illegal, and discrimination against people who have gay sex is increasingly prohibited, then what will remain as the political position of a gay person who is neither the product nor the presumed target of social and political violence, yet remains woefully underrepresented in political power? Bentham's writings on sexual nonconformity suggest another political path, one in which each person's happiness, whatever that may be, *because* of its variation from the norm, rather than despite of it, is a significant contribution in itself to the happiness of society.

Bentham was aware that his advocacy for oppressed people, especially sexual nonconformists, inspired this fearful, enraged, disgusted response, and he ultimately came to believe that the sinister interests of the powerful will always react with violent terror to any challenge of the presumed consensus. To suggest that legislators and governors must listen to marginalized persons, not only when they speak in praise of the dominant culture, but also when they criticize it from their own physical and emotional experience, is to threaten the power that authorities have to decide what is in the best interests of the community. Whether these criticisms of Bentham have been the product of ignorance or malice is beyond the purview of this work. Bentham himself wrestled with this question throughout his career, initially believing that if powerful men in public discourse could only know how counterproductive oppression of others was to their own economic and political security, they would surely abandon discriminatory laws and begin to protect the liberty of all persons. Later, Bentham came to believe that the hostility his work met with was simply "sinister interest"—the desire of the powerful to perpetuate the suffering of others, even when there is no expected benefit for themselves.

However, there is a less sinister pair of motivations that I would propose as an alternative to ignorance and cruelty as the justifications for dismissing Bentham. The first is an application of consequentialism; as the theory goes, Bentham may not have endorsed any of the actual implementations of his own ideas, such as the posthumous iterations of the Panopticon, but the fact that they came into being because of his clear and precise understanding of how to efficiently exercise power makes him morally responsible for the postmodern police state, unremunerated productivity demands on workers, mass incarceration, concentration camps, and the USA PATRIOT Act of 2001.[37] Given that Bentham analyzes the observed noxious effects of actions and ideas, it is reasonable to notice that sinister political agents have frequently exploited the mechanisms of oppression defined and analyzed by Bentham without in any way equalizing access to political power. In *Discipline and Punish*, Michel Foucault identified Bentham as the genius behind modern oppression, and it is difficult to deny the evidence that his ideas and plans were implemented to promote the control and humiliation of the populace. Forty-six years after the publication of *Discipline and Punish*, I wonder whether one might apply the same consequentialist analysis to the legacy of Foucault, whose own liberationist agenda can sometimes be difficult to find in the legacy of his work on political and social power carried on by his readers.

The second is an application of consensus epistemology; if, as David Hume argues, moral and aesthetic values are constructs that contribute to general utility by promoting social order, then Bentham's criticism of moral and aesthetic hierarchies could be read as an invitation to chaos and nihilism. If each person's unique sense of pleasure or meaning matters more than a shared sense of cultural value, then communication among members of a society would become impossible. But at no time in the modern era in the Anglophonic world could it be said that countercultural values have not proliferated and thrived, nor that the morals and tastes of the elite class are shared or even admired by anyone else. In the twenty-first century as well as in the eighteenth, low and high art vie for accolades and praise, while revolutionaries clash with advocates for deference to patriarchal authority. During the Enlightenment, countercultures proliferated in the colonies as well as the metropolis, based on alternate ideological allegiances to oppressed racial, gender, sexual, religious, and economic groups, and they each constructed their own political, moral, aesthetic, and rhetorical values.[38] As numerous literary and social historians have shown, subcultures and countercultures seem to have been so prolific and well defined during this period that it is difficult to imagine a consensus epistemology that does not acknowledge the limitations of that consensus to a small community of politically enfranchised men. And yet, it is as possible today as it was in 1750 for members of a demographically homogenous ruling class to assume that everyone shares their values but simply cannot live up to them.

Jeremy Bentham was perhaps the only philosopher of the British Enlightenment to recognize that members of these various subcultures and countercultures were not envious at failing to live "up" to the standards set by elite men, but were often the objects of the envy of elites. Adam Smith had convincingly argued in *The Theory of Moral Sentiments* that the poor sympathize with the pleasures and pains of the rich because they enjoy imagining themselves among their company. But what about disenfranchised persons who were members of communities that rejected the dominant culture for shared alternative values, aesthetics, and methods of communication? For Bentham, the man who engaged in same-sex intimacy emerged as a perfect test-case for alternative desire; a man could be in every other way a member of the ruling class, with property, connections, education, political power, and participation in the public sphere, but if it were known that he preferred sex with men to sex with women— if his taste in one respect did not adhere to the norms of other men like himself—then he was an outlaw of human nature, at the mercy of the executioner or the mob. How much more vulnerable would a woman or an enslaved or disabled person be who did not envy the tastes and values of the ruling class?

Reading Bentham's Critics

So how did things go so terribly wrong for Bentham's legacy? How did someone who devoted every moment of his efforts to the liberation of oppressed persons become a laughable oddity at best, and the evil genius of dehumanizing modernity at worst? I can speculate about six possible reasons for Bentham's failure, moving from his own limitations as a writer and philosopher, to readers who value the traditions of virtue ethics and aesthetic hierarchies more than the potential benefits of the strict aesthetic and political egalitarianism of Bentham.

1. Like most really transformative philosophical thinkers, Bentham is often a terrible writer, especially in his published work. Bentham struggled throughout his life to express himself in a way that readers could understand. He is tedious, long-winded, and apparently frustrated by the likelihood that he will be misread, even as his pen moves across the page. His first drafts contain multiple competing phrases for the same idea, entire lines or paragraphs struck out, annotated, bracketed, and left orphaned. As I discuss in chapter 5, he sometimes longed for a writing partner who could move his readers to feel the truth of his prose, the way that he himself enjoyed gothic novels by women and sexually nonconformist authors. At other times, he wrote instructions to himself about how to be more pleasant to others in conversation and rhetoric. In one series of notes dated March 23, 1795, titled "The Art of Pleasing," Bentham seems to vacillate between insisting, on one hand, that pleasing everyone is not a reasonable or desirable goal and, on the other, that greater rhetorical efficacy could be achieved by engaging with interlocutors one-on-one, rather than in large groups, especially on topics of moral sensitivity.[39] In his published writing, he can be dull, contemptuous of the reader's stupidity and vanity, and prematurely defensive. It was not until I read some of his private papers, addressed to himself, or perhaps to future sympathetic readers, that I felt the urgency of Bentham's liberationist desires. Thanks to the Bentham Project at UCL, these private papers are almost entirely publicly available for free on the Internet, and for those who have not yet learned to decipher his scrawl, they have been mostly transcribed by a global phalanx of volunteer readers.[40] Few of us are as radical about liberty as Bentham, who envisioned political liberties for children, animals, and sexual minorities such as necrophiles which are still difficult to envision, but we are perhaps the less hostile readers he imagined could one day find him.

2. Bentham was extremely fearful of being silenced or killed for his ideas, and censored himself heavily. As bold as much of his published writing was, he also published a great deal under pseudonyms—including his daring works in theology, *Analysis of the Influence of Natural Religion on the Temporal Happiness of Mankind,* and *Not Paul, but Jesus.* But

for every major published work, Bentham had stacks of notes in which he clarified what he intended to say, but felt that he could not because of the limits of intellectual discourse in his time, especially regarding sex and suicide. While *Not Paul, but Jesus* focuses on what Bentham saw as Paul's misreadings of Christ's theology, the notes for *Not Paul, but Jesus* and the planned third volume contain what can only be called a queer reading of Jesus's life as a gay suicide who came to teach children, laborers, and women how to live like free people. From his earliest writings on sexual nonconformity from the 1770s, Bentham expressed excruciating anxiety about his need to address sexual liberation in a violently homophobic culture.[41] In many of these notes, Bentham directly addresses some reader not yet born who will live in a time when his ideas are no longer criminal. In the last decades of his life, he was more able to craft clear and unambiguous arguments for sexual toleration, even if he still found it impossible to convince his contemporaries.

3. Amelioration does not stave off revolution; it hastens it. What I referred to as the "optimistic" earlier phase of his career was also when he developed ameliorationist ideas, pleading with heads of state to clarify and reduce the penal code, excise discriminatory statutes, reduce enforcement of laws against victimless crimes, and provide for briefer and more comfortable detention. In this earlier period, Bentham seemed to believe that sweeping changes to the law could be made that would make clear that the cruelty of the state to disenfranchised people was unprofitable, inconvenient, and inferior in effect to providing all citizens with security and the hope for a decent life. One of the things that I think young Bentham may not have understood about prison reform, reform of the Poor Laws, and the education of women is that their oppressors knew that if these groups were not totally dehumanized and demoralized, they would demand seats in Parliament, with torches if necessary. The happier people are, the harder it is to oppress them.

4. One must also concede that Foucault is, of course, right about the effect Bentham's work really had on the agents of power, even if it was the opposite of his intent. Modern forms of surveillance, optimization, and discipline have resulted in a culture in which most people gladly oppress themselves so the state does not even have to do the work of making us unhappy—we do that all by ourselves. What Bentham seems to have invented in the Panopticon is a scheme for deriving increased productivity from laborers without allowing them to feel as if they

actually own their bodies and pleasures. Bentham imagined a scenario in which all boats could rise simultaneously; patriarchal oppressors figured out how to use that information to raise their own boats, while turning the resentment of the oppressed against one another.

5. Vivasvan Soni's charge, that Bentham reduces happiness to mere physical pleasure, is one that may rankle the sensibilities of the philosophically inclined. Just because the opportunities for morally reflective happiness are unequally distributed should not, perhaps, mean that classical virtue ethics is politically useless, but that its benefits should be expanded to all demographic groups. I have no argument with the democratization of moral purpose, except that, as Bentham argues, the oppressed are *always* expected to prioritize moral purpose over physical gratification. Powerful people are rarely more disgusted than when they see their social inferior enjoying a flavor or a feeling that either does not appeal to them or of which they might be envious. Bentham accuses lawmakers of deriving the penal code from aesthetic disgust for other people's pleasures rather than from any measurable social noxiousness. While the people with relatively little political power are enjoined to desire the life of the mind, the people with the most power are often found desperate for decadence in the sewer. Bentham's empiricist deontology, as we will see, attempts to divorce human action from the euphemistic and dysphemistic moral language that is applied differently to people of different social condition. Who is licensed to feel physical pleasure without stigma? Only those who control the discourse about law and resources are licensed to enjoy pleasure. Until that stigma is removed, one must begin, Bentham argues, with liberation of the body.

6. On some level though, it seems clear that the most dismissive criticisms of Bentham—reducing him to a babbling philistine calculator or a sadistic flinty-eyed gaoler—come from people who have inherited the hegemonic legacy of Eurocentrism: inherited wealth, political enfranchisement, and relatively little public humiliation for their sexual and private pleasures. While Bentham was the rare white wealthy educated man who imagined all human beings as craving bodily autonomy and political representation, those whose lived experience has been homophobia, sexism, racism, imprisonment, and poverty still only rarely find themselves in the position of engaging critically with Enlightenment-era philosophy. Bentham's published and private papers

open a door that many historians of Enlightenment culture would perhaps prefer to remain shut. If it was possible for a bourgeois white man in the eighteenth century to demand a world in which women, laborers, and sexual nonconformists have access to legal redress for infringements of their autonomy, how could our current political realities have emerged differently, if people then or now had ears to hear him?

2

Aesthetics of Pleasure, Ethics of Happiness

Sexual Nonconformity and Happiness

Although most philosophers of the British Enlightenment identified human happiness as the ultimate goal of social, political, economic, and moral reform, they often disavowed the role of physical and sexual pleasure in producing happiness.[1] Jeremy Bentham's intervention in the philosophical conception of happiness was to define it as the immediate aesthetic product of pleasure, rather than the effect of a causal narrative of moral or social fulfillment. According to Bentham, the problem with a moral discourse of happiness is that, through the efforts of philosophers, religious authorities, novelists, and dramatists, happiness had become rigidly normative and narrowly defined in ways that centralized the experiences of politically enfranchised men, at the expense of those who were legally and socially denied custodianship of their own bodies. As his manuscripts from the 1770s through the 1820s demonstrate, nearly all of Bentham's published work in legal reform, moral philosophy, and theology was written alongside notes in which he analyzed sexual liberty as a test case for each of these arguments. In this chapter, I focus on the epistemological and aesthetic arguments in this work, and their relationship to sexual nonconformity as a philosophically legitimate form of aesthetic variety.

Until quite recently, Bentham's manuscripts on sexual liberty have remained largely unknown and difficult to locate. Fearful of reprisal, Bentham withheld these manuscripts from the press, and he wondered whether it was safe to keep writing these notes in which he questioned the criminality of and religious prohibition against sexual nonconformity. To question the legal authority of the state with respect to sexual nonconformity could expose him to accusations of felonious misconduct of his own. In an early series of disjointed notes on sexual nonconformity (undated, but grouped with papers from the early to mid-1770s), Bentham expressed his sense that he had been somehow chosen to do this dangerous philosophical and legal work, and that, having begun to analyze sexual variety and behavior in a systematic and open-minded way, he had made discoveries he simply could not ignore.

> A hundred + a hundred times have I shudder'd at the apprehension of the perils I was exposing myself to in encountering the opinions that are in possession of men's minds on subject:—as often have I readied to turn aside from a road so full of precipices [danger] I have trembled at the thoughts of the indignation that must be raised against the apologist of a crime that has been looked upon by many and those excellent men as the blackest under Heaven. But the dye is now cast, I having thus far pressed with undeviating fidelity the principles of general utility I at first adopted. . . . It shall not be said I at last abandon them from considerations of personal danger.[2]

It is unclear whose accusation Bentham fears, if he were to abandon his work on sexual nonconformity. He seems to feel he has been chosen by fate—"the dye is now cast"—for this work, and that perhaps future generations would think him a coward for abandoning such an important task. Bentham's notes on sexual nonconformity mostly consist of refutations of what seem to him to be exaggerated, meaningless outrage regarding adults enjoying consensual sex in private. In her analysis of Bentham's legal reform, Lea Campos Boralevi notes that Bentham's papers on sexual nonconformity (especially box 74a, in which this quotation appears) seem to constitute a coherent argument for penal reform that centralizes sexual liberty. The 2014 publication of three sets of his 1810s manuscripts in *Of Sexual Irregularities* has sparked renewed interest in Bentham's theories of sexual liberty, and provided an entry point into a vast archive of unpublished material on pleasure, sex, and the misery produced by sexual asceticism.

In his private notes over the course of his sixty years as a philosopher and legal reformer, Bentham consistently uses sexual liberty as a counterpoint to what he perceives as compulsory asceticism for women, colonized and enslaved persons, and sexual nonconformists. In one of his 1770s notes, Bentham analyzes the hatred for sexual nonconformity under the heading "End of Legislation the Greatest Happiness for the Greatest Number": "My abhorrence I feel for it say you is ungovernable [inconquerable]. The very thought is unsupportable—Mine is equal to it—What then is the inference? we shall not do it—but do not you see that if you put it upon mere sentiment [or feeling] the Man in question has just as good a reason for doing it as you have for letting it alone."[3] Bentham insists that mere moral feeling cannot impose one man's disgust onto another man's desire, no matter how strong that disgust may be. To use the law to enforce that disgust with capital punishment is to add a deterrent that is neither needed nor appropriate to the crime. Measuring the tastes of others by the standard of our own tastes as a matter of legal prosecution can only result in legal absurdities like punishing literally victimless crimes like consensual sex as felonies. The problem with using our own sexual feelings and desires to judge and regulate the desires of others is that our physical experiences of pleasure are as individual as our tastes in any of the senses. Bentham claims that sexual nonconformity is not punished with execution for any reason other than that those with political power cannot endure the difference in pleasure experienced by people who do not share their own aesthetic values.

In order to create a discourse of happiness that accounts for all members of the state, Bentham formulates a discourse of sensory pleasure that recognizes and protects aesthetic differences as a duty of proper government. Bentham demonstrates that previous conceptions of happiness in political theory and moral philosophy depended on moral reflection as a precursor to delight, which rendered enjoyment a potential matter of moral reflection and legal judgment. Instead, Bentham asserts, pleasure and pain and the intensity thereof, which cannot be measured by any objective scale, must be left as a matter of individual aesthetic response. In a manuscript from 1800, he writes, "No one man in short has any accurate and minute measure of the intensity of the sensations of any other: much less is there any such thing as an instrument that is to all persons of man a common measure for the intensity of the sensations of all."[4] Bentham determined that the greatest utility depends on the happiness of the greatest number, but that happiness in turn depended on the independent, individual perception of every member of the community to decide which pleasures they would seek, which pains they would avoid, and that these experiences of pleasure and pain should be considered as aesthetic assessments of sensory experience.

In his papers on sexuality, Bentham argues that the neoclassical, moralistic conception of happiness was conceived by politically enfranchised men for whom the happiness of politically disenfranchised persons was abstract, at best, or dangerous, at worst. Bentham feared that as long as happiness is defined according to a metric of morality (as defined by those same men) rather than pleasure, then state-sanctioned violence against women, enslaved and colonized persons, and sexual noncon-formists would perpetuate their oppression and disenfranchisement. Reproductive and sexual freedoms may seem to be trivial aspects of happiness to someone whose own sexual proclivities and reproductive decisions do not provoke lynching or exile.

Lea Campos Boralevi argues that philosophers and legal theorists should look to Bentham as the earliest philosopher to advocate consis-tently for broadening and equalizing security from oppression across the categories of women, sexual and religious minorities, the poor, colonized and enslaved people, and animals. Boralevi shows that each of these categories was singled out for special legal and extralegal cur-tailments of liberty by what Bentham refers to as the "sinister inter-ests" of enfranchised men, which take the form of paternalistic moral knowledge about what is best for the disenfranchised person. Typically, these groups of people were those to whom asceticism and self-denial were mandated as required virtues, while no such asceticism could be required of ruling-class patriarchs. From early in his career, Bentham believed that total emancipation and political enfranchisement would necessitate the end of compulsory asceticism for marginalized people. Boralevi writes, "For their own purposes, ascetic philosophers, priests, lawyers, even dramatists had created these fictions: in truth, it was not in the interest of the people—of their greatest number—that religious and sexual non-conformists were persecuted, that animals were left unprotected, and that women were kept in subjugation. . . . [W]here the formation of sinister interests is prevented by the radical reform of the political system, then these unfortunate delusions will disappear, preju-dice will no longer have a social function, and the oppressed—even those oppressed by the majority—will be emancipated."[5] In physical, aesthetic pleasure, Bentham finds a crucial liberty that is most cur-tailed for disenfranchised groups by the same nations that celebrate the liberal discourse of natural rights. Defining liberty as the ownership and custodianship of one's own body, Bentham concluded that without reproductive and sexual freedom, a human being is less free to pursue happiness than a wild beast.

The Moralization of Aesthetic Variety

A fair analysis of legal rights should begin, Bentham insisted, with analysis of the motivations, actions, and discourse of human behavior. In 1815 and 1817 Bentham published versions of his *Table of the Springs of Action,*[6] which was an attempt to diagram all possible forms of human motivation under different categories, with the neutral, eulogistic, and dyslogistic cultural associations attached to each. This table could be described as an expansion of *Leviathan,* in which Thomas Hobbes had described all possible human motivations as movement toward appetite or away from aversion.[7] In Bentham's *Table,* human motivation is derived from fourteen categories of pleasure, including those of The Palate, The Sceptre, The Trumpet, The Heart, The Pillow, and so on. Under the motive of "Sexual Interest," Bentham lists no eulogistic terms. The only terms we have for sexual desire, he notes, are tainted with opprobrium—venery, lust, lechery, and so forth.

In *An Enquiry Concerning the Principles of Morals,* David Hume had argued that the moral language we use is socially encoded with eulogistic and dyslogistic associations in order to inform us of the real utility—and therefore, moral correctness—of qualities and behaviors. For Hume, morality does not arise, as for Hobbes, from self-love or fear, but from the language we share for the purpose of benefiting society. Hume writes, "General language, therefore, being formed for general use, must be moulded on some more general views, and must affix the epithets of praise or blame, in conformity to sentiments, which arise from the general interests of the community."[8] In locating the source of moral sentiment in the de facto utility function of language, Hume fails to consider that eulogistic and dyslogistic moral language is employed by the powerful in order to inspire the powerless to willingly abandon the pursuit of pleasure.

In his analysis of Bentham's disagreement with Hume about taste, Malcolm Quinn demonstrates that Bentham applies extreme skepticism to language related to aesthetic judgment; Bentham repeatedly argues that a judgment of "bad taste" often serves as a proxy for discrimination against disenfranchised people who share that taste. Of the essays published in *Of Sexual Irregularities,* Quinn writes, "Bentham's three essays on sex and the liberty of taste suggest that discriminating judgements of taste cannot be made free of prejudice, principally because such judgements on what is 'good' and 'bad' in taste perforce reveal their roots in 'the unreflecting emotion and passion of antipathy,' which, when aroused by a difference in taste, can only be appeased by conformity, because these judgements have no basis in actual injury or mischief."[9] Quinn shows that while Hume takes the language of aesthetic judgment for granted as reflective of the real moral and social utility of the pleasure under examination, Bentham consistently interrogates the role of prejudice in forming the fictional category of "bad taste," which is discredited by the pleasure that taste creates, even if only for a small number of people. Although this analysis applies to all aesthetic judgment, it is especially egregious in the case of sexual nonconformity, as this is an instance where prejudice regarding "bad taste" has been totally conflated with moral and even legal judgment. In attempting to cleanse moral and ethical analysis of aesthetic prejudice, Bentham examines behaviors as indicative of pleasure and pain as they are experienced, rather than as a philosopher believes they should be experienced.

During the 1810s, especially, Bentham seems to have been obsessed with the problem of sexual pleasure as perhaps the chief motivation toward human happiness. If pleasure produces happiness, and happiness is the ultimate goal of human existence, then why is sexual pleasure relegated to categorical censure? In his manuscript essay "Of Sexual Irregularities" from 1814, Bentham focuses especially on same-sex male relationships, as they seem to be the sexual relationships most likely to expose participants to legal and social punishment, while also being the least likely to produce social mischief, in the form of unwanted pregnancy, coercion, or other dangers.

In addition to being legally prosecutable under the Buggery Act 1533, sodomy is, Bentham notes, the sex act most likely to be described as "unnatural," a word so closely associated with same-sex intercourse as to be euphemistic for it. The only other two examples Bentham lists of "unnatural acts" are infanticide (including abortion) and political rebellion—both of which, he notes, are the expressions of desperate people who lack legal recourse for abuse or the means for survival. Of the "unnatural," Bentham writes:

> The truth is that, by the epithet *unnatural,* when applied to any human act or thought, the only matter of which it affords any indication that can be depended upon is the existence of a sentiment of disapprobation,

accompanied with passion, in the breast of the person by whom it is employed: a degree of dissocial passion by which, without staying to enquire or to consider with himself whether the practice, and thence the conduct and character of him whose practice it is, be or be not in any way, and if in any way in what degree, noxious to society, he endeavours, by the use thus made of this inflammatory word, to kindle and point towards the object of his ill-will, the same dissocial passion in other breasts, for the purpose of inducing them to join with him in producing pain in some shape or other in the breast of him by whom the passion has been thus excited.[10]

That is, accusations of "unnaturalness" make no substantive claim regarding any real harm caused by the "unnatural" act. Rather, "unnatural" is an epithet used by what Bentham calls the sinister interests of the powerful for the purpose of inciting legal or extralegal violence against powerless or socially marginalized persons. Like a woman who must choose between abortion and death, or like an enslaved person who must choose between rebellion and death, a person who is willing to risk their life for same-sex pleasure must, Bentham concludes, need pleasure more immediately than they need safety or survival.

Why, then, is men having sex with men the quintessentially "unnatural" crime? Bentham examines the supposedly noxious effects of same-sex relations between men and finds little evidence of even potential harm. In the case of private, consensual pleasure between social and political equals, Bentham notes that same-sex intimacy is a victimless crime that destroys nothing, costs nothing, engenders felicity, forms social bonds, enriches art, expands human knowledge, curbs masturbation, and possibly even follows the example of Jesus, who, Bentham argues in several texts, was perhaps involved in—if not merely broadly tolerant of—passionate same-sex intimacies. As far as pleasures go, sexual nonconformity seems to be obviously less socially noxious than, for example, drinking alcohol or excessive eating. So, Bentham wonders, why are drunkenness and gluttony tolerated while men having consensual sex are punished with death or banishment?

In the context of an analysis of the accusation that same-sex intercourse causes "enervation," detriment to the health of the sexual partners, Bentham supposes it might be possible in some imaginable case that a person who indulges in sexual pleasure too freely may feel weakened by it.

> But under this head as under every other is—1. in the first place, whether, supposing evil to be the result, the sum of that evil is in such quantity and value as to be preponderant over the good derived from the same source: 2. in the next place, if yes, whether the net balance of difference be to such amount as to justify the employing against it the force of penal law in general, and in particular of such penal laws of extreme rigor as those which, in the civilized world in general, and in the British empire in particular, have been in use to be employed against it.[11]

In the context of the ensuing lengthy comparison between sexual non-conformity and alcohol use, Bentham demonstrates that, in the case of a vice directly related to luxury, indubitably noxious effects are in no way considered sufficient evidence to ban the practice, because they are outweighed by the widely recognized sociable pleasure created by drinking.

> By the appetite for *drink,* that, to a prodigious amount, destruction is continually resulting to health, to strength, to life, is matter of notoriety, though the exact amount is altogether unsusceptible of measurement. . . . But for drunkenness taken by itself, and considered apart from any disorders of which it may happen to it to be productive, unless it be, in the case of publicity, on the score of the pain of scandal inflicted or liable to be inflicted on the public mind by the exposure, what legislator was ever weak enough to employ against such weaknesses the force of penal law?[12]

In this comparison, Bentham suggests that the unique scrutiny applied to the supposed deleterious effects of nonconforming sex practices, as opposed to those of consumable indulgences, may be because mutual, consensual sexual pleasure between free equals is not dependent on socioeconomic status or luxury. Bentham finds that the pleasures of the palate and the bottle are tolerated precisely because they cost money, and vices associated with luxury will be tolerated in a culture that affords more freedom to persons who have more wealth. While only dyslogistic terms are associated with seeking sexual pleasure, the great drinker or eater is credited, according to Bentham's *Table,* with being a lover of "good cheer" and "good living"—the very stuff of happiness itself.[13] The insidious nature of eulogistic and dyslogistic language for vice and virtue is that it is necessarily hegemonic in its moral tautology. A specific culture's moral language—especially around "unnatural" behaviors—relentlessly perpetuates and replicates the social and political order as it is, while inciting punitive violence against already-oppressed persons.

Bentham acknowledges that sexual irregularity may, of course, include practices that are genuinely harmful to the self or to society. As examples from least to most deleterious, he offers bestiality, necrophilia, pedophilia, onanism, and rape, which violate the principle that sex acts should produce mutual pleasure between or among consenting participants. He suggests that sex between women may serve as a model for how male sexual nonconformity could be more appropriately tolerated, since same-sex women's intimacy seems to cause very little moral panic while offering apparently significant gratification to participants. Bentham considers at length that, one day, difference in sexual preferences may come to seem utterly mundane. He hopes for a future in which people will sneer at historical ascetics, just as one might sneer at the stoic Seneca for abhorring the unnaturalness of perfumes.

> The gratification which, such as it is, has been spared even by the most severe and terror-struck religionist has not been spared by the caprice of a set of heathen philosophers, or at least (for one such philosopher is quite sufficient) the Stoick Seneca. Against the inhaling the essential oil of the flower while it remains in the neighborhood of the flower, he raises no objection: but let the same substance be obtained in a state of separation from the flower, language sinks under the task of furnishing expressions strong enough to represent the enormity of the practice in its proper colours. It thus comes under the denomination of *a perfume*—and Oh! what wickedness can match the wickedness of smelling at a perfume?[14]

In his inimitable sarcastic style, Bentham mocks the ascetic extremism of Seneca with respect to perfumes as a clear parallel to his contemporaries who panic at the idea of same-sex intercourse. Someday, he hopes, anti-sexual violence will seem just as absurd as Seneca's moral loathing for perfume. Ultimately, Bentham's argument depends on the reader's response to his illustrations of the absurdity of considering persecution of sexual nonconformists as a form of moral—rather than aesthetic—disgust.

Bentham argues that sexual pleasure constitutes a sixth sense, which he calls "Sextus," and therefore it is not subject to higher-order reflection and judgment.[15] While taste in higher-order judgments like art appreciation or literary aesthetics might be subject to cultural influence, and might change in response to argument, a preference in sensory experience is nearly impossible to alter. Bentham uses the example of tobacco use: "The man to whom habit has rendered the use of tobacco a source of gratification, whether in the way of snuffing, smoking, or mastication, by nothing that any one can say to him will he be convinced that that taste of his is a bad taste. Let him see that by taking it he inflicts annoyance on those in whose presence he is taking it, you may make him abstain from it, but never can you make him in his own mind acknowledge it to be a bad taste."[16] Even if you force the tobacco user to quit, on pain of death, he will never experience revulsion at the taste or smell of tobacco. Bentham urges his reader to ask whether an immutable preference of taste can in any way be legitimate grounds for hanging or exile.

Although Bentham wrote about sexual nonconformity throughout his career, these manuscripts of the 1810s demonstrate an almost single-minded focus on the relevance of sexual nonconformity to every possible philosophical discourse. In his published work, it is less explicit, but apparent, given the context of his more recently transcribed notes from the 1810s. From 1813 to 1817 he worked on his *Table of the Springs of Action*. *Of Sexual Irregularities* was drafted in 1814. His *Deontology* was mostly drafted between 1814 and 1817. In 1815 he began the work toward the pseudonymously published 1822 text *Analysis of the Influence of Natural Religion on the Temporal Happiness of Mankind*. In the summer of 1816, he created and apparently abandoned an essay called *Sextus*, arguing that sexual pleasure was a sixth sense alongside hearing, touch, taste, smell, and sight. And in 1817 he began an outline of what would later be published in 1823 as *Not Paul, but Jesus*. In this outline, Bentham seems obsessed with proving that Jesus was a philosopher who preached and practiced the centrality of physical pleasure, and that he tolerated—if not participated in—sexual pleasure and intimacy among men. All of these texts urgently and anxiously circle the problem of sexual liberty, approaching it with aesthetics, moral philosophy, empirical observations, theology, epistemology, and economic, political, and legal analysis. The resultant body of work from this period is simultaneously stunningly single-minded and bewilderingly complex. In the long-unpublished manuscripts, especially, one finds Bentham wrestling with too many analytical tools at once for one single, haunting question: Why would anyone else care if men have sex with each other?

Pleasure and Subjectivity

In lieu of ethics based in metaphysical rights or a natural order, Bentham demanded a simple revisionist analysis of empiricism. Unlike any of the empiricist arguments between Thomas Hobbes's *Leviathan* and his own work, Bentham's writings do not instrumentalize human happiness toward some other goal, such as national security, civil manners, religious adherence, moral virtue, or economic productivity; for Bentham, human happiness is pleasure, and is the only good that must be sought for its own end. Before Bentham, the empiricists of the British Enlightenment had—perhaps unwittingly—metaphysicalized pleasure by categorizing it as a kind of a priori cultural judgment, rather than as a sensory experience in its own right. Both John Locke's *An Essay Concerning Human Understanding* and David Hume's *An Enquiry Concerning the Principles of Morals* include examples of cultural diversity in moral attitudes toward sex practices in order to acknowledge the cultural specificity of British sexual morals. Locke and Hume both use these examples to demonstrate that even pleasure and sexual enjoyment are the products of socialization and culturally specific assumptions. However, both authors, who lived in times when sexual and gender minorities continued to exist despite violent persecution, inadvertently reveal that sexual behavior cannot be entirely the product of social discipline and conditioning. Rather, Bentham argues, pleasure must be the product of sensory experience, and aesthetic preferences in the experience of that sense.

Bentham's most controversial published work asserts that pleasure is a perfectly subjective experience, not to be judged by the pleasures of others; a scent that pleases me may disgust another, and there is no objective standard by which that scent may be declared objectively pleasurable or disgusting. Whether one shares the aesthetic taste of another person or not should never serve as the basis for legal prohibition. During the latter and more cynical half of his career, Bentham began to suspect that the pleasure that powerful men take in humiliating others for enjoying their lives had become the dominant motivation for legal and extralegal violence. As Frances Ferguson writes, "The English laws governing sexuality privileged some persons' judgment (of disgust) on

other persons' pleasure, and allowed the practitioners of 'regular' pleasures to take pleasure in the sufferings visited on practitioners of 'irregu-
lar' pleasures."[17] The normativity of aesthetic judgment that emerged in
the eighteenth century elevated aesthetic consensus above even moral
or social utility, while justifying nearly limitless violence against people
whose tastes differed.

In Bentham's published work, the stakes of aesthetic disagreement
often appear much more trivial, as he feared the repercussions of addressing sexual behavior as a kind of aesthetic preference. He attempted to
demonstrate that philosophers' and legislators' descriptions of aesthetic
consensus were not based on a genuine aggregation of most people's
experience of pleasure, including the tastes of children and uneducated
people, but were instead an elitist judgment that used taste as a proxy
for legal and social disenfranchisement of specific groups of vulnerable
people. Near the end of his life, Bentham wrote, in an oft-misquoted
passage from *The Rationale of Reward*:

> The utility of all these arts and sciences,—I speak both of those of
> amusement and curiosity,—the value which they possess, is exactly in
> proportion to the pleasure they yield. Every other species of preemi-
> nence which may be attempted to be established among them is alto-
> gether fanciful. Prejudice apart, the game of push-pin is of equal value
> with the arts and sciences of music and poetry. If the game of push-pin
> furnish more pleasure, it is more valuable than either. Everybody can
> play at push-pin: poetry and music are relished only by a few. The game
> of push-pin is always innocent: it were well could the same be always
> asserted of poetry. Indeed, between poetry and truth there is a natural
> opposition: false morals, fictitious nature: the poet always stands in need
> of something false. When he pretends to lay his foundations in truth,
> the ornaments of his superstructure are fictions; his business consists in
> stimulating our passions, and exciting our prejudices. Truth, exactitude
> of every kind, is fatal to poetry. The poet must see everything through
> coloured media, and strive to make every one else do the same.[18]

Because push-pin, a children's game, can be shared and enjoyed among
people of any level of education, and it has no power to manipulate morals, we should consider its utility to be, on the whole, higher than the
arts only enjoyed by the wealthy and educated, especially those arts that

flatter the ambitious and the prejudiced. Bentham thus demonstrates that the purported consensus of aesthetic judgment fails to account for the shared tastes and enjoyments of most people; if an appreciation for music or poetry is to be used as a justification for colonialism, patriarchy, slavery, and violence against sexual nonconformists, then push-pin, at least, must be valued as relatively harmless.

When John Stuart Mill dismissively revisits this argument in his somewhat laudatory essay on Bentham in *Dissertations and Discussions* (1859), he asserts that only a Benthamite would exclusively compare the "moral" aspects of something like poetry or push-pin; the true philosopher must also consider judgments about excellence. "Every human action has three aspects: its *moral* aspect, or that of its *right* and *wrong;* its *aesthetic* aspect, or that of its *beauty;* its *sympathetic* aspect, or that of its *loveableness.*"[19] For Bentham, these three aspects of judgment are really only two, split in a different direction—the feeling, positive or negative, that arises when one performs an action, which has the potential to result in pleasure or disgust, *or* the feeling that arises when one imagines the action as performed by someone else, which is irrelevant to judgment. For Mill, in a comparison between push-pin and poetry, this judgment would, of course, be suddenly weighted on the side of poetry; the beauty and lovableness of poems spring immediately to any educated reader's mind. Mill's refutation of Bentham is an attempt to reconcile utilitarianism with Immanuel Kant's *sensus communis,* but in doing so, Mill drains Bentham's argument of its radical potential. Who decides what is beautiful, and what is lovable? And why do matters of aesthetic preference have any bearing on access to legal or social liberties?

Even early in Bentham's career, he came to realize that aesthetic judgments are manipulative because they favor the tastes of powerful people; aesthetic judgments allow elite or normative pleasures to masquerade as virtues, and so unusual or "bad" taste can be used as a justification for denying equal liberties under the law. In one of his early sets of notes on sexual nonconformity (undated, but found with papers from 1776 to 1786), Bentham contemplates the "Horror of Singularity" that seems to inform penal laws against same-sex intercourse, and blames this intolerance of difference to people with "weak and capricious temperament" who must kill or destroy anything unusual.[20] He compares the penalization of "Pederasty" (which he would later refer to as sexual nonconformity or irregularity) to outlawing scratching an itch with the wrong finger: "It is wonderful that nobody has ever yet fancied it to be sinful to scratch where it itches: and that it has never been determined to be that the only natural way of scratching is with one such or such finger, and that it is unnatural to scratch with any other."[21] Bentham wondered what possible harm could arise from someone else's unusual or nonelite taste in the means of satisfying a desire for pleasure, and whether there were any limitations on the desire of powerful men to withhold gratification from the masses.

The justification for laws against sexual nonconformity seemed to be the *aesthetic* disgust the idea of it inspires in people who have no desire to experience it. Bentham often admitted that the disgust people have for others' aesthetic preferences is real and must be taken into account, but only insofar as it is impossible for that person to limit exposure to the behavior that disgusts them. In the case of sexual tastes, there is little or no danger of the public being forced to witness or participate in sexual acts they find undesirable for themselves. He writes, "The act is odious to the highest degree and disgusting, that is not to the man who does it, for he does it only because it gives him pleasure; but to one who think of it. Be it so, but what is that to him? He has the same reasons (as far as the circumstance applies) for doing it, that I have for avoiding it."[22] He goes on to imagine a man who prefers carrion to fresh meat for satisfying hunger; no matter how little one relishes the thought of eating food that is disgusting, there is simply no demonstrable utility in punishing someone with death for enjoying something unusual. Except in the case of nonconsensual or coercive intercourse, Bentham finds no legal, social, or philosophical justification for punishing someone for gratifying physical pleasure through means that may be uncommon, unless, as he later came to believe, the powerful are gratified by keeping the bulk of the population in a state of misery and joylessness.

In Bentham's formulation, the subjectivity of pleasure is the source of its political power. If sanctionable pleasures must first be submitted to elite authorities who claim to represent the common sense of one's society, then they will almost certainly be restricted by the sinister interests of powerful people who seek to immiserate and disenfranchise groups without political representation or a voice in the public sphere. It is clear from Bentham's manuscripts that individual pleasure was a matter of deep political concern for him, as he notes that judgments about taste are used as the rhetorical foundation for colonialism, patriarchy, homophobic violence, and the abuse of children. The way these ideas appear in his published work take the form of trivial-seeming arguments, and the subsequent revisions and refutations of Bentham by scholars from John Stuart Mill to Vivasvan Soni express anxiety that allowing for a wide variety of individual, sensory pleasures as the means of facilitating general happiness is potentially devastating for public morals and culture. However, the alternative is to judge pleasure by some purportedly objective common sense of beauty and morality as defined by those who are already fully enfranchised and depend on the material oppression of most other groups of people for their livelihood and comfort.

Locke and Hume on Sexual Nonconformity

In matters of aesthetic or moral judgment, the claim to common sense has a long history of manipulation by philosophers and politicians alike. From the works of Aristotle until the publication of John Locke's *An Essay Concerning Human Understanding* in 1689, the "common sense" is generally used to signify an internal mental faculty that organizes sensations into perception, or, more expansively, the faculty that organizes perception into cognition. Philosophers of this earlier period conceived of the common sense as a sense much like smell or sight, in which a person might be more or less gifted, but from which one would typically be able to corroborate information and experience. Locke suggests that one ought to judge one's common sense by attempting to develop consensus with other people who have perceived the same object or event, and thus to define the limits of the normative community whose consensus is possible and meaningful. If one lacked the capacity for logically sorting information, then one could not arrive at consensus with others about reality. For Locke, the faculty called the common sense is something that one may have in greater or lesser capacity, and that ability or disability is measurable by the normativity of one's understanding of the sensible world.

Locke insists that, in order to verify that there is a normative communal experience of cognition, individual persons must share and collate "testimony" of their observations to discover what is incidental and what is universal about experience. "Where any particular thing, consonant to the constant observation of ourselves and others in the like case, comes attested by the concurrent reports of all that mention it, we receive it as easily, and build as firmly upon it, as if it were certain knowledge; and we reason and act thereupon with as little doubt as if it were perfect demonstration."[23] According to Locke, the closest we can get to certainty about observed phenomena is that all available accounts by various observers accord with one another in every particular. As Locke goes on to acknowledge, however, this confidence of agreement is not often the product of shared testimony. "The difficulty is, when testimonies contradict common experience, and the reports of history and witnesses clash with the ordinary course of nature, or with one another; there it is, where diligence, attention, and exactness are required, to form a right judgement, and to proportion the *assent* to the different evidence and probability of the thing; which rises and falls, according as those two foundations of credibility, *viz.* common observation in like cases, and particular testimonies in that particular instance, favour or contradict it."[24] Whether the variations in testimonies of shared experiences are the products of faulty perception, damaged cognition, prejudiced judgment, limited perspective, or inarticulate representation of the experience in language, the difficulty of comparing testimonies of actual experience is enormous. If eliciting testimonies of experience that do not conflict is so rarely possible owing to the variety of subjective experiences and the representation of these experiences in language, then how can it be said that there is a common sense, or even a common observation, of the world?

Locke describes the process of sensation in roughly the same terms as traditional Scholastic interpretations of Aristotle—a person receives sensory information through the organs of perception, and that information is then collated by what Thomas Aquinas translates as the "sensus communis" into a coherent cognitive experience, consisting of, according to Aristotle, "movement, rest, number, figure, magnitude."[25] That is, in order to have a coherent experience of a perception, some higher order "common sense" must organize sensory information. For Locke, however, the common sense does not stop there. The common sense is also responsible for organizing cognition into abstract ideas, and ideas into judgments. Since, for Locke, even our most complicated intellectual and aesthetic concepts are ultimately derived from sensory experience, this common sense is promoted to an internal faculty responsible for all possible thought.

Locke pointedly distinguishes between his use of "common sense" from the Greek phrase κοιναί έννοιαι, typically translated as "common sense," but which Locke uses exclusively to refer to the (in his account, nonexistent) innate ideas shared by rational human beings. Given the vast diversity of tastes and morals and principles all over the world, he finds that it simply cannot be true that we are born with innate ideas. Rather, a particular group of people may share values and ideas because they have similar experiences, and those experiences will, barring some infirmity in a person's common sense, yield roughly similar moral and aesthetic judgments. Only someone who is disabled in their common sense would be able to have abnormal or countercultural desires, pleasures, and judgments.[26]

For Locke, one of the most crucial arguments for the noninnateness of moral ideas is the toleration of nonprocreative sexuality in other cultures. After a discussion of various cultures in which infanticide, cannibalism, and atheism are tolerated or celebrated among the Mingrelians and Topinambous, Locke offers an example from the *Voyage of Baumgarten* in Latin, from which the following passage is translated by Peter Nidditch:

> We saw there (namely, near Belbes in Egypt) a holy Saracen sitting among the sandhills as naked as he came forth from his mother's womb. . . . This class of men have virtually unbridled liberty to enter any houses they please, and to eat, drink, and what is more have sexual intercourse; and if there are any offspring resulting from the latter, they too are regarded as sacred. . . . Moreover, that particular holy man whom we saw in that place was said to be held in exceedingly high public regard as sacred, superhuman, and of an especial integrity in that he never had intercourse with women or boys but only with she-asses and mules.[27]

If sexual morality could be so very different in Egypt—not merely that excesses are tolerated, but that bestiality, sodomy, and rape are marks of sainthood—then surely morality must be derived from experience within a social environment, rather than being universal or innate. Locke deploys this example of Egyptian Saracens in order to incite a kind of rhetorical disgust; his argument demands that any English reader must share his sense that these nonnormative sex practices are abhorrent—if not to everyone everywhere, then at least to "us," the British reader of Latin in the 1690s.

About sixty years later, David Hume would use sexual disgust in a rhetorically similar passage in *An Enquiry Concerning the Principles of*

Morals. Hume asserts in a fictional dialogue that the historical example of ancient Greece is even more morally shocking for English readers whose education in classical literature and philosophy leads them to admire the great morals of the ancients. In the dialogue, a friend, Palamedes, tells the Hellenophilic narrator about a trip he recently took to a country called Fourli, where, as he explains, sodomy is normalized and celebrated. After his host Alcheic took him to meet his beautiful boy lover Gulki, Palamedes marvels: "It gave me some surprise, that Alcheic's wife (who by-the-by also happened to be his sister) was nowise scandalized at this species of infidelity."[28] After beginning with a rhetorical invocation of sexual disgust, Palamedes goes on to discuss several other appalling Fourlian cultural attitudes regarding violence, suicide, and political assassination. The narrator stops him in a rage: "Such barbarous and savage manners are not only incompatible with a civilized, intelligent people, such as you said these were; but are scarcely compatible with human nature. They exceed all we ever read of, among the Mingrelians and Topinamboues."[29] Echoing Locke's examples of stereotypical "savages," Hume's incredulous narrator declares the toleration of same-sex intercourse to be a reason to declare the Fourlians not to be fully human.

Of course, the joke is on the narrator. Palamedes reveals that these people are "your favorites, the Greeks." "Have a care, cried he, have a care! You are not aware that you are speaking blasphemy, and are abusing your favourites, the Greeks. . . . The amours of the Greeks, their marriages, and the exposing of their children cannot but strike you immediately."[30] In a footnote to this passage, Hume adds, "The laws of Athens allowed a man to marry his sister by the father. Solon's law forbid paederasty to slaves, as being an act of too great dignity for such mean persons."[31] As in Locke's example of the Saracens, we learn from the example of sexual deviance in some other time or place that while modern English people can only feel disgust when reading of nonnormative sex, one must acknowledge that morality is socially constructed when we confront the approbation for varieties of sexual pleasure, in addition to forms of violence, in other communities, safely separated from the philosophical discourse of the British Enlightenment by space or time.

The problem with this argument is, of course, that if pleasure is entirely socially constructed and is a product of judgment, then, as Locke and Hume both suggest, there would be *no* British people who engage in or enjoy sexual difference in an increasingly sexually ascetic British culture. Unlike other criminal behaviors that might be tempting because of secondary benefits, such as getting money by stealing, sexual pleasure offers no reward except enjoyment in itself. Across the eighteenth century, in English literature, including pamphlets of propaganda, plays, and popular realistic novels, the effeminate man and the sexual nonconformist became stock characters for humiliation and censure. If, as Locke, Hume, and others so confidently insist, a British person cannot hear of sexual nonconformity without being disgusted, owing to their cultural indoctrination against it; and if trials frequently resulted in execution, transportation, or exile; and there is no secondary benefit of sex, such as money or power, then how would it be possible, from an empiricist perspective, for anyone still to enjoy it?

As I argue in the introduction, eighteenth-century philosophers from Berkeley to Kant suggest that objectivity in moral, aesthetic, or rational judgment can be achieved through our ability to imagine, rather than actually solicit, the perspectives of others. While each subjective account of experience is necessarily informed by self-interest, cognitive and perceptual ability, and limitations of time and space, a common sense of experience can be generated by an individual person, and can be compared, not to the real experience of others, but to their common sense. Thus, by refusing to imagine sexual nonconformists as participants in the public sphere, Locke and Hume simply deny their existence, despite the manifest evidence all around them.

Frances Ferguson demonstrates some of the ways that Bentham's insistence on the subjectivity of pleasure has greater liberationist potential, especially for disenfranchised persons, than Kant's theory. She shows that Kant considers judgment through an abstract imagined situation of aesthetic judgment, while Bentham examines reports of individual behaviors as evidence of actual subjective judgments. "While Kant wants to analyze the importance of the faculty of judgment, Bentham looks at pleasure from the outside, citing various love songs and historical accounts and accepting them as a plausible record of a history of pleasure that has been built up over time."[32] Ferguson notes that Kant recognizes that aesthetic pleasure is first experienced as immediate and purely subjective, before reason and outside of judgment: "[T]he pleasure in perception operates in advance of and independent of any cognition of the object, so that aesthetic judgment escapes from the trammels of the determining judgments that pure reason makes."[33] But, unlike Bentham, Kant denigrates these immediate reactions of pleasure or disgust as of no social or moral utility unless tempered by comparison to imaginary others who are not as susceptible to those subjective experiences.

Bentham's conception of pleasure could be described as an attempt to take Berkeley's invitation that ideas could be "submitted to the judgment of men who had plain common sense" seriously.[34] If the common sense of what is pleasurable or good were actually taken from real communication with individual persons who are not under the self-censoring influence of education and public opinion, then we could perhaps get a more accurate sense of the breadth of human experience. Bentham saw that human behavior does not neatly conform to normative discourses of law, religion, or philosophy. To understand human pleasure—not just one's own, or what one can imagine about others', but the irreconcilable fact of other people's pleasure—would be to understand something real about human motivation, and the perpetuation of pleasure-seeking activities despite social injunction, legal prohibition, and philosophical abstraction. If nonconforming pleasure-seeking behaviors like same-sex intimacy can survive even in the age of common sense, then the subjective experience of pleasure cannot simply be dismissed as irrelevant to the pursuit of a worthwhile existence.

Egalitarian Pleasure

The debate about the relationship between pleasure and happiness is an ancient one, articulated by Epicurus as a conflict between a specific pleasure and its consequences. In *Principal Doctrines,* he writes, "No pleasure is evil in itself; but the means of obtaining some pleasures bring in their wake troubles many times greater than the pleasures."[35] The consequences for troublesome pleasures that he imagines are not external social, moral, or legal ramifications, but an internal sense of disturbance created by excessive luxury and frantic striving. Ultimately, he concludes in the *Letter to Menoeceus,* "For it is not continuous drinking and revels, nor the enjoyment of women and young boys, nor of fish and other viands that a luxurious table holds, which make for a pleasant life, but sober reasoning, which examines the motives for every choice and avoidance, and which drives away those opinions resulting in the greatest disturbance to the soul."[36] Even one whose greatest physical pleasure may

lie in the satiation of ravenous hungers and lusts must ultimately arrive at
the conclusion that temperance, patience, and virtue are ultimately more
pleasurable than gross satisfaction of one's desires. Epicurus thus reverses
the causal relationship between pleasure and virtue articulated by Plato
in the *Symposium,* in which Socrates quotes Diotima to Agathon, say-
ing that bodily pleasure leads one toward virtue and a love for goodness
and beauty itself (that is, as abstract ideas), rather than merely physical
enjoyment.

This debate, about whether pleasure itself is an immediate reaction to
sensation or a conscious reflection on ideas inspired by sensation, was
revived in the seventeenth century during the formation of empiricist
epistemologies. Frederick Rosen notes in his study of utilitarianism that
Pierre Gassendi was instrumental in placing Epicurus at the center of
this argument, which was subsequently taken up by Thomas Hobbes
and John Locke.[37] Although both Hobbes and Locke both worked from
epistemology as the basis for wide-ranging political theory, the difference in their understanding of pleasure was a rift that led them to nearly
opposite conclusions about the purpose and function of law.

For Hobbes, appetite and aversion are the movements toward or
away from something pleasurable or painful, and those movements
are inseparable from the nature of the stimulus. "These words, *appetite*
and *aversion,* we have from the *Latins,* and they both of them signify
the motions, one of approaching, the other of retiring."[38] Memory and
expectation affect our appetites and aversions in the case of objects
not previously experienced. "But aversion we have for things, not only
which we know have hurt us, but also that we do not know whether they
will hurt us or not."[39] That is, rather than attempting to judge or understand the feeling of pleasure or pain, Hobbes examines the observed
movement—unconscious though it may be—toward sources of potential pleasure or away from sources of potential pain, as predicted from
memory and fear of the unknown. This is ultimately how Bentham
would also analyze human motivation; no matter what people might
say or report about their own feelings and desires in the public sphere,
the incontrovertible evidence of their true motivation is in their actions.

For Locke, physical pleasure and pain serve a regulatory function intended by God to lead one to virtuous (and pleasurable) self-
governance. Unlike Hobbes, Locke identifies pleasure in the perception
of the subject, rather than in the relationship between the subject and

object, pointing out that the same object that produces pleasure, such as a delicious warmth, may, from too much exposure, become the cause of terrible pain, such as a burn. "*Pain is often produced by the same objects and ideas, that produce pleasure* in us. This their near conjunction, which makes us often feel pain in the sensations where we expected pleasure, gives us new occasion of admiring the wisdom and goodness of our maker, who designing the preservation of our being, has annexed pain to the application of many things to our bodies, to warn us of the harm that they will do; and as advices to withdraw from them."[40] By shifting the cause of pain to the changing state of the subject's mind, rather than a physical attraction between subject and object, Locke transfers the judgment of pleasure from a property of the object and its relation to the self, to the person who interacts with that object and may or may not heed the warning sensations produced by God through the object of pleasure.

Hobbes determines that the appetitive relation between a subject and an object suggests a kind of meaningless, immutable attraction created by the experiential expectation of pleasure, without any expectation that the fulfillment of desire is consummated by the production of some kind of divine meaning or lesson. Pleasure, for Hobbes, may run entirely counter to norms and morals, and may even be the product of others' pain or failure, as in his example of "*Sudden glory*"—"laughter at the defects of others."[41] For Hobbes, appetite is not proof of the moral or social correctness of desire, any more than aversion is caused by the righteousness of disgust. Unlike Locke, who understands pleasure as a communication from God about the appropriate measure of positive judgment about an object, Hobbes does not conclude that judgments formed from desire and sensation, whether normative, corroborated, or not, are evidence that one has objectively or divinely valid reactions to stimuli.

In their article "Love and the Leviathan," Haig Patapan and Jeffrey Sikkenga argue that Hobbes's analysis of sexual desire and pleasure is consistently anti-Platonic.[42] Hobbes uses the word "love" to signify the presence of a pleasurable object, and "desire" to signify the absence of an object of expected pleasure, suggesting a dichotomy between love and desire that would be joined in a Platonic conception of eros. Patapan and Sikkenga show that Hobbes does discuss eros at length, but as a kind of emotional disorder in which "[e]rotic love erupts when the person believes that he can acquire the other person's love by his

own powers."[43] Thus, for Hobbes, eros is an emotion typical to people with greater social power than the objects of their desire; the lover
has not attained the reciprocation of his feelings, and yet he maintains
hope that he has or will develop the power to overwhelm his beloved's
objections. In his analysis of the *Symposium* in *Human Nature*, Hobbes
questions the supposed charity and continence of Socrates in wooing
and resisting Alcibiades; as framed by Patapan and Sikkenga, "It turns
out that Socratic charity—fuelled by an *eros* that was supposed to rise
above the body to the 'beautiful itself'—was 'merely . . . an honorable
pretense for the old to haunt the company of the young and beautiful'
(HN IX, 17)."[44] What for Plato was a description of the real properties
of beauty and desire becomes, in Hobbes's analysis, a rhetorical gambit
based in the power of social relations and conventional sexual coercion. Hobbes's conclusion, that the sublimity of virtuous eros is a mask
for power asserting itself at the expense of the less powerful, is exem-
plary of materialist critiques of virtue ethics. At the moment when love
is exalted beyond pleasure and pain and into the realm of good and
evil, it begins to serve as a cover for oppressive power relations among
socially unequal persons.

Hobbes's critique of virtue ethics does not morally distinguish between
same-sex and opposite-sex intimacies, nor does it use arguments based
in British or modern cultural supremacy to establish Socrates's fault
in the *Symposium*. Unlike John Locke and David Hume, who would
claim that the problem with ancient Greek ethics was that they were
not restrictive enough about sexuality, Hobbes instead finds fault with
virtue ethics itself, as it is used by the powerful as a proxy for oppressive coercion. That is, as he argues in response to the *Symposium,* virtue
ethics pretends to have objective knowledge of goodness, but it conveniently contributes to the satisfaction of the sensory desires of powerful
people by extracting favors, sexual or otherwise, from the less powerful.
The similarity between Hobbes's materialist critique of Plato and Bentham's materialist critique of Kant indicates a similar trace of mutual
Epicurean influence that informed Bentham's critical reading of subsequent Enlightenment philosophers, for whom virtue ethics, especially
on the matter of rigidly defined sexual and gender roles, formed the
bedrock of common-sense discourse on morality.

I do not intend to suggest that Hobbes shared Bentham's egalitarian politics; as James Crimmins has argued, there is little evidence that

Bentham found common political ground with Hobbes, and does not cite him with uncritical approval anywhere in his extensive notes or correspondence.[45] According to Crimmins, although there are significant similarities in their materialism and use of clear and precise definitions of relevant terms, there is not sufficient evidence that those ideas could have only come from Hobbes, rather than, for example, Claude Adrien Helvétius, who was strongly influenced by Hobbes and cited approvingly by Bentham. While Bentham was an aggressively polemical, radical political theorist with an active program for social and legal reform, Hobbes seems to have intended merely to describe power relations as they are, without proposing a utopian alternative, or even an ameliorative condition.

But it is clear that both Bentham and Hobbes saw that the debate between Platonism and Epicureanism in the matter of physical pleasure would always swing in favor of Platonists wherever social and political elites intend to shore up defenses against the less powerful, who might seek to gratify their own pleasures or to end their own oppression. The virtues lauded as sublime by the powerful—self-denial, stoicism, endurance, beauty—would ultimately only have to be practiced by the less powerful, while their social superiors gratified their own whims. Both Hobbes and Bentham are critical of patriarchal virtue ethics regarding sexual pleasure, in that it advocates abstinence and self-denial for women, laborers, and young people while falling suspiciously silent in regard to the sexual gratification of powerful men. If gender normativity and sexual asceticism were at the center of Enlightenment virtue ethics, it must have been because those were the social roles in which powerful men desire the most freedom and have the most to gain from others' self-denial.

Bentham's own analysis of pleasure and human motivation started in the 1790s, when he began to develop his theory of sinister interest, which he typically used to refer to the methods used by people with power to humiliate and immiserate less powerful persons so they would not challenge their oppressors. In 1795 he began a series of manuscripts that would ultimately form the basis for his *Deontology* and the *Table of the Springs of Action*. Under the heading "Virtue what," he writes, "Virtue is under every system of Morals a common name attributed to human actions considered in the light of their being apt to be repugnant to the inclination of the agent: i:e: to a certain degree and in a certain respect painful to him."[46] One of the primary reasons that Bentham rejects virtue as a meaningful moral category is that it seems only to be used as a kind of congratulation for rejected pleasure or self-inflicted pain. Without a valid objective stance from which any sense of virtue could be defined, whether divine or manufactured by imagination, Bentham exclusively understands virtue as the influence used by the powerful to restrict the will of the less powerful. Virtue could be defined as those actions which are in themselves perhaps beneficial to the community, but Bentham is wary of appropriating a term from ethical discourse that is ill matched to the pleasures for which he intends to advocate. "Utility alone, though ever so great can not be understood under the system of utility to bring an action under the denomination of virtuous. The act so useful as the act of eating. It is more than useful: it is absolutely necessary. Without it the species would soon perish. Yet neither according to the principle of utility nor under any other system was the act of eating what one liked to eat ever considered as an exercise act of virtue—ever set down in the catalogue of virtuous acts."[47] Bentham recognizes that giving oneself pleasure is no act of heroism, only self-satisfaction. There may even be times, he acknowledges, when withholding one's own pleasures in order to provide pleasure to others is of both greater virtue and greater utility for the community. But it troubles him that there are categories of human action and motivation for which we only have dyslogistic terms, or none at all.

The man who eats what he likes is no hero or saint to anyone, but it makes him happy without directly hurting anyone else, which, according to Bentham's felicific calculus, is good for society as a whole. Likewise, as he argues throughout his notes on sexual nonconformity, those who enjoy unrestricted sexual pleasure are not expressing a superior morality, but they are contributing, along with their partners, to the aggregate of pleasure and happiness. Certainly, there are times when *not* gratifying one's physical desires may be more beneficial to the community than gratifying them, but on the whole, more pleasure for people is better than less. So why are there so few positive—or even neutral— terms in English for describing actions motivated by physical desire?

By reframing pleasure, in as many varieties as possible, as the real essence of utility, Bentham hoped to obviate matters of virtue ethics (as in a neoclassical discourse of happiness) and moral sentiment (in a modern discourse of happiness) entirely from the question of right and wrong. Sexual variety, though it raises obvious problems for the consistency of argument in the works of John Locke and David Hume, poses no problem whatsoever for Benthamite utilitarianism, in which the proliferation of human pleasure, especially in a social context like consensual intimacy, constitutes the most useful action a person could perform to contribute to the health and happiness of the community.

3
Against Rights

The Libertarian Legacy

As we approach 250 years since the adoption of the US Declaration of Independence, political theorists have begun to reassess the effects of this influential statement on human rights as a justification for revolution and a foundation for civil government. In his critique of rights discourse, Lawrence Hamilton demonstrates that rights "tend to create the illusion of political power while undermining real individual political agency."[1] Hamilton notes that it is strange that the perpetuation of rights discourse on the supposedly utilitarian grounds of human happiness seems to ignore the criticism of rights leveled by Jeremy Bentham, the founding theorist of utilitarianism. In his responses to declarations of rights by the United States, France, and Spain, Bentham warned that these statements of so-called divine, natural, or human rights would ultimately undermine the legal and political means to obtaining redress for discrimination and disenfranchisement.

As his manuscripts from the 1770s through the 1820s demonstrate, Bentham consistently tested liberal rights discourse against the example of sexual liberty from legal proscription, without which the individual subject's rights to self-determination and happiness were meaningless. If the penal code prohibits individual subjects or classes of people from engaging in intimacy and pleasure with consenting adults, causing no harm or distress, then, Bentham argues, any declaration of positive "rights" or "freedoms" is absurd on its face; subjects of a state that prohibits sexual pleasure (as well as reproductive choice and license to avoid suffering) do not even have the liberty to use their bodies. Bentham's analysis of sexual liberty demonstrates that although rights discourse may be inspiring for those subjects who are unrestricted by discriminatory laws, it can only be demoralizing for those who are denied legal custodianship of their own reproduction and pleasure— especially in the cases of women, enslaved persons, and men who have sex with men. Ultimately, Bentham came to believe that demoralizing disenfranchised persons was not an unintended side effect but the primary function of liberal rights discourse. In this sense, Bentham's arguments regarding discrimination, dehumanization, and rights discourse anticipate later theories of political oppression by Hannah Arendt and Giorgio Agamben.

It is important to note that Bentham uses the word "liberty" exclusively to refer to the silence of the law on a particular subject; while "rights" and "freedoms" refer to positive assertions, "liberty" is only a negative category—liberty *from* law. Regarding Bentham's position on liberty, Frederick Rosen writes, "Most laws violated liberty either through prohibition or by requiring people to perform certain actions and coercing (or threatening to coerce) them if they did not. To criticise a law for violating liberty, as Adam Smith did, failed, in Bentham's view, to appreciate that virtually all laws violated liberty."[2] Liberal rights discourse, in which subjects of the state are guaranteed positive freedoms, but within a system of law that delineates the limits of those freedoms, often effectively discriminated against disenfranchised persons either explicitly, in the text of the law, or implicitly, in the selective execution of the laws. So-called human rights variously might not extend to convicted prisoners, to women, to enslaved persons, to children, or to sexual nonconformists—all of whom are subjects of the state, but some of whom are seen by the law as more human than others.

From his earliest writings on legal reform, Bentham observed two contradictory trends in Europe and America that suggested all was not well in modern legal discourse. A new, passionate language of natural rights was emerging in neo-Lockean political theory, while the law itself continued to proscribe liberties on the basis of prejudicial discrimination. If it is true, as Thomas Jefferson insisted in the Declaration of Independence, "that all men are created equal, that they are endowed by their Creator with certain unalienable rights," then, Bentham points out in his response to the Declaration, no government of any human being over another could ever exist. He writes, "[I]n as many instances as Government is ever exercised, some one or other of these rights, pretended to be unalienable, is actually alienated."[3] If the absolute rights of every subject were equally guaranteed by law, then the enforcement of any restrictions of individual behaviors could be challenged as an infringement of those rights, and the result would be anarchy.

But of course, not every subject has the legal or extralegal power to threaten law enforcement, and the existence of a penal code suggests that at least some groups will have their behaviors prohibited or prosecuted against their will and pleasure. Bentham was bothered by the absurdity of rights discourse, not merely because of its hypocrisy in nations of slaveholders, colonizers, and patriarchs, where the will of a few clearly still controlled the daily lives of many, but because of its cynicism. If it were true that the modern state exists only to facilitate the natural liberty of its inhabitants, then why does the law itself excessively restrict the liberty of most of those people? Bentham concluded that rights discourse is not a promise yet to be fulfilled, but a lie with the potential to invalidate the entire legal system.

Bentham and libertarian natural rights proponents draw their theories about political liberty from the same source, John Locke's *Two Treatises of Government*, though they derive very different conclusions about who has the right to overthrow tyranny, and under what conditions. In the second *Treatise*, Locke states that, in the event of one person claiming "an Arbitrary Power . . . over another to take away his Life, whenever he pleases," that is, by enslaving someone, that despot has effectively forfeited his own life by placing his subject into a state of war with him. "He renders himself liable to be destroyed by the injur'd person and the rest of mankind, that will joyn with him in the execution of Justice."[4] If the individual enslaved person does not have the physical power to kill his master on his own, then he may attempt to organize rebel forces on his own behalf. The right to self-defense in the case of mortal threat is absolute, for Locke, unless there is a higher legal authority that may be invoked to redress the wrongs that have been committed. If there is no higher legal authority, and no way to overcome the defenses of the oppressor, Locke concludes that the victim of oppression "may *appeal, as Jephtha* did, *to Heaven*,"[5] that is, for divine assistance in mortal combat. Locke describes "natural rights"—the rights of self-defense against slavery, tyranny, or death—as the worst-case scenario for an oppressed person, who is unlikely to be able to amass the violent force necessary to overwhelm the oppressor.

Rather, for most situations of interpersonal dispute of less severity than mortal combat, the appropriate appeal would be to the law, which exists, according to Locke, solely for the purpose of restricting powerful people from committing violence and abuse against the powerless:

"Where-ever Law ends, Tyranny begins."[6] Without meaningful access
to legal redress for political oppression, the natural right of self-defense
provides only for war to the death between the oppressor and the
oppressed. Libertarian rights proponents conclude from this discussion that laws may be opposed with force whenever the subjects deem
them to violate rights and can amass the might to overthrow them.
Bentham interprets Locke to mean that laws should consist only of
those that protect subjects from the tyranny of the powerful to exercise their might. When a government declares its subjects have rights
beyond self-defense, it creates a contest between legal power, which
may be overruled by exercise of those rights, and physical power, which
may be limited for certain subjects by discriminatory law, economic
violence, or social humiliation.

In his extensive writings on the law, Bentham wondered whether
the simultaneous declaration and denial of liberty are really at odds, or
whether they constitute an emergent modern legal rhetoric of oppression, under the guise of absolute freedom. These declarations of rights—
especially in the United States and France—did not instantly sweep
the legal code of discriminatory statutes; rather, they seemed to lend
a strange new force to slavery, misogyny, and persecution of same-sex
relationships. Wealthy European patriarchal men somehow retained
total legal authority under this new system of political thought, supposedly predicated on the universal rights of humankind. Any declaration of
rights, Bentham concludes, is nothing but an absurdity—or, as he titles
one 1795 essay responding to the French First Republic, "Nonsense Upon
Stilts"—as people cannot be said to have rights if the law itself proscribes
those rights and violations are subject to no legal means of redress. For
colonized and enslaved people, the poor, women, and gender and sexual
minorities—that is, the vast majority of the population of any European
or American nation in the eighteenth century—declarations of rights
could only be demoralizing, a reminder of the liberties denied to them by
discriminatory laws they had no political power to repeal, nor, like their
French and American predecessors, the military might to overthrow in
violent revolution.

In effect, rights discourse threatened to give liberty to the powerful to
oppress the victims of their prejudice without limit. The only people with
the legal means to seek redress for violation of stated rights were those
with sufficient education in the law to understand what privileges they

could draw upon and the resources to press the courts to defend those privileges. Without thorough reform of the entire legal code to eradicate and reverse statutory prejudice and disenfranchisement, declarations of rights could only serve to facilitate greater violence against those whom the law had weakened through political and economic privation.

Bentham opposed libertarian rights discourse in part because, if taken seriously, it invalidates even normal penal law. Who could prevent a man from destroying the life and happiness of those around him if his right to perfect liberty is unalienable? Near the end of "Nonsense Upon Stilts," Bentham writes, "[I]f I have a right to be upon a par with every body else in every respect, it follows that should any man take upon him to raise his house higher than mine, rather than it should continue so, I have a right to pull it down about his ears, and to knock him down if he attempts to hinder me."[7] In his sarcastic style, Bentham dramatizes the potential consequences of rights discourse that declares a divine right to lawlessness and, ultimately, the rule of force. The law cannot guarantee liberty from laws without exposing the weak to the violence and coercion of the relatively wealthy or strong. Revising the penal code to remove or reduce needless restrictions of personal liberty seemed a far more promising method of reform than declaring the existence of rights that are not and cannot be granted without enabling oppressive violence. As the dramatic rise of libertarian political violence in the twenty-first century in the United States has made clear, one's rights may extend as far as the last round of ammunition, or to the last dollar in the account.

Sex, Utility, and Legal Reform

Bentham's political, legal, and moral theory may be seen in this light as a kind of antidote to emergent European and American libertarianism, in which so-called natural, human, or divine rights were romanticized as inviolable, but only for those whose rights were not already explicitly limited by the law, or implicitly threatened in the discriminatory execution of the law. Libertarian discourse championed the rights of a man to pursue his individual destiny with little or no concern for community welfare; his rights to perfect liberty implicitly included his right to disregard the happiness of those whose labor and service would be required to facilitate his freedom. Bentham saw the need to codify a new kind of discourse of utility. As he later admitted, "utility" might have been a confusing name to apply to happiness, by which, in turn, he meant pleasure, but Bentham hoped that an appeal to the *utility* of a happy populace would help lawmakers to see the value of facilitating that happiness.[8] In Bentham's utilitarian philosophy, the liberty to seek pleasure must be legally protected for all members of the community, even if that means explicitly curtailing the liberties of the powerful to destroy or limit the happiness of those with less power.

Throughout his career, Bentham was constantly writing, revising, testing, and reformulating his theory of utility. As J. H. Burns shows in his analysis of the disappearance and reappearance of the "greatest happiness principle" in Bentham's published work, it does not seem to be true from Bentham's papers that he changed his mind about utility, happiness, and pleasure over the course of those fifty years, but that he "continued, almost to the end, to puzzle over the best way of expressing that essential formula."[9] Throughout all of Bentham's writing, one finds a nearly constant anxiety that the romantic rhetoric of libertarian rights discourse will always grind communitarian reformist concerns like "general happiness" into dust—in part because the readers of legal and political theory are usually those in whose favor the prejudices of the law have already decided. Legislators and lawmakers were the wealthy patriarchal men who benefited most from libertarian rights discourse, and the least likely to consider the communitarian utility of general happiness without prejudice.

In the 1770s Bentham began considering the problem of sexual liberty as one of the areas in which legal reform was most urgently necessary, as the prohibition of consensual sex between adults reduced the general happiness of the community without offering any measurable benefit to any members of the community. Decriminalizing same-sex intimacy could also provide a simple first step toward utilitarian legal reform, as it would not require subsequent revision of any other economic or social system. During this period, he refers to nonheterosexual (or otherwise nonnormative) sexual intercourse in his notes as "nonconformity," a term that he later would change to "irregularity" (perhaps because the former term too closely recalls one applied to dissident Protestant sects following the Act of Uniformity 1662).[10] Sexual nonconformists, as Bentham lists them, included those who participated in same-sex intercourse between men or women, multiple-partner intercourse, intercourse with animals, and sexual intercourse with dead bodies. Bentham's analysis focuses mostly on intercourse between adult men, because it seemed the clearest example of a private pleasure enjoyed by people who were in no way considered by the law to be hindered by discriminatory rules, and yet the penal code against men's intimacies demanded the most violent retribution available to the state.

Even the extreme severity of the penal code did not satisfy the desire for revenge against sexual nonconformists. In the church, in secular literature, in the theater, and in the lynch mob, the sexual nonconformist of the late eighteenth century would find nearly universal humiliation and violence, ranging from mockery to lynching. That this vast orchestra of legal and extralegal violence was arranged just to prevent a private act of consensual, mutual pleasure suggested to Bentham that sexual nonconformity was an important testing ground for modern political theories of liberty. In an undated manuscript from the 1770s, while pondering the problem of male same-sex intimacy, he writes, "The popular reason for offering so intense a punishment to such a crime is the horror in which that crime is held: now either this reason is true in fact, or false in fact: if false, it falls to the ground: if true, the greater [+ more universal] the horror the stronger the natural determent, the less occasion for the artificial one grounded by the Laws."[11] If the social (and purportedly natural) abhorrence of men's intimacy is so self-evidently violent, then the only just role for the law should be protecting the victims of extralegal mob violence, not adding to their burden of fear and misery.

From these earlier papers discussing nonconformity and pleasure with some objective distance, to his far more explicit analysis of nonconforming sexual practices in the 1810s and '20s, Bentham consistently argued that liberty must not be reduced to a dishonest rhetorical gesture, as in libertarian rights discourse, nor should it be satisfied with merely abolishing slavery while continuing to deprive, disenfranchise, and threaten formerly enslaved people. Unless the law takes up the task of protecting universal custodianship of individual pleasure, the law cannot succeed in facilitating the greatest happiness for the greatest number.

The reasons why a legislator would be motivated to pass laws against violence and theft were obvious to Bentham; the legislator's only duty in a society that promotes happiness should be to deter citizens from restricting one another's happiness. But the motivation for passing laws that restrict one citizen's liberty without alleviating another's suffering were mysterious to him. In the latter half of his life of theorizing legal reform, Bentham began to suspect that the sinister interests of the powerful profited somehow from the systematic demoralization and humiliation of the bulk of the people. Widespread human misery was not an unfortunate side effect of religion, law, or philosophy; it was the unspoken goal of every human institution. As I discussed in chapter 1, Bentham developed his theory of sinister interest in the latter half of his career, having largely abandoned his proposals to assist the governments of the United States, France, Spain, and Great Britain in restructuring their penal codes to better reflect their stated investments in liberty and human happiness.

Two hundred years later, this challenge to libertarian rights discourse may be more urgently necessary than ever. Bentham feared that declarations of human rights would ultimately limit the ability of a legislature to respond to emergent threats and abuses of social and economic power. In the United States, the Bill of Rights is still applied unequally to various demographic groups, despite increasing political enfranchisement of gender, racial, sexual, and religious minorities, even in the highest levels of legislative government. Rather than appealing to the well-being and happiness of the state as a community, lawmakers are bound by their foundation in libertarian discourse to assert that no laws will hinder the absolute liberty of historically privileged patriarchal men to amass limitless wealth and machines of violence, to seek their destiny by imposing their will on their neighbors and the environment.

Bentham charges modern governments to recognize that laws must exist to protect the weak from the oppression of the strong, and to empower legislatures to respond to social and economic threats on behalf of members of the community who may never be represented as a majority in government, even with full political enfranchisement. A healthy, functional, productive democratic populace must be one in which the liberty from law to pursue individual pleasure according to one's own conscience is secure for all, not merely for those with the money and power to fight for their rights, and is therefore subject to accessible, uncorrupted, unprejudiced legal redress under statutes that are clear, fair, and equally applied without discrimination.

From his earliest reformist writings in the 1770s to his last and most radical projects of the 1820s, Bentham consistently maintained that happiness must be the ultimate goal of human governance. It is not enough to preserve all human life indiscriminately, nor to facilitate universal education and suffrage, if the populace still lives in self-denial, despair, and misery. Nor, he argues, is happiness possible if the political subject is denied full access to sensory enjoyment, as long as that enjoyment is not predicated on the pain of another person, their equal before the law. Lea Campos Boralevi notes that Bentham's papers on sexual nonconformity were long suppressed or disguised by the executor of his will, John Bowring, resulting in an extremely limited understanding of Bentham's radicalism by his contemporaries. She writes, "Besides suggesting the need for a re-examination of Jeremy Bentham's personality, his writings on sexual non-conformity merit the greatest attention for the new evidence they provide on many crucial questions of his philosophy, and for the new light they shed on several hitherto misunderstood aspects of his thought."[12] She indicates the mislabeling of box 74 of Bentham's notes, which possibly contain his earliest analysis of sexual nonconformity, as a particularly suggestive vein for future analysis. These papers, cited throughout this book, reveal that Bentham discovered early in his career that sexual liberty and variety were to be his private test for the utility of government in providing for the happiness of its people. Knowing that he would be unable to publish any of the hundreds of pages of analysis he wrote regarding sexual pleasure, Bentham anticipated a future time when his vision for truly utilitarian legal reform could be brought to light and put to use.

Sexual Nonconformity and the Failure of Penal Law

After qualifying for the bar in 1769, Bentham found himself unwilling to pursue a career practicing the law, lest he become complicit in perpetuating its bigotry. In his first (anonymously) published work, *A Fragment on Government,* he wrote that there are two kinds of writing on any system of power—"that of the Expositor, and that of the Censor,"[13] and that anyone who merely interprets or employs the law as it is, without criticizing it is in some sense culpable for the abuses the law perpetrates on the most vulnerable citizens. As a response to William Blackstone, Bentham argues that "a bigotted or corrupt defender of the works of power, becomes guilty, in a manner, of the abuses which he supports."[14] If the law itself is prejudiced, then so is anyone who works to uphold the law rather than to dismantle and reform it. Unwilling to participate a career in which he would necessarily become complicit in the injustices of the legal code, Bentham instead devoted his life to reform—in part, advocating for a revised penal code that would be enforceable, simple to learn, and fair to all citizens.

Over the previous 150 years, nearly every other system of thought had gone through a process of modernization through simplification—sweeping away the prejudices of Scholasticism and religious bigotry in order to reestablish knowledge on an empiricist foundation of unprejudiced observation. In the natural sciences, history, economics, theology, linguistics, and the arts, the task of eighteenth-century thinkers was no longer to deduce modern instances from ancient principles, but to derive new principles from unprejudiced observation of the world. The preface of *A Fragment on Government* begins by comparing the progress that had recently been made in the natural sciences, in which "every thing teems with discovery and improvement"[15] to the relative stagnation of moral and legal discourse. It seemed to Bentham that the law had been shielded from censure by being preserved in a form that was incomprehensible without extensive esoteric education. Those who had received that education became expositors of the law, unwilling to reform it and thereby render exposition unnecessary.

In his analysis of Bentham's writings on sexual irregularity, Stefan Waldschmidt notes that Bentham accuses the legal system of having been "deliberately designed to confuse citizens"[16] about the limits of legal authority, especially in matters of sexual intercourse, with the goal of making everyone worry that some secret pleasure either is or will soon become a matter for legal retribution. For most British people, the law was illegible, complicated (rather than clarified) by commentary, and far too confusing and changeable even to be understood, much less obeyed. Prohibited sex acts were especially ill defined in the law, with no clear explanation of who the victim of the crime would be or why the punishment was so severe. Later, Bentham would ultimately conclude that the esoteric nature of the law was purposefully maintained in order to oppress the populace, but in *A Fragment on Government* and his notes from the 1770s, he still seems to believe that reform is possible, and must begin with a clearing out of all laws that needlessly restrict individual pleasure, beginning with sexual nonconformity.

In manuscripts from this period,[17] Bentham describes the central problem of English law as "voluminousness"; the law is too extensive and minute to be learned by the citizens who are its subjects. Byrne Fone notes that, during Bentham's life, "the English criminal code . . . listed over two hundred offenses as punishable by death,"[18] including sodomy and other consensual sex acts. In addition to the extensive statute law, the student of English law also had to learn to make rhetorical use of the common law—seven hundred years' worth of cases, decisions, arguments, and precedents. Every legal dispute ultimately depends not merely on whether a written law was violated as much as whether a lawyer or judge can recall and convincingly apply the circumstances of a relevant historical judicial opinion. Although the common law system was (and is) celebrated for making the law flexible to circumstance and responsive to change, Bentham points out that it also makes legal discourse impossible for amateurs to participate in. And until 1733,[19] English court proceedings had been recorded exclusively in "law Latin," a mixture of Latin, French, and English mostly unintelligible without professional training, and printed in close black-letter typeface. In *A Fragment on Government,* Bentham writes, "A large portion of the body of the Law was, by the bigotry or the artifice of Lawyers, locked up in an illegible character, and in a foreign tongue."[20] To most English citizens, the law was unreadable and unknowable. The average person did not just lack sufficient knowledge to invoke the law on his own behalf; he could not even know the law well enough to obey it.

According to William Blackstone, whose *Commentaries on the Laws of England* espoused eighteenth-century England's most humane and enlightened legal ideas, the purpose of English law was to protect, instruct, and guide the populace in how to uphold the citizen's implicit contract with the government that, in turn, keeps the peace. Rather than asserting the rights of one class of persons to oppress the rest with arbitrary rules, Blackstone insists that laws exist only to provide protection for all the individual members of society.

> And this is what we mean by the original contract of society . . . namely, that the whole should protect all it's parts, and that every part should pay obedience to the will of the whole; or, in other words, that the community should guard the rights of each individual member, and that (in return for this protection) each individual should submit to the laws of the community; without which submission of all it was impossible that protection could be certainly extended to any.[21]

Blackstone describes the "original contract" between the community and the individual as the foundation of any society of human beings who submit to authority, promising that the protection of individual rights is the ultimate purpose of law. But in the case of laws prohibiting sexual freedom, Bentham demonstrates, no rights are protected by restricting the private pleasure of nonconformists. Rather, they seem to be pure expressions of legislators' disgust for a pleasure they do not share.

In *Loving Justice*, Kathryn Temple analyzes Blackstone's romanticized notion of community as a kind of ahistorical English identity and sensibility going back to its origins. Of his "Table of Consanguinity," in which Blackstone argues that all men are in fact relatives of one another, Temple writes, "Such textually inscribed moments reinscribe Blackstone's refusal to divorce 1760s England from its past, either Norman or Saxon, and attempt to affirm community persisting over time, to bring the Saxons and the Normans into solidarity with Blackstone's present."[22] These impassioned rhetorical pleas for the family of humankind nevertheless assume a nationalist feeling of unity that must be, Bentham insists, predicated on conscious or unconscious complicity in the historical injustices of the English legal system on its least powerful subjects, who might in some instances be related, but do not all benefit from the inheritance of that legacy.

In his masterful analysis of Bentham's political thought, *Utility and Democracy*, Philip Schofield explicates Bentham's criticisms of Blackstone as a product of his extreme skepticism about extralegal fictional concepts such as "original contract" or "natural law," which imagine English common law as derived from an ahistorical oral tradition of shared moral and cultural values for which the statutory law itself serves merely as a momentary, shifting index. "The point was that the law of nature did not exist—and something which did not exist could not be known. Hence, any appeal to the law of nature in order to invalidate a positive law was either nonsense or a reflection of 'bare unfounded disapprobation' on the part of the objector to the positive law in question. No sort of government could survive in these circumstances."[23] Setting aside the fact that government does somehow continue to survive in these circumstances, Bentham correctly observes that by removing the source of the power of law from the law to some ill-defined distant past or ahistorical identitarian community, legal authorities such as Blackstone rendered the law beyond the power of the critique of the people it oppressed. If the statutory law overreaches, discriminates, or oppresses, natural law proponents respond that the law is a merely human attempt to represent ideal, immutable shared moral values in the relationship between each individual and the people as a whole.

Instead of an imaginary contract between the community and the individual, Bentham describes the origin of laws as the tastes and feelings of a legislator imposed on the populace without their consent and enforced with privation, pain, or death. In his manuscript notes from 1776 under the heading "What a Law Is," Bentham imagines the process by which a penal statute is formed, under the best of intentions:

> I am a Legislator—I have a state to govern. What I have to do is to produce Happiness in it—I set myself to work. My business is to produce happiness in it. I look around me and see a sort of act done which appears to me to produce unhappiness—How does this affect me—I wish, that it was not done—I will that it be not done. such a volition takes place within my breast. The act is robbery: I will that Robbery be not committed. This is the 1st scene in the drama. It lies within my breast.[24]

Here Bentham identifies the origin of a law not in observation of the world, where action is taking place that restricts the happiness of other individual persons, but in the feelings of the legislator who hates that action. Bentham is attempting to identify fallible human agency in legal authority; once an act is illegal, then police, judges, and jailers must enforce it, but the law may itself be the product of prejudice, spite, or self-interest, and not a temporal index of an ahistorical idealized virtue.

Bentham proposes that the will of the legislator to prevent an action should not be enough to justify writing a law against it. A law is not complete—that is, fully expressed and able to be enacted—until it is written so that it can and must be enforced whenever the law is broken, without regard to the person who breaks it: "A Law is *compleat,* that is is compleatly expressed, when the act it prohibits (to take the instance of a prohibitive law) and the punishment for it (to take the instance of a penal law) are so expressed as that, granting the act so described to have been done, no supposition can be framed, in which, according to the Will of the Legislator, the punishment in question shall not take place."[25] If it is not possible or desirable to enforce a proposed penal law in every instance of its violation, then it should not become a part of the legal code. Although this may appear to be a statement in favor of absolute law enforcement, Bentham's intention is to raise the standard by which a law can be deemed valid. A law that the state does not intend to (or cannot) enforce must exist solely as a kind of idle threat or deterrent, which in turn threatens to invalidate the prohibitive force of the penal code, or excite the violence of vigilantes and the mob.

In no case was this more obvious than in that of consensual same-sex male intercourse, a victimless crime that could only be prosecuted if one of the participants could be convinced to inform on his partner. The Buggery Act 1533 was obviously a bad law—it was an unclear, unenforceable gesture on the part of Henry VIII to recategorize ecclesiastical jurisdiction as a function of the government.[26] That is, the Catholic Church had handled sexual matters in their own way, but as Henry began to coalesce church powers for himself, one of those powers was the punishment of sexual deviance. The Buggery Act was briefly repealed by Queen Mary in 1553 as an attempt to return sexual crimes to ecclesiastical authority, but it was reinstated by Elizabeth I in 1563 as an affirmation of state authority over ecclesiastical matters.

In *The Statutes at Large, of England and Great Britain* from 1811, listed between offenses for improper treatment of wool and eels, one finds, "Forasmuch as there is not yet sufficient and condign Punishment appointed and limited by the due Course of the Laws of this Realm, for the detestable and abominable Vice of Buggery committed with Mankind or Beast," followed by a list of punishments, including death, forfeiture of property, and exclusion from the clergy.[27] No definition of buggery is offered here, though case law would clarify (*Rex v. Wiseman* 1718) that buggery includes anal sex between a man and a woman. The most obvious problem with enforcing the law is that, in the case of consensual sex acts, where there is no wronged party, there is no one who would report the crime who was not also complicit in committing the crime. Thus, the power of the Buggery Act was almost entirely symbolic; the state had no business in the bedroom. In its first 150 years, the Buggery Act was invoked only a handful of times, in high-profile cases that typically also involved political intrigue, and a mostly symbolic force.[28]

But by the end of the seventeenth century, the rise of hatred of sexual nonconformity in England had given new venom and force to the law. Around this time, paid agents provocateurs began betraying sexual partners to the magistrates for profit or legal protection. Publishers began to

sell court proceedings containing sexually explicit accounts of seduc-
tion that capitalized on the erotic fascination with—and rising hatred
of—male intimacy. By the eighteenth century, antibuggery prosecutions
had become frequent and well-funded media spectacles that enriched
informers and printers while popularizing extralegal violence against
sexual and gender nonconformists.

Even so, despite the prosecutions of many men who engaged in same-
sex intercourse during the eighteenth century, the vast majority of men
who had sex with men did so in private without exposure, though not
without considerable fear of paid informers, blackmail, and extortion.
At any time, a lover could become an agent of the magistrate, as in the
notorious account of the 1698 prosecution of Captain Edward Rigby,[29]
and the threat of being exposed as a sodomite deterred sexual nonconformists from seeking redress for theft and other crimes. As a secular
tool of social repression, the Buggery Act 1533 became newly effective
in the eighteenth century—not at preventing or prosecuting same-sex
relations, but in creating a culture of suspicion, confusion, and paranoia
that ultimately resulted in the development of a criminal underworld
for sexual nonconformists. Bentham's standard of legal completeness
suggests that there are deleterious social consequences of passing laws
that the state does not really intend to prosecute on behalf of any real
victims. In the case of sodomy, victims were invented to the measure of
the law by antisodomy activists and profiteers.

In the early 1770s Bentham began to speculate about the special case
of sodomy and other forms of what he called "sexual nonconformity"
(or "NONCONF" for short), the violent rage with which moralists address
the subject, and the potentially disastrous effect this rage has on the
penal code. After listing various moralists who have declared sodomy to
be worse than murder or raping one's own mother, Bentham scribbles
in the margin, "I who think that there are other methods of displaying
virtue than preening forth their fury . . . against a Vice of which they are
secure from the temptation."[30] What other crime or sin inspires such
superlative demonstrations of outrage? All of the evidence presented
against sodomy is hyperbole and comparison; no one seems to be able
to find any evidence that consensual sexual nonconformity causes participants any discomfort or unhappiness. To Bentham, if no corruption
is possible, because the acts are performed in private, between or among
consenting parties, and from which no costly or unwanted offspring

could be the result, sexual enjoyment should be considered one of the most beneficial and harmless activities imaginable for the happiness of the people. The legislator's volition to prohibit consensual sexual pleasure between or among adults of any sex comes not from a careful analysis of the evidence of deleterious effects on any other persons, but from personal disgust rooted in bigotry.

Despite his anxiety about persecution for his ideas, Bentham found himself unable to abandon his private commitment to analyzing sexual nonconformity, even though he knew that hatred and violence toward anyone even suspected of sympathy for men who have sex with men could result in his prosecution and possible death. By the 1810s Bentham's writings on sexual difference would come to constitute a kind of second career. Behind every major work of legal, theological, and cultural analysis that Bentham published during the latter part of his life, there are seemingly endless pages of manuscript notes in which he rigorously tested each of his ideas about human happiness and freedom against the example of radical sexual liberty.

Revolutionary Rights and Sinister Interest

For his earnest and passionate engagements with various governments on the subject of legal reform, Bentham was much more celebrated than heeded, and he grew increasingly disappointed by the failure to enact any of his suggestions. His Panopticon project, which he developed in the late 1780s, was one such attempt. Bentham designed and proposed to govern a prison colony in which the guard could develop a personal interest in the health and reform of the inmates, who in turn could experience greater protection from disease and personal security at a far lower cost to the state. His intention was, at least in part, to obviate the financial and social justifications for executing or transporting criminals who could be returned to the general populace. The scheme itself was widely praised, and Prime Minister William Pitt explored various sites for constructing the Panopticon according to Bentham's plan before it was ultimately abandoned. As I discussed in chapter 1, the Panopticon was taken up as a model of invisible social surveillance used in authoritarian and institutional settings, and became Michel Foucault's central metaphor in *Discipline and Punish* for modern forms of surveillance that manipulate subjects into oppressing themselves for an invisible audience of unknown power. Bentham's plan to improve the lives and prospects of convicted felons is now known only as a traumatic emblem of dehumanizing misery.

A similar fate seemed to befall Bentham as a legal reformer. His carefully detailed, minutely argued legal principles, arranged variously as letters, satire, philosophy, theology, drawings, charts, commentaries, pleas, and proposals, were often received with praise and gratitude for the excellence of his contributions to national discourse in the United States, France, Spain, and Great Britain. In each case, Bentham suggested how greater political enfranchisement, economic opportunity, and legal redress for the powerless would ultimately strengthen national security through the greater happiness of the people. Yet the result of these contributions was often that legislators ignored Bentham's suggestions about enfranchisement and happiness, instead focusing exclusively on strategies for consolidating power to oppress minority groups into silence.

Bentham took an eager interest in the progress of the French Revolution and the formation of the French Republic. If any nation in the world had the occasion to reform their legal code from scratch, having made a definitive and violent break from the ancien régime, it was France. In extensive letters and reports written between 1788 and 1795, Bentham urged his contacts in France not to found the new government on fictitious ideas of natural rights, but to construct a powerful new civil code that explicitly protects the liberty and happiness of all members of the French nation, including women, the poor, and colonized and enslaved people. Declarations of rights would only serve, Bentham argued, to limit the power of the legislative body to facilitate the massive social and economic shifts that would make total suffrage and political enfranchisement a reality, while exposing the young republic to potential anarchy, tyranny, misrule, and further revolutions. Although France offered Bentham French citizenship in 1792 as a sign of gratitude for his extensive contributions to legal theory in the Republic, his principle that government must work for "the greatest happiness for the greatest number" went unheeded, while the incipient social and economic instability he warned of was obviated by plunder of the colonies and economic retribution for rebellions.

In 1793, on the eve of the Reign of Terror, Bentham published an impassioned address to the National Convention of France that would later come to be known as "Emancipate Your Colonies!"[31] when it was reprinted for British readers in 1830. In this powerful document, he challenged French legislators to recognize that in holding on to colonial territories, the new French government had made lies of their own declarations of natural rights. "To give freedom at the expence of others, is but conquest in disguise: to rise superior to conquerors, the sacrifice must be your own."[32] Proceeding through arguments appealing to justice, economics, global diplomacy, and utility, he mocks the imagined protestations of the French revolutionaries, satirizing their colonial reenactment of the same tyranny they had so recently overthrown. "Think of how you have dealt by them. One common Bastile inclosed them and you. You knock down the jailor, you let yourselves out, you keep them in, and put yourselves into his place. You destroy the criminal, and you reap the profit, I mean always what seems to you profit, of the crime."[33] By treating so many far-flung colonial subjects as subhuman, unable to claim the so-called natural rights of French people, France had, as he describes it, declared war against its own body, turning healthy limbs into cancerous "excrescences"[34] that would ultimately attack in self-defense. Bentham attempts to reason with the Republic that French territory must only include those citizens it can and will treat equally under the law, or else they will have begun a cycle of perpetual political violence as each disenfranchised group comes to claim their so-called human rights.

In "Emancipate Your Colonies!" Bentham enumerates the necessary consequences of denying rights to certain demographic groups while righteously declaring those same rights to be universal. To enslaved and colonized persons and other disenfranchised French people, what could declarations of rights mean? In a 1795 essay, "Nonsense Upon Stilts," Bentham presumes that the 1791 Declaration of Rights was nothing more than a retroactive justification for the Revolution. He warns the French legislators that, whatever the original intent of creating such a document, the people of France will read that Declaration as a real and binding promise, to be fulfilled for all citizens, or else the government must be overthrown again. He imagines how that Declaration will fall on the ears of the oppressed: "*People, behold your rights: let a single article of them be violated, insurrection is not your right only, but* 'the most sacred of your duties.'"[35] A nation with a declaration of rights must be prepared to withstand constant challenges to the rule of law, both from enfranchised persons who insist on the absolute right to tyrannize and oppress others, as well as from those who have been denied full personhood under discriminatory laws. The French Republic would be forced either to facilitate the means of liberty for all French territories and persons, or it must limit its borders to a community whose happiness it can legitimately facilitate so that another revolution would be unnecessary.

Twenty-seven years after the French Republic ignored his demand that they emancipate their colonies, Bentham would try the same argument again, at much greater length, with the government of Spain. These letters, titled "Emancipation Spanish" and "Rid Yourselves of Ultramaria,"[36] were sent between 1820 and 1822, during the period when the 1812 constitution was restored by Ferdinand VII, under pressure from a military mutiny. The constitution of Spain replicated the libertarian rights discourse of the French Republic, while rejecting the course of overturning the antiguo régimen through revolution. Meanwhile, with vast colonial territories spanning the globe, Spain felt it necessary to partially enfranchise certain colonial subjects, including indigenous persons, but not enslaved Africans or their free descendants. In these sets of letters, Bentham explained in much greater detail why holding on to territories abroad and exploiting enslaved persons would necessarily create constitutional crises, as the partial enfranchisement of colonial subjects would result in challenges to imperial authority. "Spaniards!" he writes, "Your Constitutional Code is a mixt mass: a compound of sugar and arsenic it may be stiled. From the nourishment, would you distinguish the poison? Would you rid your body politic of it?"[37] Without cleansing the nation of dependence on colonial labor and resources, and converting those relationships to equal trade between political entities, Spain's liberal constitution can only become a kind of poison to the health of the peninsular nation. Where natural rights are declared to be universal in the same document that violates them, the rule of law will, Bentham predicts, dissolve into anarchy, as the oppressed are left with no option but to overthrow their oppressors, as they are directed to do by the constitution itself.

In the cases of the United States and France, declarations of natural rights were used retroactively to justify the violence of their revolutions, but the new laws developed after those revolutions did little to provide legal redress for future abuses of power. In the United States, France, and Spain, the new constitutions explicitly limited the power of the legislature to create and reform laws, holding the enumerated "rights" to be sacred and inviolable for those not explicitly disenfranchised on the basis of race, class, or gender. In Locke's political theory, natural rights are by definition *extralegal* motivations to self-preservation; without the protection law should provide to prevent the strong from tyrannizing the weak, victims of oppression have recourse only to organized violence and prayer. By declaring natural rights as an addendum and precursor to the legal code, constitutions founded on the basis of declarations of rights render law subservient to the use of violence, rather than a means of balancing the power of various members of the community.

Bentham, who spent his entire career pleading with governments to abandon their ill-considered declarations of rights, nevertheless found that Locke's definition of natural rights had tremendous political force for those persons whose survival was literally threatened by discriminatory laws. In the cases of enslaved and colonized persons, women, and men who had sex with men, their natural right to survival had been proscribed by laws that denied them custodianship of their own bodies, on pain of death. In the spring of 1814, Bentham wrote an essay intended as a criticism of the penal code under the heading "Of Sexual Irregularities— or, Irregularities of the Sexual Appetite." In this essay, Bentham draws a direct comparison between political rebellion, abortion or infanticide, and same-sex intercourse, on the basis that all three are deemed "unnatural"—crimes so unbearably evil that the law recruits citizen surveillance and incites extralegal violence to assist in deterrence and punishment. What all three of these crimes have in common, Bentham argues, is that those who commit them are acting not unnaturally but, ironically, as a practice of their only natural right, the right to defend their own lives. The enslaved person has the right, according to Locke, to kill his master, as he is in a "*State of War continued, between a lawful Conquerour, and a Captive,*"[38] so that either man has the right to kill the other if he can, until the regular force of law is restored to prevent them from harming one another as equals.

In the case of infanticide, Bentham evokes a startling comparison between the mother of an illegitimate child, hounded out of society and denied comfort and safety, and a survivor of shipwreck floating on the ocean and despairing of life. "If, on the occasion of a shipwreck, seeing another person, a stranger, saving himself upon a plank, the woman were to beat him from it and take his place, in this case the act of self-preservation thus performed would not by any person, whether disapproved or no, be termed an unnatural one."[39] The mother who, in conditions of terrifying social violence and privation, sees some way to preserve her own life at the cost of her child must at least be an object of pity. Compassion would insist that the crime of infanticide was aggravated by social violence that should be mitigated by law, so that future violence against illegitimate infants could be prevented. So, too, Bentham insists, the crime of buggery must be viewed as a form of self-preservation. Whatever the impetus to engage in same-sex intercourse may be, the law against it only intensifies the social violence of the powerful against marginalized people, instead of mitigating that violence. The rule of law exists in order to prevent the powerful from exercising their will over others in complete freedom, and so any law that intensifies that violence is both redundant and needlessly cruel.

Bentham again links sexual irregularity to abortion in a series of notes from January 1818, in which he suggests that the sinister interests of the powerful are invested in maintaining steady reproduction, against the will of people who have neither the means nor the desire to raise children. If women are prevented from aborting children, people are forbidden from nonreproductive methods of sexual intercourse, suicide is a crime, and even human castration is forbidden, then the bulk of the people will necessarily be reduced to a state of guilt, desperation, misery, and hopelessness.

> 46. Pleasures of the bed may be excluded from all but the power necessary to maximise population and from them every particle of those pleasures over and above what are necessary to the production of that maximum.

> 47. For excluding pleasure of the bed from non-[family?   ] the surest operation. But by preventing desire this would exclude pain of unsatisfied desire. Hence for self castration Origin was designed a heretic for the same reason[40]

Nearing the end of his most concentrated reasoning on sexual pleasure, Bentham concluded that elite men in law, philosophy, and religion were conspiring, not merely to eradicate nonreproductive sexual pleasure, but to force people to endure as much unsatisfied sexual desire as possible, and declaring the pain of self-denial to be the highest kind of virtue.

After nearly fifty years of concentrated analysis of the institutions of law, religion, and philosophy, Bentham concluded that the creation and perpetuation of pain for the bulk of the people is the true goal of the sinister interests of power. At some times and places, that power has taken the form of autocratic tyranny. But Bentham recognized the same impulse even behind the sublime rhetoric of the new constitutional democracies; behind the curtain of natural rights hid the specter of anarchy, tyranny, and mob rule. The law must only exist to protect the liberties and pleasures of people who would otherwise be little more than lifelong victims of the powerful—the stranger, the laborer, the unwed mother, and the sexual nonconformist.

4

Bentham's Queer Christ

Queer sexuality today could be described as defiantly useless. In the face of modern heteronormative bourgeois discourse, in which sexual desire serves to perpetuate patriarchy by producing legally contracted family relations, and to yield offspring who can then be ensconced in the normative symbolic order of capital and production, queer theorists have largely ceded the grounds of utility in order to argue that sex can, and often must, do nothing—not produce children, legal contracts, or any kind of futurity at all, as in Lee Edelman's powerful formulation. Edelman writes, borrowing from Auden, that "queerness makes nothing happen."[1] Queer sex, rather, is defined as that which refuses to instrumentalize pleasure for the replication of either hegemony or human life. In *No Future*, responding to the politicization of queerness by mainstream parties and officials, Edelman writes, "Queerness thus comes to mean *nothing* for both: for the right wing the nothingness always at war with the positivity of civil society; for the left, nothing more than a sexual practice in need of demystification."[2] Politicized sexuality must offer either a promise of continued reproduction into the future, or a promise to dissolve into an ever-widening liberal normativity that benignly swallows difference with toleration. Queerness persists in the form of a refusal to be eradicated or assimilated for the convenience of political narratives of progress.

   If the utility of living as we currently understand it is to produce more life and project the present into the future, it is only because of the emergence of reproductive futurity as a nationalist project that began in the eighteenth century. Michel Foucault traces this history in *The History of Sexuality*, volume 1, as a narrative of increasing nationalistic obsession with harnessing the reproductive potential of a "population," not merely in terms of health and survival but in terms of future growth through the management of desire. Foucault writes, "Of course, it had long been asserted that a country had to be populated if it hoped to be rich and powerful; but this was the first time that a society had affirmed, in a constant way, that its future and its fortune were tied not only to the number and the uprightness of its citizens, to their marriage rules and family organization, but to the manner in which each individual made use of his sex."[3] In Foucault's reading of the rise of compulsory heterosexuality in Europe across the modern era, sexual feelings became part of a truly public discourse through popular literature and entertainment, which allowed for that discourse to be manipulated by powerful interests for the production of the future state. If the cultural context in which sex happens—through architecture, education, and popular entertainment—can make heterosexual procreation seem to be the only purpose of life, while devaluing the bodily autonomy of women, laborers, and sexual nonconformists, then, Foucault argues, the state legitimizes its authority by requiring the bulk of the populace to sacrifice their bodily autonomy to keep on manufacturing the future.

In *The Child to Come*, Rebekah Sheldon traces the uncanny twentieth-century reverberations from that pseudoscientific discourse, which emerged out of a culture of rapid urbanization and industrialization. Reproduction became increasingly imperative in a moment in which the present was becoming frightening, dehumanizing, and unrecognizable. Characterizing the discourse of compulsory reproduction, Sheldon writes, "Reproductive futurism, then, is a two-sided salvation narrative: someday the future will be redeemed of the mess our present actions foretell; until then, we must keep the messy future from coming by replicating the present through our children."[4] The special category of the child, as an uncanny surface for projecting global and national anxiety, emerged at precisely the same time as the nationalistic project of reproductive futurity. As Sheldon argues, the child became a figure that is simultaneously infinitely vulnerable and precious *and* doomed to endure the dehumanizing circumstances of a future devoid of pleasure. The child becomes, in Sheldon's phrasing, a "retronaut, a piece of the future lodged in and under the controlling influence of the present."[5] As one of the many victims of reproductive futurism, the child who did not ask to be born to the mother who did not want to be a mother with the father who did not want to be a husband finds that life exists in order to project the misery of the reluctant family into a future it manufactured so that someone else's account books will one day come out in the black.

While queerness resists the productivity narrative of political economy, it is, and perhaps always has been, more at ease in the rhetoric of paradox and apocalypse in religious discourse. Kathryn Bond Stockton argues in *God between Their Lips* that the refusal to participate in heterosexual coupling and its symbolic gestures leaves the queer subject outside empiricist discourse. Instead, Stockton shows, queer writers who attempt to address physical pleasure end up, perhaps ironically, mysticizing it—borrowing the language of spiritual ecstasy as an alternative to the economics of production and exchange that dominate heterosexist discourse. She writes, "Spiritual discourse is discourse on what exceeds human sign systems; discourse on where human meanings fail; discourse on escapes from discourse; and, most importantly, culturally constructed discourse on escapes from culture, though from the present standpoint these escapes are always incomplete and deferred."[6] To describe queer pleasure, which has no metaphorical or physical offspring, is to suggest a signifier for some other sublime mystery, viewed in part, for a moment, as a universe of plentiful excess. Queerness, then, may be figured as a kind of introverted monasticism, turning away from the limitations of earthly exchange, productivity, and public rhetoric to experience sexual pleasure as the language in which divine knowledge is written. Compulsory heterosexualism is not an equal and opposite injunction toward a different kind of sublime pleasure, but a demonstration of obedience to the nationalist, heteronormative, capitalist obligation to make the future profitable through procreation.

In the midst of the development of modern industrial London, in January 1818 Jeremy Bentham referred to this compulsory reproductive injunction as manufacturing children to become a "receptacle for pain"—persons whose lives are not conducted by their own will and pleasure, never to be, as Locke puts it, "*Proprietor of his own Person.*"[7] In the context of this demand for more life in the future, Bentham insists that no one is responsible for making children—especially not the laboring women and men whose lives could only be embittered and impoverished by coerced reproduction. As for the purported ill effects of same-sex intimacy on the population, Bentham writes that it "is upon the face of it so palpably absurd that it is not easy to speak of it with that seriousness which the importance of the subject demands. Not more absurd would be the apprehension of the effect of a famine as about to be produced by the taste for chewing tobacco."[8] That is, an aesthetic preference for same-sex intercourse has never prevented anyone from having the children they want. Such an accusation could only make sense if literally every single sex act that could potentially be performed must result in the formation of a baby in order to produce a new generation to do the labor so that we can be allowed to die. But of course, as Bentham goes on to note, the population of living persons is already treated as excessive, expendable, and doomed to miserable lives and early deaths. The fiction of nationalistic futurity is no better reason for a person to sacrifice all hope of happiness than the fiction of heavenly rewards for self-denial, nor the fiction of Stoic satisfaction for a life endured without physical pleasure.[9] In the context of these overlapping nationalist, religious, and philosophical forms of asceticism, Bentham found little evidence of any eulogistic language for nonreproductive, noneconomic pleasure in eighteenth-century discourse, aside from in popular literature by women and sexual nonconformists, which I discuss in chapter 5, and in the example of the life and teachings of Jesus.

Bentham's criticism of Christianity as a religion is thorough and unambiguous. As a student at Queen's College, Oxford, Bentham was required by the Test Act 1674 (25 Car. II. c. 2) to profess allegiance to the Thirty-Nine Articles of the Church of England in order to take his B.A. in 1763, and he found this obligation deeply offensive. In his studies of the law, he found the influence of religion on the penal code to be absurd, and the use of scripture to justify oppression and discrimination disturbing. In the latter decades of his career, after he had largely ceased to hope to gain influence over legislators, Bentham began to publish extensive criticisms, under his own name and pseudonyms, in which he attacked the influence of religion on law and public life. In 1817 he published *Swear Not at All,* quoting Jesus on the unethical practice of requiring public oaths. For Bentham, as for Cordelia in Shakespeare's *King Lear,* a required oath is inherently dishonest, as it turns private belief or knowledge into a theatrical performance of honesty, no more to be trusted than a confession extracted under torture. In 1818 he published *Church-of-Englandism and Its Catechism Examined,* a blistering criticism of the inculcation of the church's values in the education of children. Forced to recite church dogma as a kind of payment for useful knowledge, children were learning that duplicity and hypocrisy were the price of social and economic security. In 1822 he pseudonymously published a pamphlet titled *An Analysis of the Influence of Natural Religion on the Temporal Happiness of Mankind,* in which he attacks the liberal deist appeals to "Providence" and "the Creator" as a vague way of invoking a benign, all-powerful "Being" as a threat or a bribe, without attesting to any particular scriptural basis for belief. And in 1823 he pseudonymously published a small part of his massive manuscript work on Christian scripture, *Not Paul, but Jesus,* in which he meticulously compares and analyzes Christian and Hebrew scripture in order to demonstrate that Paul, by turning the philosophy of Jesus into an ascetic, discriminatory religious doctrine, appropriated the liberationist, revolutionary fervor of the followers of Jesus in order to promote a hierarchical global order that demands the perpetual misery and cruelty of its followers.

In all of these works, Bentham consistently refers to "the religion of Jesus" as the ideas he draws from reading the teachings of Jesus directly, without the influence of any other scripture or religious tradition based on Jesus. In doing so, Bentham defends a reading of the life of Jesus as a singular eulogistic example of individual pleasure and will that caused no harm to others, and produced neither offspring nor economic value to society. In Bentham's unmistakably queer reading of the life of Jesus, Jesus's great contribution to humanity is the example of someone who did absolutely nothing except enjoy his own life and contribute to the enjoyment of others. Promising his followers an ever-renewing source of physical and spiritual comfort, and providing them with excessive nutrition and delight, Jesus attempted, according to Bentham's reading, to teach his followers, not to internalize the worries of the powerful that they might not hold on to their power forever, but to anticipate with joy a time when the future would no longer be manufactured in the image of present injustice. To live exuberantly, seeking present pleasures to assuage present pains, is all that Bentham's Jesus asked of those he taught.

I propose a friendly addendum to the monasticism of queer discourse in the form of a Benthamite reconsideration of utility itself. If queer sex is to be contrasted with "doing," then, I wonder, what is the point of doing anything? What is the end to which utility is assumed to serve as an ideological vector into the present? For David Hume and other Enlightenment philosophers, utility was a matter of common sense—benefiting society as a whole, by which they always seemed to mean the reproductive and economic security of free white men. For Jeremy Bentham, the summum bonum of utility was not economic productivity, or the perpetuation of human life, or the maintenance of bourgeois culture, but the greatest happiness for the greatest number, which he insisted must account for the happiness of women, children, disabled people, laborers, colonized people, and—with particular emphasis—sexual nonconformists. Happiness, Bentham asserted, may be derived from a wide variety of endeavors, but the very surest and least destructive means to human happiness must be nonreproductive sexual pleasure.

Although Bentham's writings on sexual nonconformity span the length of his career, his defense of nonreproductive forms of sex during the 1810s began to draw upon his increasing interest in (and strong opinions about) religious discourse. During this very productive period in Bentham's published work, he was simultaneously writing several manuscripts that gathered evidence and forcefully argued for the total decriminalization and social toleration of private consensual sex. Having answered the question of sexual liberty to his own satisfaction in his work on liberal rights, the penal code, popular discourse, and aesthetic theory, Bentham began to take religious arguments against same-sex intimacy seriously. Why would *Jesus* care if consenting equals have sex with each other?

Bentham's Secularity

One of the most hotly debated aspects of Bentham's philosophy is to what degree he was or was not an atheist. That he passionately and consistently argued for a total separation of church and state is obvious. During the formation of the Church of England in the 1530s, many formerly ecclesiastical statutes were transformed into legal statutes and became moral imperatives in the English penal code. Bentham proposed to assist the British and United States governments in cleansing the penal code of the influence of religious asceticism, with the understanding that, whatever political purpose those laws had once served, they now only prevented people from harmlessly enjoying their lives. J. E. Crimmins posited that Bentham's secularity was not merely a matter of legal principle, but was motivated by a desire "to eliminate the notion of religion itself from the mind."[10] That is, Crimmins, along with many other secularist Benthamites, suggests that the ultimate goal of secular government is not justice, equality, or well-being, but the inculcation of atheism.

Philip Schofield notes that Crimmins and other secularist utilitarians may have significantly overstated the matter of Bentham's supposed atheism. Although it is obvious that he had no pious or even recognizably religious reading of scripture, and vociferously criticized the asceticism demanded by Jewish law and by Paul in Christian scripture, as well as by deistic proponents of virtue ethics in the form of "natural religion," Bentham was clearly moved by the life and teachings of Jesus as written in the Christian gospels. Schofield concludes from his analysis of Bentham's complex treatment of Christian scripture and religion that "Bentham was 'secular' not in the sense that his starting point was a rejection of religious belief, but in that his starting point was independent of religious belief. It was a starting point from which religious belief itself could be analysed."[11] Bentham did not argue from an a priori position of the nonexistence of any god, but from the a priori position that more widespread happiness would be good. Schofield convincingly argues that the existence or nonexistence of a god is somewhat irrelevant to Bentham's primary purpose, which is to consider religious discourse as one of the forms of fictional power that, along with philosophy and law, have been employed by persons with sinister interests to increase misery by convincing people to deny themselves pleasure. Bentham nowhere takes a definitive position on God, per se, but instead focuses on the ways that men with power use fictional ideas of God and the afterlife to frighten people into conformity, obedience, and asceticism.

Delos McKown likewise argues that Bentham's hostility to Christianity as it is practiced begins from a principle of human happiness against which systems of morality, law, and governance, including performance of religious duty and ritual, may be measured. Any religion in which God is simply a projection of a would-be tyrant's resentments is clearly not based on the principle of human happiness. But that does not mean that eighteenth-century latitudinarian deism, which was promoted as a potential end to the petty squabbles between various religious sects, was any more equipped to provide for the happiness of the bulk of the people. In one of his 1770s manuscripts on the utility of religion, Bentham debates with himself about what to make of the goodness of God:

1 God is not good [is not a benevolent being] if he prohibits our possessing the least atom of [clear] happiness which he has given us the physical capacity [faculty] of attaining.

2. If we cannot depend upon his benevolence we cannot depend upon his Justice, we can not depend upon any of his moral attributes.

3. If God is good, he prohibits nothing [whereby] the clear stock of happiness ever be increased: if he is not good, that is, if he prohibits any act whereby the clear stock of happiness can be encreased, we can still find no motive for abstaining from any such act in any prohibition of his: By taking away his Benevolence his [whole] moral character, his veracity is destroy'd we have no reason to suppose he will punish from his declaring that he will punish: nor that he will reward, from his declaring that he will reward.[12]

Whatever ideas of God had been promoted as a corrective to the restrictively dogmatic theology of the pre-Enlightened era, Bentham feared that they did not solve the fundamental problem of God, which is that, if he is powerful, he is demonstrably not good to or for human beings during their lives. If God is omnipotent, then either he has refused to prevent pain, or he enjoys inflicting pain on us, and entertains himself by asking us to inflict pain on ourselves.

In *An Analysis of the Influence of Natural Religion on the Temporal Happiness of Mankind,* Bentham's manuscripts on so-called natural religion were organized, edited, and brought to press under the pseudonym Philip Beauchamp by his colleague George Grote, who shared Bentham's concern about the deistic forms of Christianity that had begun to appear in liberal political discourse. As McKown points out, even these vague liberal deist notions of Providence are exactly as harmful to the happiness of the people as any angry supposedly pagan god who demands human sacrifice and threatens annihilation. McKown writes, "It was sufficient (for [Bentham]) that the almighty Being mentioned above exercises such overwhelming power that human beings can never resist or modify it. For all anyone can ascertain from his definition, natural religion does not require that this everlasting Being be the 'Maker of Heaven and Earth,' only that the Being at issue is in a position to dispense pains and pleasures to humans in an infinite and future state of existence."[13] Bentham found that the liberal deists had not, in fact, developed a new idea of God as a truly benevolent being, but had simply reduced God to nothing more than a vague projection of their own patriarchal, heterosexist, colonialist desires for power.

In this work, Bentham attempts several thought experiments based on the ideas of natural religionists, whose idea of God seemed to be an incomprehensible observer of human action who, without getting involved in human affairs, keeps accounts of the good and evil he sees and prepares some kind of reward or punishment based on the sum of their actions. As for the attributes of this God, Bentham lists "[a] power to which we can assign no limits—an agency which we are unable to comprehend or frustrate."[14] As a thought experiment, Bentham imagines a human agent with power to which we can assign no limits, who would necessarily be a horrific tyrant if he acted in his own interests, or a cruel miser if he withheld help from the interests of his subjects. As for his incomprehensible nature, Bentham writes that it "is in human affairs termed *caprice,* when confined to the trifling occurrences of life; *insanity,* when it extends to important occasions. The capricious or the insane are those whose proceedings we cannot reconcile with the acknowledged laws of human conduct—those whose conduct defies our utmost sagacity of prediction."[15] Going further, Bentham imagines this incomprehensible, all-powerful being let loose among us: "What if we figure him, like the insane Orlando of Ariosto, roaming about with an invulnerable hide, and limbs insensible to the chain! What if, still farther, he be entrusted with the government of millions, seconded by irresistible legions who stand ready at his beck! Can the utmost stretch of fancy produce any picture so appalling, as that of a mad, capricious, and incomprehensible Being exalted to this overwhelming sway? Yet this terrific representation involves nothing beyond surpassing might, wielded by one whose agency is unfathomable."[16] Whenever religionists invoke a supernatural authority, Bentham simply asks how that authority would strike us, as described, if it were housed in the body of a person. Would that person promote the happiness of others? Which others? Why those others? Why not all?

In his analysis of the effects of this antidoctrinal "natural religion," Bentham laments that, rather than using the rhetoric of religion in order to promote a truly liberationist idea of human liberty and happiness, it seemed to exist only to preach asceticism and useless privations. He writes, "That branch therefore, at least, of religious injunctions, which is termed *our duty to God,* must be regarded as detrimental to human felicity in this life. It is a deduction from the pleasures of the individual, without at all benefiting the species. It must be considered, so far as the present life is concerned, as a tax paid for the salutary direction which the branch termed *our duty to man* is said to imprint upon human conduct, and for the special and unequalled efficacy, within which these sanctions are alleged to operate."[17] If denial of pleasure is a tax demanded by God, then, Bentham argues, this God does not want us to be happy, nor for us to live in a peaceful or productive society. The useless privation of pleasure creates factitious antipathies, dangerous resentments, joyless lives, and early deaths. If this is one's image of God, he argues, then it is a cruel god who does not deserve to be worshipped. Throughout the work, Bentham shows how this supposedly benevolent deistic notion of God as an omnipotent supernatural judge of the afterlife is not invoked to promote liberty for the oppressed, the enjoyment of the sensual body, or the love of other people, but merely to terrify the populace out of acting on their own desires, and to redirect the petitions of the oppressed to a being outside the visible universe, rather than to the flesh-and-blood oppressor that sits before them, whether in the household, the school, the plantation, the factory, the courtroom, or the prison.

"Natural religion" had become, Bentham feared, a kind of euphemism for the modern liberal form of oppression, which asks individual subjects to oppress themselves in ways that are convenient for those in power—not because it is demanded by some particular scripture, or because one will be rewarded by their Maker at some point after death, or even simply because the self-denying person will be perceived as socially admirable in a culture that resents noneconomic pleasure to the point of punishing it with death. Rather, in the modern state, the disenfranchised person is asked, through "duty to God" or "duty to Man," to conform to self-discipline and regulation of pleasure with the promise that a reward will come someday, in a form yet to be determined. By framing happiness in neoclassical terms of abstract moral satisfaction that require one to abstain from physical pleasure, the ruling class can continually deny even basic sexual and reproductive freedoms to disenfranchised persons.

Bentham's intense appreciation for Jesus is that, if he is a representation of God in human flesh, he is nothing like the incomprehensible tyrant madman that the deists' god would be on earth. He is not capricious, inconsistent, withholding, or resentful of pleasure. What powers he has are used to comfort, soothe, heal, and provide sensual enjoyment to others, and much of his teaching as reported in scripture offers

advice on how it might be possible to enjoy the modest sensory pleasures available in one's own life without causing violence or privation for
others. Jesus warned against sinful resentment, envy, worry, miserliness,
self-righteousness, cruelty, ambition, and so forth—all expressions of
concern about one's status relative to that of others. In the Sermon on
the Mount as presented in Matthew 5, 6, and 7, Jesus offers a kind of
philosophy of minding one's own business, and not using fear (whether
real or fabricated) as an excuse to deprive others of resources, or even to
deny oneself pleasure:

> Behold the fowls of the air: for they sow not, neither do they reap, nor
> gather into barns; yet your heavenly Father feedeth them. Are ye not
> much better than they? Which of you by taking thought can add one
> cubit unto his stature? And why take ye thought for raiment? Consider
> the lilies of the field, how they grow; they toil not, neither do they spin:
> And yet I say unto you, That even Solomon in all his glory was not
> arrayed like one of these. Wherefore, if God so clothe the grass of the
> field, which to day is, and to morrow is cast into the oven, shall he not
> much more clothe you, O ye of little faith? (Matt. 6:26–30)

Anxiety about resources, concern for social status, and disgust for the
pleasure of others are three of the main distractions Jesus identifies that
lure the faithful away from real righteousness, which is uninterested in
power, unconcerned about the future, and responsive to the sensory
pleasures provided by life. The divinity of Jesus seems to have been
irrelevant to Bentham, for whom the existence or nonexistence of God
remained unimportant; rather, Jesus was quite clearly an advocate of
utilitarianism, in Bentham's understanding of it. In a "religion of Jesus,"
one could imagine enjoying one's own pleasures and allowing others to
enjoy theirs without feeling the need to prevent, restrict, or spoil their
access to those pleasures—if only Paul had never written his commentaries to decentralize pleasure from the religion of Jesus.

Bentham's extensive writing on what he refers to as "the religion of
Jesus" describes an alternate reading of the Christian gospels that imagines a different legacy for Christianity, as if it never fell under the doctrinal influence of the writings of Paul. Across what are now two published
volumes of *Not Paul, but Jesus,* as well as the notes in his outline, *General
Idea of a Work . . . ,* Bentham argues for a radical reanalysis of the life and

teachings of Jesus that emphasizes human flourishing, the reduction of suffering, facilitation of sensory and emotional pleasures, and the end of legal and social discrimination against disenfranchised or economically dependent groups such as women, children, disabled people, laborers, the poor, sex workers, and sexual nonconformists.[18] Bentham argues that the "religion of Jesus" implied by scripture is the direct opposite of the religion of Paul that was adopted as "Christianity" and the culture that emerged from those "Christian" principles. Without ever asserting that there is or is not a God, Bentham nevertheless seems to acknowledge that the Christian religion, as a fiction that guides human action by providing a hierarchy of values, could have been a very different force in the world from what it has been in reality.

Bentham on the "Religion of Jesus"

In *Swear Not at All,* a pamphlet containing one of his earliest arguments on the "religion of Jesus," Bentham used evidence from scripture to demonstrate the hypocrisy of demanding oaths to the state. "Thus repugnant to one of the plainest precepts of Jesus,—to that one which may perhaps be stated as being the most pointed and specific of all the precepts of Jesus,—how happens it, it may be asked, that, under a religion calling itself the religion of Jesus, the use made of this ceremony should have been so abundant?"[19] If Bentham's primary goal had been, as Crimmins argues, to put an end to religious thought altogether, what could be the purpose of this argument from scripture about the anti-Christian nature of British law? I do not argue that Bentham himself "believed" in God, but that he found something compelling in the teachings and life of Jesus, which, as he continually reminds his reader, were consistently at odds with any demands to vow allegiance to state or social authority, and would certainly forbid making any such oath a requirement of citizens for political or legal participation.

In *Church-of-Englandism,* Bentham likewise compares the compulsory nature of state religious education to the teachings of Jesus, who, Bentham asserts, promoted individual will and liberty in all things. He writes:

> In this state of things,—the religion, which in these same schools is thus taught, is it the religion of Jesus?—Not it indeed—it is a quite different thing. Of this proposition, the proof rests—not on any points of

detail—not on inferences drawn, on such or such particular subject, from such or such particular texts. It applies not to this or that opinion— to this or that word. It goes to the whole together. The ground it rests upon is the broadest of all grounds: viz. that, administered as they are, and as above they have been seen to be administered, the portions of discourse thus forced into the minds, or at least into the mouths, of these poor children, form altogether a *substitute*—not a mere—*additament*, but a complete *substitute*—to the religion, which would be composed of the discourses of Jesus.[20]

Nowhere does Bentham assert the real divinity of Jesus, nor does he insist that Jesus is or is not the son of God. But it is plain that Bentham has something quite concrete in mind when he refers to "the religion of Jesus," a religion that has perhaps never been practiced as such, but would have the potential to cleanse the law of unnecessary proscriptions of bodily custodianship, as well as of compulsory ideological training.

Bentham's appeal to the teachings of Jesus may seem hypocritical, coming from someone who had spent his entire life fighting the influence of religion on government. It could be read as a mere commonplace, citing the authority of Jesus as a means to his own rhetorical end, the cessation of government-required oaths. But in the case of oaths as well as sexual liberty, I am inclined to think that, far from paying lip service to Jesus, Bentham was deeply influenced by the teachings of Jesus as an antiauthoritarian radical who promoted the authority of individual conscience and will rather than obedience to power. In matters of sensory pleasure—especially in food and sexual pleasure—Jesus was a pioneer of aesthetic variety, in Bentham's analysis, and his life's work was to model a life of earnest physical pleasure that harmed no one while producing no offspring or economic value. Rather than reading Jesus as the sacrifice whose death atones for the sins of the world, Bentham sees Jesus as a martyr for nonprocreative, unproductive enjoyment of his body, the greatest utilitarian who ever lived.

Bentham feared that the message of Jesus had been perverted, first by Paul and then by others, into a religion of self-denial, for the purpose of holding the lives of the masses hostage to the political will of a few. As he laments, even the more recent turn toward secular liberalism in the eighteenth century did little to mitigate oppression, as women and the poor were still politically disenfranchised. The slaveholders in the

United States and the colonizers in France had fought bloody revolutions for "freedom," only to consolidate power for a slightly different group of white patriarchal tyrants. Asceticism had flourished in eighteenth-century Britain, at a time when popular literature had taken over from sermons as a source of moral instruction, particularly with respect to sexual behavior. But instead of liberating gender and sexual minorities from oppressive religious doctrine, the secularization of morality had made sexual asceticism the most urgent priority of social discipline.

In 1817 Bentham began an outline of what would later be published pseudonymously in 1823 as *Not Paul, but Jesus.* The published version of *Not Paul, but Jesus* would be a 400-page refutation of Paul's authority as an interpreter of Jesus's teachings. In it, Bentham lists every factual and doctrinal inconsistency between the writings of Paul and those of other early Christians, as well as Jewish law, demonstrating that the character of the Antichrist as a kind of hobgoblin nemesis comes exclusively from Paul, and that various prohibitions on bodily enjoyment, including sexual irregularity, come from Paul. But in his extensive notes for the work *Not Paul, but Jesus,* it is clear that Bentham had intended to write and publish two more parts of the work. According to the editors of *Of Sexual Irregularities,* "In Part II he would deal with the implications for sexual morality, and therefore for happiness more generally, of adopting either the principle of utility or the principle of asceticism, and in Part III with the respective sexual attitudes and practices of Jesus and St. Paul."[21] Nothing has survived of Bentham's notes for the second part, but in the third part, Bentham intended to focus much more on Jesus as an advocate for practitioners of nonconforming sexual practices, as well as people who engage in polygamy, promiscuity, birth control, abortion, suicide, and other "eccentric" acts of self-determination. Bentham feared bringing this work to print in his virulently homophobic time and place, and so he intended to gauge the response of the public to the first part alone.

As he began his extended analysis of what would become *Not Paul, but Jesus,* Bentham was simultaneously exploring the supposedly "moral" problems that arise from noneconomic forms of pleasure. He notes that Jesus's teachings are remarkable for their moral indifference to a variety of sexual practices, while being clearly and starkly opposed to violence or retribution against those accused of sexual deviance. In *Of Sexual Irregularities,* a series of manuscript notes analyzing the problem of aesthetic normativity and cultural hierarchies that privilege so-called mental pleasures, Bentham describes Jesus:

> Jesus, from whose lips not a syllable favourable to ascetic self-denial is, by any one of his biographers, represented as ever having issued. Jesus who, among his disciples, had one to whom he imparted his authority and another in whose bosom his head reclined, and for whom he avowed his love: Jesus who, in the stripling clad in loose attire, found a still faithful adherent, after the rest of them had fled: Jesus in whom the woman taken in adultery found a successful advocate: Jesus, on the whole field of sexual irregularity, preserved an uninterrupted silence. Jesus was one person, Paul was another.[22]

Bentham understands the "religion of Jesus" to be a kind of Epicurean activism, something like a performance of experiencing and facilitating pleasure, in defiance of legal and economic powers that expect some classes of persons to live miserably so that elites can hoard resources. According to Bentham, Jesus was entirely antipatriarchal, anticolonialist, and anticapitalist—not that he promoted violent political revolution, but that he urged his followers not to conform their individual capacity for pleasure to the asceticism demanded by earthly authority. "Render unto Caesar what is Caesar's" suggests that one should probably, for example, pay taxes, but also to remember that while money belongs to the state, the body and will of a person do not. Bentham's religion, if one can call it that, is not that God is good, but that good is God.

Bentham's reference to the "stripling clad in loose attire" is one of the gospels' most suggestive mysteries for queer readers of Christian scripture. Mark, the first written and shortest of the four biblical accounts of Jesus's life and teaching, includes an account of his betrayal and arrest in Gethsemane in the middle of the night. A mob led by the high priest had come on information from Judas Iscariot to arrest Jesus while he was praying. Jesus mocks them for bringing weapons. "Are ye come out, as against a thief, with swords and with staves to take me?" (Mark 14:48). (It is worth noting that Bentham often asks the same question of the homophobic lynch mob; what is the reason for *so* much violence, in excess of the peaceful crime of enjoying one's own life?) As the disciples flee, the author of Mark adds, "And there followed him a certain young man, having a linen cloth cast about his naked body; and the young men laid hold on him: And he left the linen cloth, and fled from them naked" (15:51–52). The stripling, or *neaniskos* (νεανίσκος—Bentham insists that "young man, as in the authoritative translation, makes him too old"), is wearing a *sindona* (σινδόνα), a thin muslin cloth inappropriate for street wear and more commonly used to wrap dead bodies—as Bentham notes, "the garment at once fine and costly," though "so thin and incompleat an attire as a sign of the profession in either sex," suggesting that the stripling was perhaps a sex worker.[23] Christian exegetes have struggled to understand why this practically naked man is found with Jesus in Gethsemane. Later in Mark, a neaniskos in a sindona is sitting in Jesus's tomb after his resurrection. This person is not identified as an angel, nor is he identified as someone with whom the reader of Mark should already be familiar.

For Bentham, the neaniskos serves a very particular theological purpose in the context of the book of Mark—to contrast the faithfulness of a male sex worker (who not only remains awake with Jesus but even engages in playful naked fun with the mob brought by Judas) with the faithlessness of Peter, who had promised his fidelity to Jesus but denied knowing him the moment it would no longer improve his relative status. Bentham claims that he began to notice the curious fact that Jesus would spend his last hours as a free person in the company of a male sex worker rather than with his better-known disciples after it was suggested by someone who wrote with a query to the *Monthly Magazine*— perhaps another fellow inquirer into the "religion of Jesus" as Bentham understood it.

The person in the sindona has served as a tantalizing clue to those who are hopeful to find evidence of Jesus's queerness. As an unmarried man who, according to the Gospels, surrounded himself with social outcasts, promiscuous women, laborers, and children, mostly colonized people living under Roman rule, Jesus has often inspired what we would call queer readings of his life and teachings—interpretations that emphasize the radical political positions that feel so familiar to more recent utopian and liberationist projects. In 1973 Morton Smith published what he claimed was a letter from Clement of Alexandria describing a longer version of Mark—later referred to as "Secret Mark"—in which Jesus raises the young man in the sindona from the dead, and the man falls in love with Jesus and begs to be with him. After six days, Jesus invites the young man to spend the night with him and to come to him in his graveclothes. The veracity of these nested accounts—Morton Smith's, Clement's, and the author of Mark's—is in perpetual doubt even still. Wishful thinking about the young man in the sindona long pre-dated Morton Smith's discovery, which cast doubt on its validity. Bentham would not have heard of Secret Mark, of course, but the same-sex intimacy suggested by the presence of the man in the sindona at Gethsemane seems clear enough to him without it.

I suggest that what matters about the idea of the young man in the sindona is not the historical accuracy of this story; surely we can accept that the legacy created by scripture is far too important for the history of global culture and discourse to simply forget about any narratives, persons, or utterances in scripture that cannot be empirically verified. Rather, the young man in the sindona matters in exactly the way religious scripture has always mattered—as a shared text for interpretation, analysis, debate, and even as a screen for projection. We may learn in the midst of that projection that the traced outlines of queer desire lay rather smoothly down on the narrative of Mark. From Bentham's reading of the young man in the sindona, one might notice that Bentham is doing wishful thinking of his own—not merely making a rhetorical case to readers who may be deluded by Christian thinking, but reflecting what seems to be his own desire, represented throughout these manuscripts from the last two decades of his life, to find evidence in the life of Jesus for toleration for sexual nonconformity, or even participation.

Bentham did not lay the blame for the rise in sexual discrimination at the doorstep of Christianity, as it seemed clear that asceticism had, in some sense, replaced biblical Christianity as the dominant moral discourse of the late eighteenth century. "Sin" had become synonymous with sexual sin, "virtue" with chastity (especially for women), and "pleasure" with sexual deviance. In his manuscript *Sextus,* Bentham offers an extended analysis of religion as a kind of self-portrait of desire, reflected back as enforced sacrifice. "To draw his picture of the Almighty, man looks in his own glass, and with a little heightening pourtrays his own image."[24] According to Bentham, in each place and time when religion has emerged, the sacrifices demanded by the gods have been chosen on the basis of whatever aesthetic hierarchy has been established; the greatest and most refined pleasure that the priests can imagine becomes the holiest of all sacrifices. "Of all pleasures, the most exquisite were the pleasures of the sexual appetite. Of all objects of sacrifice, these were best adapted to the nature of a God of the most refined class—of a God taken at the highest pitch of refinement and civilization."[25] The sacrifice of sexual pleasure for holiness is something that every believer can participate in, and perhaps even use to heighten their sexual appetite, just as a religious fast makes the next meal more delicious.

However, Bentham demonstrates, the sacrifice of one's own pleasure is never quite as delicious as the sacrifice of someone else's. In the case of sexual nonconformity, the required sacrifice adds the relish of antipathy to the practice of self-denial, and Bentham suggests that the sinister interest that motivates hatred for men who have sex with men is the product of this special variety of self-denial. "The more vehemently I should dislike to do what he does, the greater the punishment he deserves. . . . In the ordinary case, the pleasure sacrificed is a man's own pleasure: in this case, it is another man's pleasure. Giving meat of one's own to be roasted for a dinner to God and Priest would cost money: taking a man and roasting him costs nothing: and moreover it makes a spectacle."[26] Here, Bentham indicates Paul as the writer who gave license to this particular form of Christian cruelty, relishing in judgment of sexual sins committed by others that he himself had no intention or desire to commit. The violence of antipathy against men who have sex with men, in particular, takes up most of Bentham's baffled speculation. He points out that excessive drinking causes far more harm to a person and their society than same-sex intimacy, but he notes, mobs do not form to attack drunks—their pleasure costs money, which entitles them to their enjoyment. Perhaps the mob that came to crucify Jesus brought weapons with them not because they feared his violence, but because they feared their own desire for joy.

Must Sex Mean Something?

The difficulty of addressing queer sexual pleasure—for Bentham, and I think for us, too—is that it is so closely aligned with luxury or privilege, an excess of joy that serves no other purpose. In her analysis of Georges Bataille, Kathryn Bond Stockton demonstrates that his representations of nonreproductive sexuality celebrate "[a]ny outlay (Bataille in no way minds the word *wasting*) of money or energy or life itself—outlays that (happily) do not serve, that indeed defy, the ends of production; these would be wastings such as 'luxury,' 'mourning,' 'competitive games,' 'artistic productions,' and 'perverse sexual activity (i.e. deflected from genital finality).'"[27] Stockton reads Bataille's celebration of this wasteful luxury of sex as a pointedly Marxist critique of economic forms of luxury consumption, framed defiantly in capitalist terms. Ironically celebrating the negative terms of capitalistic "bad behavior" and repurposing them through a kind of Satanic rhetoric, Bataille (and Stockton) attempt to reframe queerness as the righteous enemy of capitalist productivity.[28] But, Bentham argues, if queer sex were a luxury good, if it cost money or resources to enjoy queer sex, no one would begrudge the pleasure, because it would be pleasure within the symbolic order of capitalist hegemony and bourgeois entitlement. What if pleasure for its own sake, which takes nothing away from anyone else, is its own utility—a spring rather than a well—because it is inexhaustible, infinitely divisible, like a couple of loaves of bread divided among thousands, leaving baskets of excess behind.

In his recent essay "What Is Sex For?" David Halperin uses Aristotle's analysis of sex and eros to consider the utility of nonprocreative sex within the framework of psychological and emotional satisfaction. If casual sex were, in fact, merely a form of mechanical physical pleasure, then why, he asks, is there such an elaborate culture of exaggerating the emotional potential of the sexual encounter, as in, for example, a bathhouse playing Adele's broken-hearted ballad "Someone Like You" as a soundtrack for anonymous pleasure? Using Aristotle's analysis of erotic logic, perhaps as a way of bypassing the oppressive modern logic of compulsory heterosexuality altogether, Halperin suggests that sex is certainly *for* something outside itself—a need to be seen and recognized by the other, if not a need to be loved. He lists several possible ways of seeing the purposes of nonreproductive sex: "The possibility that the reason we want to have sex is in order to attain some goal that lies beyond sex; the possibility that sex is not in fact the telos of erotic desire and does not fulfill it; the possibility that erotic desire aims at something other than sex; and the possibility that the act of sex makes sense only when it makes no sense—when it is undertaken for the sake of some purpose that sex, by itself, in and of itself, cannot achieve."[29] But surely the cultural context in which men are seeking sex in a bathhouse (however global) is relevant to the choice of Adele's "Someone Like You" as a soundtrack. That we still live in the modern era, in which seeking same-sex partners for sexual pleasure—especially in public—is subject to extraordinary social, legal, and economic violence, and that nearly all queer-identifying adults have developed sexual consciousness in defiance of that violence, may have something more to do with the mournful erotic frisson of sex procurement than the fully normative discourse of ancient Greek pederasty, in which, as Halperin notes, eros was generally a tragic sentiment because of the insuperable differences in age, beauty, and power between partners.

In a book chapter addressed to David Halperin, Valerie Traub notes that ahistoricity in queer theory marks one prominent strategy currently serving the ends of queer discourse, but she argues that this may be a counterproductive strategy for those of us who intend to recover queer histories from the normative discourse that has cloaked them in the silencing heterosexist platitudes of scholarship, so righteously dismantled by Eve Kosofsky Sedgwick in *Epistemology of the Closet*.[30] Traub acknowledges that any academic scholarship on historical queerness has been done in defiance of academic injunctions to "historicize," under the heteronormative assumption that all queer history must simply be the product of wishful narcissistic projection, rather than a genuine recovery of discourse that has perhaps been heterosexualized by modern scholars who, whether purposefully or not, have cast the veil of their own narcissism or bigotry over historical texts. However, Traub argues that experiments in anachronistic, metaleptic queer inquiry (e.g., "homohistory") cede too much epistemic ground to heteronormativity; by willing a recognition of the transhistorical presence of "the homo" throughout time, one fails to demand that nonreproductive sexual practices, with all their attendant cultural, countercultural, and extracultural modes of self-determination, can be analyzed in their alterity and historically specific substance. Traub writes, "Might historical alterity not sometimes offer its own pleasures (as well as accurately describe certain pre- and early modern modes of intelligibility)? . . . Not every diachronic or chronological treatment of temporality need be normativizing, nor is every linear arc sexually 'straight.'"[31]

Traub's call for queer historicism is a respectful call for the recognition of difference even in the midst of historical analysis inspired by a desire to find ancestors, or at least predecessors—evidence that "we," however constituted, have always been "here." I have to admit that in my initial encounter with Jeremy Bentham's queer reading of the life of Jesus, my initial reaction, informed by emergent discourses of "homohistory," was to dismiss it as the wrong sort of queer history, invested as it is with the epistemics of historical evidence and alterity where a plain assertion of transhistorical identification with Jesus might have been more effective. Why attempt to convince anyone of the "truth" of a reading of the gospels that is not even predicated on an assumption of the truth of scripture in general, or even an assertion of the existence of God or divinity of Jesus? Bentham's reading of the neaniskos in the sindona is unconcerned with these matters of epistemic certitude; he simply describes the scene as *fun,* an event that he sees as an allusion to the desire of the men of Sodom to have intercourse with the visiting angels. "Seeing the stripling in this attire and in this company, some of the striplings or 'young men,' who, in order to partake of the sport or *fun,* as the phrase is, whatever it might prove, had joined themselves to the multitude, regarded him, as it should seem—cloathing and the wearer together, as a sort of prize: without incurring any such guilt as that of inhospitality, and perhaps without need of violence, the design formed by them on the person of the wearer might in one sense be not unnaturally of the same complexion as that formed by the inhabitants of the devoted city upon the two mysterious beings who were at once men and angels."[32] Whether the author of Mark intended to suggest a connection to the events at Sodom or not, Bentham is registering the similar strangeness of a mood of sexual play in the context of devastating and cosmically tragic destruction. As to the plausibility of his reading, Bentham writes, "There stands the matter upon the face of the Gospel history. If, in the unperverted sense of the word natural, any one there be that can find a more *natural*—or in a word, a more *probable*—interpretation, let him declare it."[33] A queer understanding of history need not read our own cultural assumptions about nonconformist sex onto the past, nor must it predicate itself upon a heteronormative historiography and theology that must first know where the author stands on, for example, the doctrine of the trinity. At least in these manuscripts for *Not Paul, but Jesus,* Bentham models a kind of queer historiography that is deeply interested in alterity and historicity, but will not be forced by the demands of contemporary discourse to profess faith in public before earning the right to say anything else.

Unlike the prophet Elijah, or John the Baptist, whose public works were spectacles intended to indicate the presence of the divine to convince nonbelievers, Jesus instructed those who followed him not to tell anyone that he had lessened their suffering, or their hunger, or provided good wine to drink—not to force pleasure to indicate or mean something beyond itself. The lilies of the field neither toil nor do they spin, and are arrayed beyond Solomon's glory, but, after all, they don't go around bragging about it. Bentham's skepticism about both secular and religious cultural norms during his life was that there seemed to be no discourse available for noneconomic, unironic enjoyment of physical pleasure as an end in itself. During his long career, Bentham focused on the oppression of sexual nonconformists alongside that of enslaved and colonized people, women, prisoners, the poor—but as he came to the last questions of his career, his attention turned to Jesus, because he, as Edelman writes, "makes nothing happen," which, in a world of infinite commodification, rapaciousness, and despair, is like a kind of miracle.

5

Politics and Poetics of Liberty

Literary Influences

Bentham's career as a philosopher spans the most radical era in European history, from the mid-1770s to 1832, as egalitarian movements based on the will and political action by and for disenfranchised persons challenged patriarchal monarchic rule, slowed the trade of enslaved Africans, expanded educational opportunities for women and working-class people, and resulted in political independence for a few particularly powerful colonies. However, between the American Revolution and the Polish November Uprising, counterrevolutionary violence such as the Peterloo Massacre chilled Jacobin optimism in England, where incremental legislative gains for liberationists seemed only to shore up the political and economic power of elites, while laborers and working-class women adapted to the emerging but limited roles available to them in the nineteenth-century supply chain. Political gains in the colonies, such as Haitian independence, were embittered by European economic violence, and by the 1830s the people in power all over Europe looked remarkably similar to those who had been in power in the 1770s, though in long trousers and mostly wearing their own hair.

During this period, English literature had its own revolution, as the aesthetic values of the Enlightenment—the realistic middle-class novel, neoclassical poetry, benign deistic observations on human nature, and the comedy and tragedy of heterosexual desire gone wrong—splintered into a wide variety of new experiments in aesthetic excess. The 1740s–60s balancing act of light and dark, good and evil, laughter and tears, gave rise in the latter eighteenth century to maximalist aesthetics that invented and challenged genres, rediscovered the marvelous and the horrific, and found something in sublime terror to rival the pleasures of clear-eyed daytime sociality. Gothic novels and their parodists, heretical and atheistic Romantic poetry, domestic fiction with a global conscience, and representations of obsessive desire found surprising combinations of readers, as did so-called philosophical novels that imitated the fiction of Voltaire, Denis Diderot, Jean-Jacques Rousseau, and Johann Wolfgang von Goethe. By putting challenging, liberationist political ideas in the mouths of literary characters, English Jacobin novelists such as Robert Bage, Mary Wollstonecraft, William Godwin, Elizabeth Inchbald, and Charlotte Smith hoped to awaken the political consciousness of readers who had little material or intellectual access to works of philosophy or the parliamentary record. By using the form and aesthetics of popular genres like gothic and domestic fiction, these authors introduced readers to the need for political intervention in gender discrimination, class oppression, the penal system, and the violence of colonialism. Meanwhile, Romantic poets, including Samuel Taylor Coleridge, William Wordsworth, and Percy Bysshe Shelley, not only made political statements in their work but also became public advocates for local and global political causes, even responding directly to the political philosophy of Jeremy Bentham.

In the context of so much radical political writing emerging in the accessible guise of narrative and poetic art, Bentham's contemporaneous work as an English philosopher with no literary gifts can seem almost redundant. Perhaps the most common criticism leveled at Jeremy Bentham by nineteenth-century commentators was that, despite his stunningly radical politics, ethical clarity and consistency, and analytical precision, he is simply not worth reading because he lacks an aesthetic sensibility. His unlovely prose is neither rhetorically compelling nor morally inspiring, and reflects his insensitivity to true beauty, without which the whole edifice of Benthamite utilitarianism seems to have crumbled for the post-Romantic reader. As I discussed in chapters 1 and 2, Bentham's immediate critics, including Charles Dickens, Karl Marx, Friedrich Nietzsche, and John Stuart Mill, focus on his paucity of imagination and the hyper-rigorousness of his analysis as disqualifying him from having a valid aesthetic theory, which is especially damning because Bentham's understanding of aesthetic variety forms the foundation of his protosociological understanding of human motivation in *Deontology*.

Bentham was bitterly aware of how unpleasant his writing was to others, compared to the friendly commonsensical style of the great novelists and philosophers of the Enlightenment, and compared to the sublime rhetoric and poetics of the Romantics. Bentham complains throughout his work that his own writing style is tedious and unconvincing, wishing that he had the artistic style to engage readers' hearts as well as their minds. However, it is clear from Bentham's manuscripts that he was an avid reader of fiction, not merely as part of his analysis of contemporary discourse, but primarily for pleasure. He was drawn especially to gothic novels and domestic fiction by politically radical women and sexual nonconformists, rather than to the sublime poetry of Wordsworth, Coleridge, or Shelley, no matter how radically their politics manifested. And while most of the philosophical writing he published in his lifetime was rigorously unaesthetic, almost purposefully repetitive, plodding, and meticulous, alternating between non-sentence lists and page-long snarls of multiply subjugated clauses, his manuscript notes contain stunning flights of fancy, sentimental outbursts of compassion and moral outrage, utopian fantasies for the future, and modest imitations of his favorite literary prose.

In my early research on the possible influences of eighteenth-century fiction on the philosophical rhetoric of the Enlightenment, I was surprised to find that philosophers who clearly drew on popular fiction for inspiration never seemed to acknowledge the influence, even when major arguments from fiction were lifted wholesale as *empirical evidence* of a particular social phenomenon. The most egregious example I found was in David Hume's use of the "Of Love" chapter from Henry Fielding's *Tom Jones* as a sentence-by-sentence rhetorical pattern for the appendix "Of Self-Love" in *An Enquiry Concerning the Principles of Morals*. Knowing what intellectual magpies eighteenth-century novelists often were, I had assumed after reading both texts that Fielding had plagiarized Hume's work as the basis for an argument about how to make observations of private feelings by accounting for the manifest actions of others, but the dates were wrong; Hume was writing his *Enquiry* in the two years following the publication of *Tom Jones*. As I argued in an essay on Fielding's influence on Hume, both writers drew ideas from Joseph Butler's *Fifteen Sermons* from 1726, but sharing a source text does not account for the depth of the similarities between Fielding's passage and Hume's, which nearly constitutes a paraphrase.[1] While Fielding openly avows that Jonathan Swift and William Shakespeare serve as literary precedents for his observations about vanity, moral sentiment, and epistemology, Hume cites no literary sources at all.

It is a frequent failing of Enlightenment philosophical analysis that the philosopher's purported observations of human nature seem at times exclusively to be drawn either from popular novels or from fictional narratives devised by the philosopher himself, whose access to the private sphere would otherwise be limited to the example offered by his own home. Like the "man of common sense" I discussed in the introduction, human nature in the eighteenth century seems nearly exclusively to be a fiction based on other fiction, mostly realistic middle-class novels, with narrow rules about what is plausible, what conforms to normative expectations of gender and class, and what is salutary for supposedly vulnerable readers—that is, politically disenfranchised persons whose behavior must be carefully disciplined.

Bentham, on the other hand, did not limit his literary reading to the normative or the realistic, and leveled extensive criticism at the pernicious influence of mid-century literary authors on moral sentiment. Although authors as different as Henry Fielding, Tobias Smollett, and Samuel Richardson held conflicting views about the limits, purposes, and aesthetics of fictional narrative, Bentham found much of the fiction of this era to be disturbingly heteronormative, inciting extreme expressions of disgust for sexual and gender nonconformists, especially for women who express their own sexual desires and men whose behavior is legible to others as effeminate. As realistic novels began to supply fictional evidence of the supposed private desires and moral quandaries of girls and servants—people without the means to represent themselves in the public sphere—the British discourse of moral sentiment extended further into private feelings and behaviors, including those of people who lived mostly in private.

In this chapter I discuss some of the recent scholarship on normativity—especially sex and gender normativity—in mid-eighteenth-century British fiction, and then I look at some examples of Bentham's readings and imitations of literature published in his lifetime. Then I turn to the reaction of Romantic poets to Bentham, in the context of Bentham's rejection of poetry as a means to liberationist political ends.

Aesthetic Heteronormativity

Recent studies of heteronormativity in the British eighteenth century have focused on the rise of moral sentiment in literary, popular, and political culture that was contemporary with, and in some sense predicated upon, the development of modern compulsory heterosexual gender roles. In the introduction to their edited volume *Heteronormativity in Eighteenth-Century Literature and Culture,* Ana de Freitas Boe and Abby Coykendall and write, "Heteronormativity congeals into a fully fomented hegemony by the end of the eighteenth century, reaching its apex roughly midway through the nineteenth century; however, it never becomes so completely entrenched as to curtail dissent from its own dictates or to prevent the materialization of alternate sex/gender configurations—whether those resurfacing from earlier periods or those emerging in defiance of, or simply heedless to, its mandates."[2] As their volume goes on to demonstrate, the manifestations of resistance to heteronormative and gender normative social and legal forces do find subtler and more encrypted forms of expression across this crucial period, maintaining a sense of mourning or longing for older periods of sexual aesthetics in which rigid adherence to emerging, nationalistic categories of masculinity, femininity, and reproductive sexuality were not yet on the horizon. A sexual nonconformist of Bentham's era did not need to go back to classical pederasty to find literary representations of same-sex intimacy and nonreproductive desire; as recently as the seventeenth century, the social and legal restrictions on public gender performance and sexual asceticism were not yet meaningfully in place.

In the seventeenth century, many English poets and dramatists echoed the assertion by Michel de Montaigne in "On Friendship" that the truest form of love is between social and gender equals with no family or legal obligations to one another. While heterosexual coupling might be fine for making children, preserving family relations, and even some low form of enjoyment, "Friendship, on the other hand, is enjoyed even as it is desired; it is bred, nourished, and increased only by enjoyment, since it is a spiritual thing and the soul is purified by its practice."[3] Although Montaigne claims that "our morality rightly abhors" the pederasty of the Greeks, he suggests that the real moral problem with pederasty is the social inequality of the partners, rather than any particular objection to same-sex intimacy.[4] Similar expressions are found throughout seventeenth-century English homosocial love poetry, Restoration comedies, and early feminist poetry and prose, in which the faithlessness and lack of virtue among one or the other sex are why the speaker or character insists that true intimacy is only possible with one of their own sex. But in the eighteenth century, a shift in the sexual rhetoric and aesthetics of English literature gives the preference to heterosexual coupling, and even the intimation of the possibility of sexual or gender nonconformity is treated as a matter for humiliation and violence.

In *Making Love,* Paul Kelleher analyzes the rise of compulsory heterosexual coupling in popular fiction and Shaftesburian moral sentiment during this same period. He demonstrates that while laws and religious injunctions against same-sex intimacy long predate the British novel, the rise of popular novels in the eighteenth century—especially sentimental fiction about desire and marriage—was concurrent with increasing hostility toward gender and sexual minorities.

> Understood as the erotically charged love of husband and wife that simultaneously embodies a sexual and a moral orientation, sentimental heterosexuality presents itself as a private, intimate form of relation uniquely equipped to unify and stabilize a host of social, political, and economic transformations that characterize modernity, including the rise and spread of the public sphere, contract-based governance, interest-driven sociability, bourgeois empowerment, and commodity capitalism.[5]

Kelleher argues that popular literature presented British readers with comfort in the form of the promise that carefully policed heterosexual monogamy would provide sentimental stability and, thereby, moral certainty in the face of rapidly shifting social conditions and values. While seventeenth-century English literature expressed social relations as a matter of political polemic, philosophical debate, and homosocial rhetoric, the emerging category of the novel in the eighteenth century rebranded popular literature as an arbiter and teacher of proper moral feeling, with a new duty to incite disgust for nonnormative behaviors that did not serve the interests of economic and political power. To experience desire outside the confines of the marriage bed was framed by later eighteenth-century fiction as inviting not only personal sexual chaos but also social and political upheaval.

In *Effeminate Years,* Declan Kavanagh traces the division of political subjects in the latter half of the eighteenth century into legitimized, heteroerotic, masculine men, and others whose failure or refusal to perform masculinity disqualified them from participation in public discourse. Kavanagh demonstrates that while Englishness, masculinity, heterosexuality, free commerce and finance, public discourse, the right to privacy, and even cleanliness emerged as a coherent politicized aesthetic of power, the opposite terms—Irish-/Scottishness, effeminacy, homosexuality, taxation, clubs, unwilling exposure, and filthiness— became abjected categories linked by suspicion and accusation. Writing of John Wilkes's particular influence on the development of this political aesthetic, Kavanagh writes, "Wilkesite political discourse was deeply xenophobic and antieffeminate, and its contribution to the coeval, intensely imbricated emergence of heteronormativity and the public sphere in the eighteenth century was to make the sexual, indeed the heterosexual, private as opposed to public or political."[6] Although Wilkes championed the antieffeminate heterosexual as a preferred aesthetic in order to expand the political influence of working-class English men, with the goal of purportedly radical political ends, the cost for women, sexual nonconformists, and non-English political subjects was dire, as their exclusion from the public sphere was cemented on the basis of an *aesthetic* association among masculine English men, crossing class divisions, that now explicitly excluded the feminine and the effeminate as objects of disgust and humiliation. This politicized conception of the politically active, publicly honorable, heterosexual English man seems to have arisen in part as a result of increasingly heterosexualized representations of love in popular literature.

Jeremy Bentham's writings on the violence of heteronormativity were responding not only to the capricious enforcement of the Buggery Act 1533, and to the violence of homophobic mobs, but also to the emergence of compulsory marriage and fear of effeminacy in the popular culture of the preceding century, which he saw as inciting violence and lending venom to legal prosecutions of same-sex intimacy. Over the course of the eighteenth century, realistic British fiction gradually abandoned its origins in salacious sex and crime fantasies and became the arbiter of moral judgment, particularly with respect to the sexual behaviors of young women and nonnormative men. At a time when secularization, liberalization, and religious toleration were spreading throughout Europe and its colonies, British attitudes toward sexuality were becoming virulently censorious, in step with concurrent developments in popular aesthetics and politics.

In his analysis of deterrents to same-sex relationships, Bentham points out nothing yet devised has succeeded in preventing men from having sex with other men. Despite the vast social and legal apparatus for dissuading men from forming these relationships, he writes that it is "an appetite the gratification of which has been and continues to be sought by such multitudes constantly at the risk and frequently to the sacrifice of life."[7] The persistence of same-sex intimacies in a culture entirely hostile to sexual liberty suggests to Bentham that the mechanism of pleasure itself has been grossly misunderstood, and its importance wildly under-estimated. Bentham saw that, on one hand, the experience of pleasure—especially sexual pleasure—needed to be acknowledged and analyzed as having a crucial causal role in human happiness, but also that, on the other hand, violence against sexual nonconformity needed to be exposed as an attack on nothing more than a difference in preference of taste.

Bentham argues that sexual behavior—especially nonnormative sex—must be protected from violence precisely because it is causally irrelevant to the welfare of the populace, except as a source of private pleasure and social intimacy. Bentham notes that violence seemed only to be able to deter public displays of nonnormative sexuality, but that in order to inhibit private sex, the hatred of same-sex and female desire had been encoded in the characters and plots of eighteenth-century fiction. Thus the inhibition of private desire became most complete when the self-ordained moralists turned their attention from observable behaviors to aesthetics, and effectively brought sexual asceticism into the bedroom under the cover of the comic novel.

In his manuscript *Sextus,* Bentham analyzes several examples from popular fiction—Tobias Smollett's *Roderick Random* and Henry Field-ing's *Joseph Andrews* among others—in which a character represented as a sexual or gender nonconformist is beaten, humiliated, or exposed. "Not inconsiderable is the number of Novels and other works having amusement for their object, in which the danger of loss by the intro-duction of a topic which no person charged with the care of the youth of either sex would naturally expose to the view of a pupil, much less feel disposed to satisfy the curiosity which the darkness of the allusion can not fail to excite, has not been sufficient to let slip the occasion of giving vent and increase to the popular antipathy of which these pro-pensities are the object."[8] What other crime, Bentham asks, is fodder for both laughter and capital punishment? Why do authors so willingly expose young readers to desires they believe to be the most dangerous to human society? These conflicting attitudes toward sexual nonconfor-mity are often held by the same individual persons, and that hypocrisy, he argues, is evidence that there are fundamental category inconsistencies in our analysis of sexual morality.

Bentham's reading of the heteronormative turn in eighteenth-century aesthetics reveals that he also suspected popular authors of using literature to teach readers to feel disgust and fear for sexual and gender nonconformists. Bentham worried that these fears resulted in moral bloodthirstiness to see violence committed against nonconforming persons, and that popular literature was actively inciting that violence.

> Of the violence of that antipathy, whether real or affected, of which the propensities in question have, in the British isles, beyond all other countries, been the object—of the violence of that thirst which nothing less than the heart's blood of the intended victims marked out for slaughter by the dissocial appetite has hitherto been able to satisfy—the principal causes have now been brought to view: and in the view thus given of them it has been seen that, in the number of them, no such quality in it as that of a tendency to make in any shape a defalcation from the aggregate sum of human happiness has place: and that, in one word, in this dissocial and misery-engendering affection, whatsoever fault there is has for its seat the breasts, not of those who are the objects of this antipathy, but of those who harbour it.[9]

To Bentham, the moral crisis of late eighteenth-century Great Britain was not, as popular authors would have it, same-sex desire, but violent fear and hatred for sexual difference. Bentham's analysis focuses on those British authors who incite aesthetic disgust for sexual and gender nonconformists as a way of forcing an aesthetic difference to yield to a morally imperative—and even deadly—solution at the hands of vigilantes.

The conflation of aesthetic and moral sexual values could, in effect, be considered one of the chief aims and effects of eighteenth-century British popular culture. Since the end of the seventeenth century, drama and fiction critics had turned their primary attention from the formal qualities of art to the purported effect they would have on readers perceived to be vulnerable. In his 1698 book *A Short View of the Immorality of the English Stage,* the theater critic Jeremy Collier enumerated the crimes supposedly promoted by theatrical comedy of the period, focusing particularly on positive and neutral representations of sexual desire in women and of implied sexual relationships between men, urging playwrights and performers alike to consider themselves personally morally responsible for the subsequent sins of their audience. "And since you make others thus *Faulty,* how can you be *Innocent* your self? All the People undone There, will lay their Ruine at your Door. The Company are all Accessary to the Mischeif of the Place. For were there no *Audience,* we should have no *Acting.* And therefore those who joyn in the Crime, will ne're be parted in the Punishment."[10] As the theater became a site for sexual reform, taking on the burden of advertising patriarchal sexual morality, moral discourse in turn absorbed the urgency and immediacy of aesthetic disgust. According to the drama historian Laurence Senelick, the disgust that surrounded gender and sexual minorities by the end of the eighteenth century made late seventeenth-century comedies all but incomprehensible within a few decades; the once-appealing sexually fluid fop character, represented as an immoral but clever libertine, comes later to signify not merely a criminal but an object of personal loathing and aversion.[11] The actor who plays a murderer on stage does not leave the theater morally tainted by his performance, but the actor who plays a sexual nonconformist may find himself an object of investigation.

In the 1690s the Society for the Reformation of Manners began aggressively persecuting homosexuals and prostitutes. The 1698 publication of *An Account of the Proceedings against Capt Edward Rigby* attempted to expose the methods of a sodomite in recruiting young men for homosexual relations, and the pamphlet sold widely, helping to spur the formation of dozens of antisodomitical organizations that vowed to expose, humiliate, and prosecute offenders. As so-called molly houses and other communities arose to protect sexual minorities from an increasingly hostile culture, they also became targets for blackmail and raids. Throughout the eighteenth century, in English literature, including pamphlets of propaganda, plays, and popular realistic novels, the sodomite became a stock character for humiliation and censure. In his account of the persecution of sexual nonconformists of the eighteenth century, Louis Crompton notes that a stark rise in the persecution of sexual nonconformists in England began around 1772, just as Bentham began to write about sexual nonconformity. "It was not only the hangings that dismayed Bentham. Foreign visitors to England were struck by another form of punishment for homosexual offenses. This was the pillory. Convicted men were placed in the pillory and exposed to the wrath of the mob, who were allowed to pelt them. Such events attracted thousands, sometimes tens of thousands of spectators."[12] Persecution of same-sex intimacy was not merely a function of the magistrate or the preacher; in Bentham's own lifetime, homophobia was, in every possible way, a form of entertainment. If, as Locke, Hume, and others so confidently insist (as discussed in chapter 2), an English person cannot hear of same-sex intimacy without being disgusted, owing to their cultural indoctrination against it, and if trials of sodomites frequently resulted in execution, transportation, banishment, or pillory, and if the mere suggestion of effeminacy was enough to discredit a man from public life, it becomes difficult to imagine what claim to resentment or personal injury the attackers of sexual nonconformists could possibly make.

Bentham's Literary Reading

The desire to collaborate with a sympathetic literary author must have been a great temptation for Bentham, who repeatedly expressed frustration with the inability of readers to follow his abstruse and often necessarily tedious arguments. Throughout his career, Bentham complained of being perceived as somehow both too boring and too scandalous for his contemporaries. In the 1823 preface to *An Introduction to the Principles of Morals and Legislation,* Bentham writes, "Dry and tedious as a great part of the discussions it contains must unavoidably be found by the bulk of readers, he knows not how to regret the having written them, nor even the having made them public."[13] Like most of the works Bentham published under his own name, *An Introduction to the Principles of Morals and Legislation* mostly consists of refutations of possible reasons why a reader would be inclined to disagree with him, a defensive style of argument that ultimately expends more rhetoric on insulting detractors than on winning followers.

Bentham feared that the small number of readers who were capable of and willing to follow his argument would result in a split legacy of those who really understood his work and those who stopped with the general idea of it.

> The narrower the circle of readers is, within which the present work may be condemned to confine itself, the less limited may be the number of those to whom the fruits of his succeeding labours may be found

accessible. He may therefore in this respect find himself in the condition of those philosophers of antiquity, who are represented as having
held two bodies of doctrine, a popular and an occult one: but, with this
difference, that in his instance the occult and the popular will, he hopes,
be found as consistent as in those they were contradictory; and that in
his production whatever there is of occultness has been the pure result
of sad necessity, and in no respect of choice.[14]

Bentham would prove quite accurate in his prediction of an occult following—the academic circle of avid Benthamite utilitarians seems to
gain a few members every so often, as one or another of us find the
aspects of Bentham's work that touch on the struggles and joys of our
lives—but his hope for a general appreciation of his argument that is at
least parallel to the occult understanding has not yet come to fruition.
While some of that disparity could be blamed on the sinister interest
of some of his critics who feared the liberty and enfranchisement of
women, laborers, and sexual minorities, it seems clear that a great deal
of that failure must be blamed on the inaccessibility of his writing,
which is often more impassioned in excoriating negative examples than
in praising positive ones.

    In his attacks on injustice, Bentham could be viciously sarcastic; his
moral outrage manifested as incredulousness at the stupidity and cruelty
of colonizers, misogynists, slaveholders, jailers, and homophobes, who
seemed happy to undermine their own material interests for the spiteful
satisfaction of denying freedom and pleasure to others. In 1793 Bentham
wrote to the National Convention of France on the self-destructive "use-
lessness" of colonialism, repeating, "Emancipate your colonies!" while
mocking the absurdities used to justify their perpetuation. After the
introduction, Bentham frames the entire argument as responses to objections phrased as if in the voice of a panicking colonizer: "*Oh! but they are
but a part of the empire and a part must be governed by the whole.* Part
of the empire, say you? Yes, in point of fact, they certainly are, or at least
were . . . but whence came it to you? Whence, but from the hand of despo-
tism."[15] Likewise, in the 1822 book *Rid Yourselves of Ultramaria*, Bentham
spends hundreds of pages exhorting Spanish readers to heed the title of
the book and emancipate their colonies, without any kind of rhetorical
commonplacing that would establish a mutual understanding of the situation. Bentham finds no excuse to sympathize—even rhetorically—with

sinister interests that use hegemonic platitudes like "natural rights," "duty to God," or "common sense" to justify the perpetuation of oppressive power against political, gender, racial, and sexual minorities. The resulting texts are, as he seemed to realize, practically unreadable—especially by the men who might have the education required to understand his arguments against metaphysical libertarian "rights." In his writing on sexual nonconformity, Bentham bemoans the total lack of eulogistic or even neutral discourse to draw from in contemporary literature on the subject of men who have sex with men, and finds he only has ancient examples to draw from.

In a stunning moment of painful self-awareness, Bentham writes in his notes that he does not think he can make his argument legible to a society so steeped in antipathy for sexual nonconformists—and so hostile to pleasure seeking altogether—and that he dares not publish any of it. Rather, as he writes, Bentham desired a writing partner who could lend him not only a more skillful pen but also an aesthetic investment in sexual irregularity:

> In this state of things it will hardly be matter of wonder, that the author is desirous of finding, in an appropriate social intercourse, an external support for his faculties under a burthen of such a magnitude:—a sort of partner, in whose honour, in point of secresy and all other points, he could confide, and by whose sympathy he might be cheered and supported: a co-operator, in whose literary talents whatever deficiency there may be in his own might find a supply: who, in his own person, might find an amusement in giving form and order, and superior expression, and perhaps additional quantity, to the materials which are in readiness to be supplied: by whose opulence or influence a foster-father for the work might eventually in some other quarter, perhaps, be found.[16]

In fantasizing about the possibility of intellectual community with a queer author, better suited to the task of communicating with a hostile public, Bentham turns not to philosophers or theologians but to "the author of the History of the Caliph Vathec,"[17] that is, William Thomas Beckford. *Vathek* had been published in 1786 while Beckford was in exile for having been exposed in a sexual affair with William Courtenay. At the time of Bentham's writing, Beckford had returned to England to find he was shunned. Bentham goes on to wonder how much more "amusing" his own work would be, how much more pleasant for readers, if only Beckford could help him render his ideas into a legible, sympathetic text. Until then, he fears there is an "inexorable prohibition"[18] on completing these essays for a public audience.

Beckford's *Vathek* is a gothic Oriental tale of religious heresy, the pleasures of sin, and demonic torture that would serve as a turning point in the development of the gothic genre; much like Matthew Gregory Lewis's 1796 novel *The Monk, Vathek* uses nonempiricist gothic conventions to explore new depths of human depravity in the context of supernatural agents of power. Beckford might seem an odd choice of ally for someone like Bentham, whose own writing is so rigidly empiricist, and often stultifyingly dull. However, it is clear from several of Bentham's manuscripts that he was an avid reader of gothic novels, a genre that was often mocked in its earliest iterations for being anti-intellectual, aesthetically irrelevant, hysterical in sentiment, provocative of delusional thinking, and written for silly girls. In the morally serious realistic fiction of the mid-eighteenth century, as Laurie Langbauer argues, "women have no real place" and must humiliate themselves in order to deserve heterosexual marriage as the only possible happy ending.[19] The new aesthetic landscape opened up by the gothic not only placed female and sexually nonconforming subjectivities at the center of the narrative but also explored the vast variety of licit and illicit desires, self-destructive obsessions, and inchoate longings that characterize the lives of people traumatized by lifelong disenfranchisement and economic and legal violence.

The depth of Bentham's pleasure in literary reading is apparent in a set of notes from 1794 in which he compares various kinds of "moral compositions," that is, literature that has the potential to shape the moral sentiments of the reader, including lives, characters, and histories of people who have lived, as well as novels, romances, and epic poems about the lives of fictional characters.[20] Bentham begins to imagine that the most morally moving kind of literary art would be drama, if only it could allow for a much broader range of characters, settings, spans of time, and so forth, "taken from a novel and exhibiting the whole contents of the Novel" without the traditional limitations of theatrical adaptation. He suggests that by using music, breaks for dancing, massive casts to represent every character, and no limit on the number of acts, such a performance could unite the liveliness of drama with the epic scale of the novel, with "[d]rama to be taken from one of Miss

Burney's or Mrs. Smith's novels—for instance Emmeline." With so many
contemporary novelists to choose from, it seems important that both of
Bentham's examples of novelists whose work would be gratifying to see
acted out in such great detail are women—Frances Burney and Charlotte Smith—but especially that the novel he specifies is *Emmeline, the
Orphan of the Castle*, a four-volume gothic novel from 1788 in which
a young woman insists on her independence in the face of increasing
pressure to marry against her will. That is, as his example of a moral
that should be shared through an elaborate and expensive new kind of
performance, Bentham thinks of texts that movingly represent women's
will and pleasure, which many other readers of his era criticized as pernicious for the moral health of young readers.

In the case of Charlotte Smith and William Beckford, the gothic
served as a genre that could offer a meaningful critique of the heteronormative marriage plot so common in eighteenth-century realistic fiction. Bentham does not specify which of Frances Burney's four novels
he thought should be represented on the stage in this way, but all of
Burney's work offers critical responses to the marriage plot, incorporat-
ing aspects of the gothic while depicting her female heroines under tremendous stress caused by patriarchal, encroaching, opportunistic men
and the women who want to please them.

Since Horace Walpole's *The Castle of Otranto* was published in 1764,
the gothic genre offered an aesthetic alternative to realistic fiction not
only in its exotic locations and suggestions of supernatural influence
but also in its young women characters who suspect they are the victims of masculinist conspiracy and are ultimately validated. In *Queer
Gothic*, George Haggerty argues that the gothic is in some sense inherently queer, in that by aesthetically privileging encounters of chaos
and terror outside normal reality, even gothic novels that do end with
a neatly resolved heterosexual marriage never seem to fully recover
from their encounters with alternate possibilities of desire. "The gothic
novel achieves this interpretative license precisely because it reflects in
perhaps predictable, but nonetheless often powerful, ways the anxiety
that the force of culture generates. In its excess, gothic fiction thereby
challenges the cultural system that commodifies desire and renders it
lurid and pathological."[21] In the case of Burney, Smith, and Beckford,
the gothic clearly serves to dramatize the anxiety of heteronormativity
and compulsory participation in the patriarchal social order. Bentham

seems to have been consistently drawn to literary writers who use engaging narrative styles to imagine the human will outside the demands of heteronormativity and conformity to traditional gender roles.

As for the best-known male novelists of the eighteenth century, I have already discussed Bentham's low opinion of Fielding and Smollett. His criticism of Samuel Richardson is somewhat more measured, but worth mentioning here. In a note from 1776, Bentham analyzes the title character of Richardson's *The History of Sir Charles Grandison* from 1753, which Richardson devised in part as a response to Fielding's morally ambiguous Tom Jones. Richardson was widely praised by eighteenth-century readers for offering a morally coherent male protagonist in the context of so many works of fiction in which men—even protagonists—are depicted as more or less effective sexual predators. Unlike Fielding's Tom Jones, who obeys the dictates of his desires and inclinations, both moral and immoral, Sir Charles Grandison obeys the dictates of religion, citing his Christianity as the inspiration for his heroic endeavors to rescue a young woman, Harriet Byron, from the clutches of the villain Sir Hargrave Pollexfen. His adherence to the Church of England causes his betrothal to an Italian Catholic woman to fail, and he ultimately marries Harriet. In representing a character who disobeys his own inclinations under the command of a higher authority, Richardson attempted to depict virtue that exceeds the merely personal and is instead the product of humility before divine commands. Bentham clearly disagreed with Richardson's depiction of "true" virtue, declaring Grandison to be little better than a hypocrite.

> Why is Sr Charles Grandison out of nature? because to such an attachment to the reigning superstitions [manifests a weakness of mind that] as renders a man an object of contempt, he joins on many occasions such a conduct [and receives on all occasions from the rest of the characters in the story such applauses] as manifest a strength of mind that renders a man an object of admiration.
>
> What is the reasoning that secretly passes in men's minds upon the observance of such a character? Either he is not sincere, in which case he is a knave, and uses this as a cloke [puts on this character] to cover his designs from the weak whose understandings have been perverted & broken by the terrors of this Sanction: he is sincere and is [himself] one of those weak persons.[22]

Bentham goes on at some length to show that characters who cite religion as the cause of their actions must always seem absurd and hypocritical. He imagines the audience of a play watching as the hero soliloquizes on the particular points of scripture that influenced his actions, rather than the feelings that he is experiencing. "They would turn from him with contempt as undesignedly ridiculous, or with aversion as hypocritical, or with disgust, as out of na[ture]."[23] Bentham feels that Richardson and many other authors of moral fiction simply overestimate the influence of religion on human behavior. If we were to see books such as *Sir Charles Grandison* acted out in the manner in which Bentham would like to see *Emmeline,* it would be unbearable for audiences.

This comparison reveals something startling about Bentham's aesthetics. The primary charge leveled at Gothic fiction such as Beckford's and Smith's was that it was unrealistic, sometimes in the sense of relying on the supernatural, with demons and magic and ghosts, and at other times in the sense of moral sentiment, with young women asserting their own will in the face of extraordinary threats of violence. And yet Bentham had no problem enjoying *Vathek* and *Emmeline.* He draws the line, aesthetically speaking, before texts that purport to offer the reader an important moral lesson that is ultimately revealed to be social, legal, and economic power demanding obedience from those whose desires threaten patriarchal supremacy. In those works, he sees nothing but the hypocrisy of sanctimony and bigotry in the guise of entertainment.

One last example I will note that serves as evidence of Bentham's literary reading and aspirations is a truly bizarre manuscript, in the midst of a series of notes on sexual nonconformity, in which Bentham seems to be attempting an imitation of Laurence Sterne. Sterne's *The Life and Opinions of Tristram Shandy* was serially published from 1759 until 1767, just before Sterne's death, and constitutes one of the most outrageous narrative experiments ever accomplished in the English language. Despite the text's extraordinary difficulty and strangeness, it nevertheless became, and remains, one of the most beloved of all English novels, not least because its narrator perpetually interrupts his own narrative in order to describe manic delusions, neurotic obsessions, and humorous accounts of his own struggles—not in writing, but in trying to *finish* writing.[24] One cannot help noticing that Bentham was, like many admirers of Sterne, a graphomaniac who seems to have compulsively written down every thought he had, no matter how digressive, distracted, repetitive, unprintable, or absurd. In a manuscript labeled "Castrations to . . . by the Demon of Socrates," which I can only describe as *very weird,* Bentham writes:

> To account for the mutilated appearance of these papers, it is necessary I [the Author] should make the reader acquainted with a very strange accident which befel me [the Author] the night before they were to have been committed to the Press. My eyes were just closed for sleep, when on a sudden a being of more than mortal splendor stood before me. I am that Angel, said he, who in days of yore cut the black speck out of the heart of Muhomet. It was I, and not the recording Angel, who stood in readiness with an opportune tear and blotted out Uncle Toby's oath.
>
> Thy heart hath also its black specks, thy papers have passages which need expunging much more than Uncle Toby's oath. With that, methought I felt my side open with an hideous wound into which the cruel Angel plunged without farther ceremony his searching hand. The torture produced by this operation forced from me as may be imagined a loud shriek, which awaken'd me. The next morning [on taking up my manuscript for the last time] what was my surprise to find the writing vanished in a multitude of places correspondent to the deficiencies that will be observed in the [?] copy. What was still more mortifying, I found and still find all attempts to restore them, perfectly unavailing. I felt as if by a kind of mental palsy all that part of my memory had perished within me. I still continue in that unfortunate, or as perhaps I might rather to call it fortunate condition.[25]

Bentham goes on to imply that he is telling this account as a way of warning the reader to be doubtful of anything published that looks like it is his but is not, expressing concern about the "sharks" who would try to imitate his work or imply that they are publishing something of his. "Should then any trash of that sort be at any time disgorged from the press, and my friends or my enemies should be for asking, as is natural, is this yours? the answer is already given."[26] This passage strikes me, much like many of Sterne's digressions, as simultaneously in jest and painfully sincere. Bentham ultimately expresses keen anxiety about what would come to press, under what name, and what his legacy will be, but in a playful, Shandean episode that imagines the Demon of Socrates editing his manuscript while he slept.

The reference to *Tristram Shandy* is particularly sweet. In the sixth volume, the narrator Tristram recounts a story of his beloved Uncle Toby—a man of great heart but no common sense—attempting to comfort a soldier dying of sickness in a local inn. Toby insists repeatedly that the man is about get well and return to his regiment, but his servant and companion Corporal Trim repeatedly reminds him that the man's death is inevitable:

> ——He shall not drop, said my uncle *Toby,* firmly.——A-well-o'day,—do what we can for him, said *Trim,* maintaining his point,—the poor soul will die:——He shall not die, by G—, cried my uncle *Toby.*
> —The ACCUSING SPIRIT, which flew up to heaven's chancery with the oath, blush'd as he gave it in;—and the RECORDING ANGEL, as he wrote it down, dropp'd a tear upon the word, and blotted it out for ever.[27]

Like Uncle Toby, Bentham often seemed to need a benevolent reader to excuse his heretical and blasphemous expressions, his digressions and ejaculations, by laying a tear of compassion on a text that could only seem offensive if taken in an unsympathetic spirit.

I cannot claim to understand what Bentham's purpose was in writing this passage, claiming that the Demon of Socrates took all the errors out of his work. Perhaps he was embarrassed by the number of corrections he had to make in the manuscript—though the preceding pages show no more corrections than are typical for Bentham, who was constantly amending his own prose for clarity or precision. Like Sterne's *Tristram Shandy,* this passage comes off as something like a joke, but about something that the writer does not, in fact, find funny—an iteration of what James Kim describes as "sentimental irony" in *Tristram Shandy:* "irony and sentimentality placed in a mutually constitutive, dialogical relationship."[28] Kim suggests that Sterne's use of sentimental irony is a way of exuberantly expressing melancholia in response to emasculation. "Threatened with emasculation, Sterne emasculates himself; he fashions a new self that has already accommodated the threat of phallic loss, thereby making emasculation seem like just another part of the script, part of the role that the self is so expertly fashioned to play."[29] Bentham seems especially drawn to literature that does not sentimentalize straightforward gender dynamics or class relations based in pity; rather, like Sterne, Bentham never celebrates power relations as the powerful wish to be seen, but instead conceives of those power rela-tions as having always been a fiction of potency to which no man (or author) can really live up. At precisely the moment that he is writing a series of manuscripts comprising his most daring and mature ideas about sexual nonconformity, in the face of threats of violence and cen-sorship, Bentham imagines what someone would say, peering over his shoulder, and if they would steal this work and publish it to expose him. Just as Sterne used many of these passages of sentimental irony to com-municate his sense of having been humiliated by critics, Bentham too takes some kind of refuge in this mournful and strange act of literary self-fashioning.

Romantic-Benthamite Inclinations

Bentham's arguments seem to have had some significant influence on Percy Bysshe Shelley and other Romantic reformers, for whom poetry was only one of many methods for attempting to transform public dis-course. Though the political Romantics varied widely in their extremely different political methodologies, desired outcomes, and theoretical frameworks, they all seem to have shared the sense that modern society, such as it is, is deeply antithetical to the way it should function in an ideal world. Much like Bentham, many of these poet-reformers can be difficult to categorize using simple political terms such as political par-ties, or even radical or conservative, as many of them employed neo-classicist rhetoric in order to make deeply modern claims for legal and political progress. Like Bentham, many of these reformist Romantic poets were educated at Oxford or Cambridge, and drew on their learn-ing in historical law and culture to demand rectification of what they saw as the perversion of democracy by Christianist and moralist ideas. Yet, on the topic of sexual liberty, only William Blake and Lord Byron seem to have been able to advocate in their poetry for an understanding of sexual pleasure that extends to women or to same-sex partners.

Louis Crompton's landmark study on sexual nonconformity in this era, *Byron and Greek Love*, places Bentham directly in the context of a wide variety of Romantic poets, novelists, and reformers of this period, including William Beckford, whom Bentham had named as a possible collaborator. Crompton reads extensively in Bentham's arguments on sex alongside the poetry of Lord Byron and William Blake, as well as other sexual nonconformists of late eighteenth- and early nineteenth-century England. Although deep philosophical differences split Bentham even from his sometime allies Leigh Hunt and Percy Shelley on matters of legislative reform, Crompton notes a deep vein of common interest between Blake's prophetic poetry on sexual liberty and Bentham's queer reading of Jesus, as well as between Byron's homoeroticism and Bentham's defenses of sexual variety. This affinity of radically reimagined sexual values in relation to larger matters of legal and religious liberty among Byron, Bentham, and Blake—three otherwise stunningly distinct writers—manifests in Crompton's account as a moment of tremendous potential for radical change regarding sexual persecution. As Crompton was the first reader of Bentham to put long passages from these long-hidden manuscripts into print, it is moving to find them placed in the context of these extraordinary poems, in whose company Bentham may seem slightly awkward. In general, Bentham seems to have kept his distance from the Romantic poets, whose radicalism was often tainted by classicism and traditionalism.

As Philip Connell observes, William Hazlitt in particular excoriated the Lake poets William Wordsworth, Samuel Taylor Coleridge, and Robert Southey in 1818 as having abandoned any real sense of opposition to autocracy: "sort of shuffling on the side of principle, and tenaciousness on the side of power, seems to be the peculiar privilege of the race of modern poets."[30] In comparison, Hazlitt praises Bentham for having erred in suggesting that a tyrant could enact legislative reform and then publicly apologizing for this error in judgment. Connell notes that Hazlitt's comments on the political limitations of supposedly radical poetry "seem like a quite direct allusion to Bentham's devastating critique of the 'pestilential breath of fiction' pervading the English legal system, and suggest that, at least in the late 1810s, Hazlitt was prepared to concede both the political expediency of Bentham's jurisprudential radicalism, and the corresponding practical redundancy of 'poetic' utopianism."[31] Just as Bentham had written in *The Rationale of Reward* (which had originally been published in 1811 in French), poets were continually at risk of overreaching their grasp; by being absorbed in their own subjective perspective, and infusing the empirical world with passion and imaginative interest, poetry could not be a reliable conduit of moral or political value. Perhaps in reaction to these comparisons, there were certainly many poets of Bentham's era who saw him as a kind of useful nemesis.

Samuel Taylor Coleridge saw himself as belonging to the "Old Tory" movement of the early nineteenth century, calling for a return to supposedly ancient British values, as reinterpreted by William Blackstone and other legal historians. As an adherent of Kant, Coleridge was identified by John Stuart Mill in his 1840 essay on Coleridge as having a very similarly systematic method of thought to Bentham's, rigorously establishing first principles in order to produce arguments, though, as Mill notes, Bentham and Coleridge departed from those first principles in the opposite direction from each other.

> Bentham judged a proposition true or false as it accorded or not with the result of his own inquiries; and did not search very curiously into what might be meant by the proposition, when it obviously did not mean what he thought true. With Coleridge, on the contrary, the very fact that any doctrine had been believed by thoughtful men, and received by whole nations or generations of mankind, was part of the problem to be solved, was one of the phenomena to be accounted for. . . . Bentham's short and easy method of referring all to the selfish interests of aristocracies, or priests, or lawyers, or some other species of impostors, could not satisfy a man who saw so much farther into the complexities of human intellect and feelings.[32]

In his comparisons between Bentham and his contemporaries, Mill consistently concludes that Bentham was fatally prejudiced against aristocratic men and authority figures, preventing him from detecting the truth or value of the ideas promoted by people with wealth, education, and authority over others. Coleridge, on the other hand, was capable of admiring and appreciating the legacies of intellectual tradition and aesthetic excellence that informed his judgment. Bentham would of course note that any hierarchy of excellence or traditional value system is in itself a fatal intellectual prejudice that can only result in the further oppression of those without access or means to participate as equals in the public and political sphere.

However, Ben Pontin notes in his study of environmental law that Coleridge and Bentham perhaps agree far more—at least in the case of preservation of nonhuman resources—than might be expected from Mill's assessment. Pontin suggests that Coleridge and Bentham together constitute two of the most important early voices in British environmental law, as they both championed a kind of individualistic understanding of the relationship of the subject to the nation that would later be used for communitarian, even authoritarian purposes. He writes, "It is concluded that 19th-century environmental law is grounded in a powerful alliance of Bentham and Coleridge's ideas. These ideas converged around the protection of nature from polluting industrial enterprise (and other human threats) to provide a pluralistic and resilient philosophical foundation for various relevant laws."[33] Although Bentham's apparent lack of interest in poetry in general seemed also to extend to a lack of interest in poets, no matter how political, it does seem that some Romantic poets saw Bentham as a sympathetic spirit—though, perhaps, too radical for the ultimately rather modest reforms they advocated as possible or desirable at present.

William Wordsworth seems to have been the most immune to Bentham's political radicalism, writing a poem "To the Utilitarians" in the year after Bentham's death to chide his followers for their dehumanizing, economical thinking, offering a counterproposal to guide political thought. Rather than "Fact" ruling "Imagination," as Wordsworth accuses the Benthamites of proposing, "Reason" must join hands with "Faith," because otherwise a discourse of human rights is impossible. James P. Henderson shows that Wordsworth saw Bentham as a nemesis because of his insistence that the law must allow for the will and pleasure of individual persons, while Wordsworth saw this as merely promoting "selfishness." Wordsworth resented Bentham's claim that push-pin is better than poetry if more people can enjoy it, as I discussed in chapter 2, and felt that his advocacy for the poor was wrongheaded and destructive. Henderson demonstrates that the real difference between Wordsworth's and Bentham's positions is most obvious in the case of beggars. "Bentham maintained that beggars imposed two 'mischiefs' upon those who came in direct contact with them—the pain of sympathy and the pain of disgust. However, Wordsworth celebrated the old beggar's power as a social agent."[34] While Bentham felt that it was important for the emotional health of the community as well as for the mendicant to move beggars into housing and reasonable work situations, Wordsworth argued that the beggar serves an important social role, to arouse tender sympathies in the people who pass. That is, while Bentham thought of both the beggar's interest and that of the people around him, Wordsworth is thinking of the satisfactions of condescension more than the suffering of the person exposed to the elements. For Bentham, preserving some persons in a state of abject misery simply so that a more comfortable person can enjoy observing that misery is the height of sinister interest—precisely the same cruelty that animated violence against sexual nonconformists and the systematic abuse of women.

Henderson notes that Wordsworth and Bentham were both equally invested in their accounts of the lives of the poor as based in empirical observations of real persons in all their variety, while each saw the other as performing a kind of dehumanizing abstraction—poets using the "the poor" as a condescending morality play, and the utilitarians using "the poor" as a line item in an account book. Although they shared the goal of liberating "the poor" from truly abusive policies that would inevitably immiserate the working class, Wordsworth felt that, without religious faith and "reason"—the poet's "common sense"—the utilitarians could not be trusted to devise policies in the best interests of the people they all claimed to wish to see made happy. Meanwhile, Bentham found that the self-importance produced by faith and reason could only pervert one's political goals by creating the delusion that a selfish interest must really have been inspired by the interests of everyone else.

Percy Bysshe Shelley seems to have been somewhat more aligned with Bentham in his goals for political reform, perhaps because of their shared interests in secularism and sexual liberty. In a letter to Leigh Hunt regarding his manuscript of *A Philosophical View of Reform,* Shelley describes the work as a kind of systematic plan for political reform, philosophically considered: "It is boldly but temperately written—and I think readable. It is intended for a kind of standard book for the philosophical reformers politically considered, like Jeremy Bentham's something, but different and perhaps more systematic."[35] Ultimately, Shelley objected to the impenetrability of Bentham's style, but unlike Wordsworth, Shelley, who could be rather impenetrable himself, did not let aesthetic differences prevent him from seeing the liberationist potential of utilitarian thinking. According to Kenneth Neill Cameron, the only substantive difference between the political views of Shelley and Bentham is that Bentham, unlike Shelley, was not prepared to abolish the military altogether, and Shelley, unlike Bentham, was unprepared for female suffrage, which he felt was asking for too much too soon. Shelley writes, "Mr. Bentham and other writers have urged the admission of females to the right of suffrage; this attempt seems somewhat immature.—Should my opinion be the result of despondency, the writer of these pages would be the last to withhold his vote from any system which might tend to an equal and full development of the capacities of all living beings."[36] For Bentham, universal suffrage was simply the most obvious means of solving the crisis of disenfranchisement. If men could vote without having to prove themselves to have "common sense" or a public spirit, but merely a sense of their own interests in the world, then women should have the right to represent their own interests in the public sphere as well. While some radicals simply could not imagine allowing women to participate in politics until the world was more culturally ready for women in politics, Bentham felt that the question becomes inconsequential the moment women have political power; as fully enfranchised persons, they would instantly become a majority of the voices in the public sphere, and so men's reactions to that enfranchisement would be comparatively irrelevant as a matter of democratic rule.

Shelley likewise could not bear the idea of wide social toleration for same-sex intimacy. Though he envisioned far greater sexual freedoms for heterosexual men and increased toleration of women's complicity in male desire, Shelley made clear in *A Discourse on the Manners of the Ancient Greeks Relative to the Subject of Love* that no such toleration could possibly extend to acts of same-sex intercourse between men, which he apparently objected to on aesthetic grounds. James Bieri writes, "Shelley's repeated expressions of revulsion in *A Discourse* for the unnamed anal intercourse included 'ridiculous,' 'disgusting,' 'detestable violation,' 'gross,' 'unrefined,' and an 'operose and diabolical . . . machination.' Rejecting 'that a lover' would 'associate his own remembrance' of love 'with images of pain and horror,' Shelley proposed that Greek male lovers achieved sexual gratification by using fantasies to trigger emissions."[37] Louis Crompton writes about Shelley's comments on male same-sex intercourse, "How Shelley reconciled the traditional concept of 'natural law' with his own erotic hedonism is not clear."[38] For all the vaunted "imagination" of the male Romantic poets and their "radical" vision for a new society built on greater equality and access to power, none of them seem to have been able to imagine—much less tolerate— equality on the basis of gender and sexuality. Held back by eighteenth-century aesthetic hierarchies and common-sense liberalism, they could not envision a world in which the emotions of men did not dictate the limits of freedom for everyone else.

Philip Connell identifies the one sense in which the Romantics were perhaps more "radical" than Bentham, in that Shelley and William Godwin both saw anarchism as the only true solution to the injustices of law. While Bentham pleaded for legal reform—a rigorous process of excising myth, superstition, tradition, and aesthetic matters from the law in favor of a clear, legible, greatly reduced code of statutory laws—Shelley and Godwin demanded the end of laws altogether, to be replaced entirely by a kind of common sense of communitarian justice. "There was, however, one fundamental issue upon which Bentham clearly diverged from both Shelley and Godwin, since as Michael Scrivener has pointed out, Bentham's principal perspective was that of the legislative reformer, while Godwin's philosophical anarchism sought to collapse all public law into a fluid and enlightened form of regulative 'opinion.' As we have seen, Bentham did give a central place to the 'moral sanction' of public opinion as an important tool of the 'indirect legislator.' Nevertheless, the methodological focus of his work remained centred upon legislative codification and, to that extent, was irreconcilable with Godwinian anarchism."[39] While an idealized form of absolute self-regulation might have appealed to Bentham in principle, he felt in practice that there was no way to prevent the common sense of the masses from being dominated by a small number of people who could manipulate public discourse. The judgment of "everyone" would as easily fall under the influence of fearmongering and bigotry as would any form of rule by aristocrats.

Bentham does not bother to write much about the pernicious influences of Romantic poetry on the normativity of the populace, but he remained skeptical until the end of his life that poets were capable of the kind of unselfish observation of real human life that is necessary for formulating political ideas that are not calculated to benefit themselves exclusively. If pity is the most benevolence they could imagine for people suffering and starving in the streets, or aching with frustrated desire and misery, or forced to reproduce against their own wishes, then their enjoyment of their own pity would only prevent them from working to ameliorate the suffering that gave rise to that delicious feeling. As Bentham shows, pity is always aesthetically next door to disgust, and both are aesthetic reactions based in condescension and objectification. By refusing to project his own emotional and aesthetic life onto the persons he observed, Bentham remained able to account for the differences of pleasure manifested in the behaviors of those around him. Though the disinterested gaze of the utilitarians has since been put to the use of capitalist and nationalistic discrimination and cruelty, it is possible to imagine that Bentham could have succeeded in making a very different world possible—one in which the pleasure of an individual, no matter how rare, is worth protecting from the violence of those who resent its uncommon sense.

Conclusion

Historians of sexuality are unlikely to stumble onto Bentham's papers on sexuality in the normal course of an education in British culture and ideas. Our best-respected philosophical and literary minds have made short work of him, and for all we know from biographers and his correspondence, Bentham was odd but not particularly queer, so he has not been recovered by scholars seeking accounts of historical lesbian, gay, and transgender experiences. As a legal reformer, Bentham's triumphs were modest; as a social reformer, his initial success has undeniably led to the invention of new forms of oppression that have been catastrophic for the happiness of the disenfranchised persons he advocated for. In many ways, Bentham's legacy might serve as a warning to would-be allies of oppressed people; when a self-appointed liaison negotiates with the agents of power in their own language, rather than amplifying the voices of oppressed persons speaking for themselves, those agents of power may only learn more effective means of exercising their control. Although Bentham lived at a time when sexual nonconformists could not defend themselves in the public sphere without the threat of death or exile, there were certainly women and formerly colonized and enslaved persons who did write and speak on their own behalf in public.

The innovation of Bentham's that inspired my passion for this project was his theory that if our bodies are not our own, then we have no liberty, not even the bleak comfort of self-defense. If we cannot all enjoy our bodies—protect, nourish, and move our bodies, choose whether to have children and with whom we share pleasure—then it is irrelevant to speak of having rights. Rights mean nothing to people who are not permitted to survive the rage of the police, or even a passerby. Bentham's contemporaries seemed to find his focus on bodily pleasure utterly absurd; for fully enfranchised men, born to wield the scepter of common sense, the pleasures of their own bodies were merely by the way—a matter of sickness or health, hangover and gout, desire and regret. They could not identify personally with a kidnapped and displaced African person, forced to labor for a stranger's wealth under the threat of death, nor with the woman denied an education, coerced into bearing children for a man who beats her. By focusing on men who have sex with men, Bentham hoped to devise an irrefutable philosophical proof that British men in positions of legal, philosophical, and religious authority could understand. A difference of taste cannot justify killing a man. What bodily differences could possibly justify causing needless suffering to most of the population? Which "human rights" are women, enslaved and incarcerated people, disabled people, children, and sexual nonconformists human enough to enjoy?

At present, private same-sex intercourse is no longer the most urgent priority of social and legal discipline. I am writing at a time when same-sex intimacy is no longer effectively illegal in my country since the 2003 Supreme Court decision *Lawrence v. Texas,* despite active laws banning same-sex intimacy in sixteen states.[1] In June 2020 the Supreme Court, though packed with conservative justices, decided that gender or sexual nonconformity is no longer sufficient cause for terminating a person's employment.[2] Although LGBTQ+ people are still targeted for extra-legal, social, and economic violence, sweeping legal and institutional reforms of the past twenty years have made it possible for many more people to live their lives in less fear, believing that the law will at least not add to the burdens of discriminatory treatment. It remains unclear to what extent protections for LGBTQ+ people will be upheld by courts, as the case law has continued to reveal intransigent discrimination among judges, but the battle for aesthetics has been largely successful. Representations of same-sex desire and transgender lives in mainstream entertainment are becoming more common, but of course, therefore, also subject to the same pressures of normativity via racism, classicism, and gender conformity that have shaped mainstream representations of heterosexuality and cisgender identity.

If Bentham is right about sexual nonconformity and the politics of taste, then greater toleration for same-sex pleasure is potentially the first step on the way to truly widespread legal and social reforms for disenfranchised people. He believed that if men with power could be convinced to stop persecuting people on the basis of their sexual partners, and nonheterosexual people could represent their own interests in the public sphere and in politics, it could be the first step in eradicating the influence of sinister interests from positions of power. The legislator who cannot openly govern from a sense of pure resentment and cruelty regarding sexual difference, and who must protect the liberties of others to enjoy their pleasures in their own way, may also be convinced to respect the full humanity of women, laborers, children, disabled persons, and other groups underrepresented in the public sphere. Bentham's felicific calculus allows us to sidestep the problem of moral sentiment in arguing for true social and legal equality. It does not matter how the few people with power feel about the pleasures of the many; whether they resent or are disgusted by those pleasures cannot be the basis for prohibition. It does not matter if the few people with power sympathize with the happiness of others, or have compassion for their sorrow; the only duty of power is to make their happiness possible. And if those with power are not able to do that, they must be replaced. Using the example of sexual nonconformity, Bentham shows us why we cannot trust a tiny minority of self-interested persons—who control the government, the economy, the church, and philosophical discourse—to decide whose pleasures are a crime.

NOTES

INTRODUCTION

1. Booth argues that the narrator of *Tom Jones* is not merely the voice of the author, which is very different in each of Fielding's novels, but a kind of imagined objective perspective for the world of the story—not an avatar of moral perfection, but a superhumanly *reasonable* judge of characters. "In a fictional world that offers no single character who is both wise and good . . . the author is always there on his platform to remind us, though his wisdom and benevolence, of what human life ought to be and might be." Wayne Booth, *The Rhetoric of Fiction,* 217.
2. Immanuel Kant, *Critique of Judgement,* 123.
3. A typical example from Locke: "He would be thought void of common sense, who asked on the one side, or on the other side, went to give a reason, 'why it is impossible for the same thing to be, and not to be.'" *An Essay Concerning Human Understanding,* 76.
4. George Berkeley, *Three Dialogues between Hylas and Philonous,* 117, 120.
5. Bentham, *A Comment on the Commentaries,* 393.
6. Ibid., 459–60 note k.
7. Bentham, *An Introduction to the Principles of Morals and Legislation,* 12.
8. UN General Assembly, "Universal Declaration of Human Rights," 217 (III) A (Paris, 1948), http://www.un.org/en/universal-declaration -human-rights/, Article 1.
9. Philip Goodchild, *Theology of Money,* xi.
10. Adam Smith, *The Theory of Moral Sentiments,* 220.
11. John Locke, *Two Treatises of Government,* 290.
12. Ibid., 269.
13. Ibid., 298.
14. Ibid., 183.
15. Smith, *Theory of Moral Sentiments,* 255.
16. Ibid., 242.
17. Kant, *Critique of Judgement,* 123.
18. Immanuel Kant, "An Answer to the Question: What Is Enlightenment?," 58.
19. Jürgen Habermas, *The Structural Transformation of the Public Sphere,* 107–8.
20. Jeremy Bentham MSS, University College London (UCL), xiv. 8 (1800).
21. Locke, *Two Treatises,* 298.

22. Louis Crompton, *Byron and Greek Love,* 20.
23. Bentham, *An Introduction to the Principles of Morals and Legislation,* 283.
24. D. Christopher Gabbard, "From Idiot Beast to Idiot Sublime," 377.
25. Locke, *Two Treatises,* 141.
26. David Hume, *An Enquiry Concerning the Principles of Morals,* 100.
27. David Hume, *Political Essays,* 86nl.
28. Richard H. Popkin, "Hume's Racism Reconsidered."
29. John Immerwahr, "Hume's Revised Racism."
30. Robert Palter, "Hume and Prejudice."
31. The recent statistics provided by the American Philosophical Association for the year 2018 are difficult to analyze, since, of 8,266 registered members, only a quarter to a half responded to voluntary survey questions on demographic data points, while 93 percent of those members responded to questions about their employment status on the same survey. Even if the responses to demographic questions were somehow representative, among full (i.e., nonstudent, nonemeritus) members of APA, including part-time and contingent staff, 72.4 percent self-identified as male, and 78.8 percent self-identified as "White/Caucasian." In addition, 5.7 percent of all APA members self-identified as LGBTQ+, and 4.5 percent self-identified as disabled. *Demographic Statistics on the APA Membership, FY2016 to FY 2018.* https://cdn.ymaws.com/www.apaonline.org/resource /resmgr/data_on_profession/fy2018-demographic_statistic.pdf.
32. Eve Kosofsky Sedgwick, *Epistemology of the Closet,* 128.
33. Michael Warner, *Letters of the Republic,* 112.
34. [Samuel Johnson], *Taxation no Tyranny,* 89.
35. [Jeremy Bentham], "Short Review of the Declaration," 120.
36. Jeremy Bentham, "Emancipate Your Colonies!"
37. Jeremy Bentham, *Colonies, Commerce, and Constitutional Law.*
38. Bentham MSS, UCL, clviii. 231 (14 August 1811).
39. Bentham offers a four-part test for the worthiness of any scheme of punishment; it must not be *groundless* (undeserved), *inefficacious* (impossible or unlikely to prevent mischief), *unprofitable* (too expensive), or *needless* (because the mischief is unlikely to reoccur). Without any such test for appropriate punitive measures, Bentham finds that the penal code swells with violations for which enforcement is absurd, cruel, or ruinous. Bentham, *An Introduction to the Principles of Morals and Legislation,* 158–59.
40. The first iteration of this table that I find in Bentham's manuscripts is titled "Dimensions of Happiness" from 1800, and suggests a plan for a larger work outlining the ingredients, dimensions, definitions, axioms, values, diagnostics, and sensory attributes of happiness. Bentham

MSS, UCL, xiv. 1–9 (1800). By 1805 the table would become the "Table of Motives" (Bentham MSS, UCL, xiv. 21 [1805]) before evolving into *A Table of the Springs of Action,* published in 1815. Jeremy Bentham, *A Table of the Springs of Action,* in *Deontology,* 1–115.

41. Frances Ferguson, "Not Kant, but Bentham."
42. Ibid., 581.
43. In his manuscript "Sextus," Bentham lists several popular literary works by men—especially Tobias Smollett's *Roderick Random* and Henry Fielding's *Joseph Andrews*—in which an expression of same-sex desire or gender nonconformity is met with retributive violence committed by the triumphantly heterosexual protagonist. "Sextus," in *Of Sexual Irregularities and Other Writings,* 85–86.
44. Bentham mentions his love of gothic fiction and women novelists in several manuscripts, as discussed at length in chapter 5.

1. The Trouble with Bentham

1. Bentham, *A Comment on the Commentaries,* 393.
2. Charles Dickens, *Hard Times,* 10.
3. Frances Ferguson, "Envy Rising," 896.
4. Ibid., 898.
5. Kathleen Blake, *Pleasures of Benthamism,* 144.
6. The concerns of the reform movement were perhaps best articulated by John Howard in his 1777 work *The State of the Prisons in England and Wales,* which described overcrowding, excessive suffering, untreated disease, filth, and hopelessness as the products of poor funding, mismanagement, financial corruption, and cruelty.
7. Bentham MSS, UCL, cxv. 1–5 (1791).
8. Michel Foucault, *Discipline and Punish,* 200.
9. Frances Ferguson, *Pornography, the Theory,* 72.
10. Anne Brunon-Ernst, *Utilitarian Biopolitics,* 4.
11. Vivasvan Soni, *Mourning Happiness,* 256.
12. Ibid., 395.
13. Bentham, *Deontology,* 79–86.
14. Jeremy Bentham [as Philip Beauchamp], *Analysis of the Influence of Natural Religion,* 142.
15. Faramerz Dabhoiwala, review of *Of Sexual Irregularities,* by Jeremy Bentham, *Guardian,* June 26, 2014.
16. Bentham MSS, UCL, lxxiv. 14 (c. 1774).
17. Bentham, *A Comment on the Commentaries,* 393.
18. Champs, *Enlightenment and Utility,* 3.

19. See chapter 3 for more on the legal history of the Buggery Act.
20. Bentham MSS, UCL, lxxiv. 6 (c. 1774).
21. Bentham, *An Introduction to the Principles of Morals and Legislation,* 15 note d.
22. Jeremy Bentham, *Not Paul, but Jesus: Vol. III,* 108.
23. Bentham MSS, UCL, cxxxix. 35 (3 January 1818).
24. Stefan Waldschmidt, "Bentham, Pater, and the Aesthetics of Utilitarian Sex," 366.
25. Bentham leaves a wide blank space in the manuscript here, suggesting, perhaps, the powers of the church, society, law, etc., combined?
26. Bentham MSS, UCL, cxxxix, 35 (3 January 1818).
27. Bentham MSS, UCL, clxi.b. 234 (14 November 1817).
28. Eric O. Clarke, *Virtuous Vice,* 63–64.
29. Kevin Floyd, *The Reification of Desire,* 16.
30. Karl Marx, *Capital,* 758.
31. Ibid., 759n.
32. Friedrich Nietzsche, *Beyond Good and Evil,* 156–57.
33. See chapter 2 for an extended analysis of Mill's response to Bentham's statements about push-pin in *The Rationale of Reward* (1825).
34. Bentham MSS, UCL, xv. 105 (16 April 1821).
35. Samuel Delany, *Times Square Red, Times Square Blue,* 189–90.
36. Floyd, *Reification of Desire,* 151.
37. The Uniting and Strengthening America by Providing Appropriate Tools Required to Intercept and Obstruct Terrorism Act (H.R. 3162).
38. Recent historical and historicist studies of eighteenth-century British/ colonial subcultures and countercultures are so numerous as to exceed the capacities of a footnote, but I draw the reader's attention to a selection of notable studies, arranged in reverse chronological order, that describe communities whose rejection of the normative values of the supposedly dominant culture produced alternate systems of semiotic, semantic, and rhetorical meaning. Ula Lukszo Klein, "Eighteenth-Century Female Crossdressers and Their Beards"; Bryychan Carey, *From Peace to Freedom;* Laura Rosenthal, *Infamous Commerce;* Erin Mackie, "Welcome the Outlaw"; Rictor Norton, *Mother Clap's Molly House;* Randolph Trumbach, "Sex, Gender, and Sexual Identity in Modern Culture"; William Dillon Piersen, *Black Yankees;* Pat Rogers, *Grub Street.*
39. Bentham MSS, UCL, xiv. 15 (23 March 1795).
40. See the Transcribe Bentham project at http://transcribe-bentham.ucl.ac .uk/, where scans of nearly all of UCL's collection of Bentham's manuscripts are readily available for reading.
41. These writings are quoted at length at the beginning of chapter 2, Bentham MSS, UCL, lxxiv. 3 (c. 1774).

2. Aesthetics of Pleasure, Ethics of Happiness

1. For example, John Locke defines pleasure as a lesser degree of pain, concluding that the pursuit of pleasure serves as a regulatory function to produce disappointment and make one long for the perfect pleasure of eternal life with God. Locke, *An Essay Concerning Human Understanding*, 131, 216–19. Bentham assesses the relative pain and pleasure of each sense separately, concluding, for example, that "the pleasure of the sexual sense seems to have no positive pain to correspond to it: it has only a pain of privation, or pain of the mental class, the pain of unsatisfied desire. If any positive pain of body result from the want of such indulgence, it belongs to the head of pains of disease." Bentham, *An Introduction to the Principles of Morals and Legislation*, 47.

2. Bentham MSS, UCL, lxxiv. 3–4 (c. 1774).

3. Bentham MSS, UCL, lxxiv.a. unnumbered (c. 1774).

4. Bentham MSS, UCL, xiv. 8 (1800).

5. Boralevi, *Bentham and the Oppressed*, 178.

6. In Bentham, *Deontology*, 1–115.

7. In part 1, chapter 6, of Thomas Hobbes, *Leviathan*, 27–35.

8. Hume, *An Enquiry Concerning the Principles of Morals*, 115–16.

9. Malcolm Quinn, "Jeremy Bentham on Liberty of Taste," 619.

10. Bentham, *Of Sexual Irregularities*, 6.

11. Ibid., 28–29.

12. Ibid., 29.

13. Bentham, *Deontology*, 79.

14. Bentham, *Of Sexual Irregularities*, 63–64.

15. As the editors of *Of Sexual Irregularities* note, Bentham's immediate source for this "sixth sense" of sexual pleasure was probably Georges-Louis Leclerc, comte de Buffon, who wrote in his *Natural History of Birds*, "But there is a sixth sense, which, though it intermits, seems, while it acts, to control all the others, and excites the most powerful emotions, and awakens the most ardent affections:—it is love" (29). Buffon is not the first to suggest the existence of a sixth sense of "love" or sexual pleasure; in *Anatomy of Melancholy*, Robert Burton credited Julius Caesar Scaliger with inventing the sixth sense of "titillation" (22). Scaliger, in turn, seems to have gotten the idea for a sixth sense of sexual excitement as a response to Girolamo Cardano, whose *De Subtilitate* (1550) formed the basis for Scaliger's critique in *Exercitationes exotericae de subtilitate* (1557). Cardano does not name a sixth sense and asserts definitively that there are only five senses in book 13; on the contrary, his extended analysis of erection and reproductive intercourse in book 12 suggests that sexual desire arises from a combination of internal heat and moisture,

habit, mental stimulation, and arousal of the five senses, not an independent sixth sense. John M. Forrester, ed., *The "De Subtilitate" of Girolamo Cardano*, vol. 2.

16. Bentham, *Of Sexual Irregularities*, 77.
17. Ferguson, "Not Kant, but Bentham," 579.
18. Jeremy Bentham, *The Rationale of Reward*, 206.
19. John Stuart Mill, *Dissertations and Discussions*, 387.
20. Bentham MSS, UCL, lxxii. 189.1 (c. 1776–1786).
21. Ibid., 189.2.
22. Bentham MSS, UCL, lxxii. 201.2 (c. 1776–1786).
23. Ibid., 584.
24. Ibid., 585.
25. Aristotle, *De anima*, 418a17, quoted in Aquinas, *The Commentary of Saint Thomas Aquinas on Aristotle's Treatise on the Soul*, 31.
26. By turning the common sense into a faculty that one may have in greater or lesser capacity, as with any other sense, Locke invents a new kind of ableist discourse that has sweeping ramifications for the political and social disenfranchisement of marginalized populations. As a justification for oppression, this description of common sense naturalizes the marginalization of social others; rather than justifying oppression openly using racial and gender categories, religious dissent, or a person's status as a laborer, the charge that a person or population lacks common sense could be leveled at anyone who disagrees with the agents of their oppression. Unless one shares the aesthetic and moral values of the oppressor, one is deemed insufficient in the common sense required to enter public discourse regarding one's own oppression. In the later eighteenth century, abolitionists like Olaudah Equiano and Phillis Wheatley expounded on antislavery politics using the most elite literary aesthetics of their era in order to establish their credibility within the common-sense aesthetic discourse of their oppressors.
27. Locke, *An Essay Concerning Human Understanding*, 823.
28. Hume, *Enquiry*, 186.
29. Ibid., 188.
30. Ibid.
31. Ibid.
32. Ferguson, "Not Kant, but Bentham," 582.
33. Ibid., 584.
34. Berkeley, *Three Dialogues*, 120.
35. Epicurus, *The Essential Epicurus*, 70.
36. Ibid., 66.
37. Frederick Rosen, *Classical Utilitarianism from Hume to Mill*, 19–25.

38. Hobbes, *Leviathan,* 28.
39. Ibid.
40. Locke, *An Essay Concerning Human Understanding,* 130.
41. Hobbes, *Leviathan,* 32.
42. Haig Patapan and Jeffrey Sikkenga, "Love and the Leviathan."
43. Ibid., 815.
44. Ibid., 818.
45. "First, regardless of the confident assertions of numerous historians of political thought, it is arguable that the alleged influence of Hobbes on Bentham remains questionable. As we have seen, with the exception of five scattered asides in a vast volume of published and unpublished writing, Bentham never discussed the work of Hobbes in any meaningful way." James Crimmins, "Bentham and Hobbes," 687.
46. Bentham MSS, UCL, xiv. 16 (8 September 1795).
47. Ibid.

3. AGAINST RIGHTS

1. Lawrence Hamilton, *The Political Philosophy of Needs,* 7.
2. Frederick Rosen, "Bentham and Mill on Liberty and Justice," 122.
3. [Jeremy Bentham], "Short Review of the Declaration," 120.
4. Locke, *Two Treatises,* 383.
5. Ibid., 386.
6. Ibid., 400.
7. Bentham, *Rights, Representation, and Reform,* 398.
8. Bentham discusses the limitations of the word "utility" in many places in his published and unpublished writing. This discussion is perhaps clearest in his manuscript notes for *Not Paul, but Jesus,* where he admits that "utility" is a confusing word to apply to happiness because it shares no etymological relationship with happiness or pleasure: "The use of the word *utility* labours under this inconvenience, viz. that not, in the language of the logician, being a *conjugate* of either the word happiness, or of the word pleasure, or of the compound appellatives absence of pain or exemption from pain—i.e. in the language of the grammarian not being derived from the same *root,* it affords not any immediate or certain indication of the relation between the idea associated [with] it and the ideas respectively associated with those several locutions. Unhappily the language affords not any locution by which that purpose so desirable can be accomplished: nor, upon a long and diligent search, could any one more apposite than the one here employed—*utility*—be found. By the word *utility* what is directly designated is the property which an object has of

being the cause of the other considered in the character of an effect: by an useful action—an action of which utility is a quality—is here understood an action which has for its effect, or at any rate for its tendency, the augmentation of the stock of pleasures or, what is correspondent and may be equivalent, the diminution in the stock of pains" (Vol. 3, 11).

9. J. H. Burns, "Happiness and Utility," 56.

10. Act of Uniformity 1662 (14 Ca 2 c 4).

11. Bentham MSS, UCL, lxxiv. 5 (c. 1774).

12. Boralevi, *Bentham and the Oppressed*, 67.

13. Bentham, *A Comment on the Commentaries*, 397.

14. Ibid., 398.

15. Ibid., 393.

16. Waldschmidt, "Bentham, Pater, and the Aesthetics of Utilitarian Sex," 366.

17. See, e.g., Bentham MSS, UCL, lxxiv. 3 (c. 1774).

18. Byrne Fone, *Homophobia*, 254

19. The Proceedings in Courts of Justice Act 1730 (4 Geo 2 c 26).

20. Bentham, *Fragment*, 411 note r.

21. William Blackstone, *Commentaries on the Laws of England*, 47–48.

22. Kathryn Temple, *Loving Justice*, 86.

23. Philip Schofield, *Utility and Democracy*, 54.

24. Bentham MSS, UCL, lxx. 3 (1776).

25. Ibid., 8.

26. An Acte for the punishment of the vice of Buggerie (25 Hen. 8 c. 6).

27. *The Statutes at Large, of England and of Great Britain*, 145.

28. Paul Johnson and Robert M. Vanderbeck write, "There is general agreement that the enactment of the BA 1533 was not motivated solely by theological ambitions but, rather, represented a secular expression of political power by Henry VIII," and that the act was originally intended to serve as a threat to seize the property of Catholic priests, who were assumed (according to anti-Papist stereotypes) to practice sodomy. *Law, Religion, and Homosexuality*, 33.

29. *An Account of the proceedings against Capt. Edward Rigby*.

30. Bentham MSS, UCL, lxxiv. 3 (c. 1774).

31. In Bentham, *Rights, Representation, and Reform*, 289–313.

32. Ibid., 291.

33. Ibid., 292.

34. Ibid., 305.

35. Ibid., 320.

36. "Ultramaria" was a term Bentham used for describing overseas Spanish territories in the Americas and Southeast Asia.

37. Bentham, *Colonies, Commerce, and Constitutional Law*, 92.

NOTES TO PAGES 104–118   169

38. Ibid., 284.
39. Bentham, *Of Sexual Irregularities*, 7.
40. Bentham MSS, UCL, cxxxix. 35 (1818).

4. BENTHAM'S QUEER CHRIST

1. Lee Edelman, "Learning Nothing," 125.
2. Lee Edelman, *No Future*, 28.
3. Michel Foucault, *The History of Sexuality*, 26.
4. Rebekah Sheldon, *The Child to Come*, 35.
5. Ibid., 4.
6. Katherine Bond Stockton, *God between Their Lips*, 7–8.
7. Bentham MSS, UCL, cxxxix. 35 (3 January 1818); Locke, *Two Treatises*, 298. See chapter 1 and the introduction for further discussion of these passages.
8. Bentham, *Of Sexual Irregularities*, 25.
9. Bentham is clear that religion is not the only source of ascetic delusions, which are also shared by secular philosophers. "Without hope from heaven or fear from hell—without equivalent in any shape other than the gratification afforded in that same way to the passion of pride—a set of heathen philosophers—the Stoics—gave up, or professed at least to give up, these in the lump, with a whole multitude of other pleasures: pleasures in the choice of which not more consistency was manifested than in so many other sacrifices." Bentham, *Of Sexual Irregularities*, 76.
10. James E. Crimmins, *Secular Utilitarianism*, 15.
11. Philip Schofield, "Political and Religious Radicalism," 291.
12. Bentham MSS, UCL, lxx. 25 (1776?).
13. Delos McKown, *Behold the Antichrist*, 21.
14. Bentham, *The Influence of Natural Religion*, 44.
15. Ibid., 45.
16. Ibid.
17. Ibid. 68.
18. An authoritative edition of *Not Paul, but Jesus* is forthcoming from the Bentham Project's partnership with Oxford University Press. Meanwhile, the 1823 text published under the name Gamaliel Smith is readily available. Volume 3 has been published by the Bentham Project under a Creative Commons license. Bentham's preparatory writings on Jesus appear throughout the 2014 *Of Sexual Irregularities* volume, but mostly in his *General Idea of a Work, Having for One of its Objects the Defence of the Principle of* Utility, *so Far as Concerns the Liberty of Taste, against the Conjunct Hostility of the Principle of* Asceticism *and the Principle of* Antipathy; *and for its Proposed Title, Proposed on the Ground of Expected Popularity,*

or at Least Protection against Popular Rage,—Not Paul, but Jesus, in *Of Sexual Irregularities.* And his controversial writings on "natural religion" appear in Bentham, *Analysis of the Influence of Natural Religion.*

19. Jeremy Bentham, *Swear Not at All,* 77.
20. Jeremy Bentham, *Church-of-Englandism and Its Catechism,* 82–83.
21. Bentham, *Of Sexual Irregularities,* xxiv.
22. Ibid., 15.
23. Bentham, *Not Paul, but Jesus: Vol. III,* 189–90.
24. Bentham, *Of Sexual Irregularities,* 72.
25. Ibid., 73.
26. Ibid., 75.
27. Kathryn Bond Stockton, *The Queer Child,* 228.
28. In *Paradise Lost,* John Milton's Satan declares, upon seeing the newly created world for humans:

> So farewel Hope, and with Hope farewel Fear,
> Farewel Remorse: all Good to me is lost;
> Evil be thou my Good; by thee at least
> Divided Empire with Heav'ns King I hold
> By thee, and more then half perhaps will reigne;
> As Man ere long, and this new World shall know.
>   (Book 4, lines 108–13)

For many queer theorists, this kind of Satanic position with respect to the injunction to procreative sexuality has long been the only rhetorical framing available in a discourse in which the production of the future is the only imaginable good. Ultimately, I fear that, by ceding the grounds of goodness itself to heteronormativity, which is not a particularly stable or even very old social norm, queer people have necessarily embraced villainy—"Divided Empire" with reproductive heterosexuals, at best— rather than demand space for an alternative aesthetics of sexual utility.

29. David M. Halperin, "What Is Sex For?," 30.
30. Sedgwick, *Epistemology of the Closet,* 52–53.
31. Valerie Traub, *Thinking Sex with the Early Moderns,* 73.
32. Emphasis Bentham's. Bentham, *Not Paul, but Jesus: Vol. III,* 191.
33. Ibid., 193.

5. POLITICS AND POETICS OF LIBERTY

1. Carrie Shanafelt, "The Rhetoric of Consensus," 85–106.
2. Ana de Freitas Boe and Abby Coykendall, eds., *Heteronormativity in Eighteenth-Century Literature,* 14–15.

3. Michel de Montaigne, *Essays*, 94.
4. Ibid., 95.
5. Paul Kelleher, *Making Love*, 197.
6. Declan Kavanagh, *Effeminate Years*.
7. Bentham, *Of Sexual Irregularities*, 43.
8. Ibid., 85.
9. Ibid., 23–24.
10. Jeremy Collier, *A Short View of the Immorality of the English Stage*, 271.
11. Laurence Senelick, "Mollies or Men of Mode?"
12. Crompton, *Byron and Greek Love*, 21.
13. Bentham, *An Introduction to the Principles of Morals and Legislation*, 4.
14. Ibid., 5.
15. Bentham, *Rights, Representation, and Reform*, 292.
16. Bentham, *Of Sexual Irregularities*, 122.
17. Ibid.
18. Ibid., 123.
19. Laurie Langbauer, *Women and Romance*, 90.
20. Bentham MSS, UCL, xiv. 14 (17 November 1794).
21. George E. Haggerty, *Queer Gothic*, 10.
22. Bentham MSS, UCL, lxx. 37 (1776).
23. Bentham MSS, UCL, lxx. 38 (1776).
24. Most recently, the experimental writer Eileen Myles, in "Comedy of Heirs," wrote a passionate encomium to the pleasures of *Tristram Shandy*, a novel that seems to find especially appreciative readers among socially and sexually nonnormative graphomaniacs.
25. Bentham MSS, UCL, lxxiv. 17.1 (c. 1774).
26. Bentham MSS, UCL, lxxiv. 17.3 (c. 1774).
27. Laurence Sterne, *The Life and Opinions of Tristram Shandy*, 341.
28. James Kim, "'Good cursed, bouncing losses,'" 4.
29. Ibid., 14.
30. Qtd. in Philip Connell, *Romanticism, Economics and the Question of "Culture,"* 223.
31. Ibid., 224.
32. John Stuart Mill, "Coleridge," 120.
33. Ben Pontin, "Environmental Law-Making Public Opinion in Victorian Britain," 763.
34. James P. Henderson, "Beggars," 434.
35. Qtd. in Kenneth Neill Cameron, "Shelley and the Reformers," 74–75.
36. Qtd. in ibid., 80.
37. James Bieri, *Percy Bysshe Shelley: A Biography*, 71.

38. Crompton, *Byron and Greek Love*, 296.
39. Connell, *Romanticism, Economics and the Question of Culture*, 221.

Conclusion

1. *Lawrence v. Texas*, 539 U.S. 558 (2003).
2. Three cases were decided together on June 15, 2020: *Bostock v. Clayton County, Georgia; Altitude Express, Inc. v. Zarda;* and *R. G. and G. R. Harris Funeral Homes Inc. v. Equal Employment Opportunity Commission*, 590 U.S. _____ (2020).

WORKS CITED

An Account of the proceedings against Capt. Edward Rigby, at the Sessions of Goal Delivery, held at Justice-Hall in the Old-Bailey, on Wednesday the seventh day of December, 1698, for intending to commit the abominable sin of sodomy, on the body of one William Minton. London: F. Collins, 1698.

Aquinas, Saint Thomas. *The Commentary of Saint Thomas Aquinas on Aristotle's Treatise on the Soul.* Trans. R. A. Kocourek. St. Paul: College of St. Thomas, 1946.

Bentham, Jeremy [as Philip Beauchamp]. *Analysis of the Influence of Natural Religion on the Temporal Happiness of Mankind.* Ed. Delos McKown. Amherst: Prometheus, 2003.

———. *Church-of-Englandism and Its Catechism Examined.* Ed. J. E. Crimmins and Catherine Fuller. Oxford: Clarendon Press, 2011.

———. *Colonies, Commerce, and Constitutional Law: Rid Yourselves of Ultramaria and Other Writings on Spain and Spanish America.* Ed. Philip Schofield. Oxford: Clarendon Press, 1995.

———. *A Comment on the Commentaries and A Fragment on Government.* Ed. J. H. Burns and H. L. A. Hart. Oxford: Clarendon Press, 1977.

———. *Deontology, Together with A Table of the Springs of Action and Article on Utilitarianism.* Ed. Ammon Goldworth. Oxford: Clarendon Press, 1983.

———. *An Introduction to the Principles of Morals and Legislation.* Ed. J. H. Burns and H. L. A. Hart. Oxford: Clarendon Press, 2005.

———[as Gamaliel Smith]. *Not Paul, but Jesus.* [Vol. 1]. London: John Hunt, 1823.

———. *Not Paul, but Jesus: Vol. 3.* Ed. Philip Schofield, Michael Quinn, and Catherine Pease-Watkin. London: The Bentham Project, UCL, 2013.

———. *Of Sexual Irregularities and Other Writings on Sexual Morality.* Ed. Philip Schofield, Catherine Pease-Watkin, and Michael Quinn. Oxford: Clarendon Press, 2014.

———. *The Rationale of Reward.* London: John and H. L. Hunt, 1825.

———. *Rights, Representation, and Reform: Nonsense Upon Stilts and Other Writings on the French Revolution.* Ed. Philip Schofield, Catherine Pease-Watkin, and Cyprian Blamires. Oxford: Clarendon Press, 2002.

———[unsigned]. "Short Review of the Declaration." In *An Answer to the Declaration of the American Congress* by John Lind. London: T. Cadell, J. Walter, and T. Sewell, 1776.

———. *Swear Not at All: Containing the Exposure of the Needlessness and Mischievousness, as Well as Antichristianity of the Ceremony of an Oath.* London: R. Hunter, 1817.

———. *Writings on the Poor Laws.* Vol. 1. Ed. Michael Quinn. Oxford: Clarendon Press, 2001.

Berkeley, George. *Three Dialogues between Hylas and Philonous.* Ed. Jonathan Dancy. Oxford: Oxford Univ. Press, 1998.

Bieri, James. *Percy Bysshe Shelley: A Biography: Exile of Unfulfilled Reknown, 1816–1822.* Newark: Univ. of Delaware Press, 2005.

Blackstone, William. *Commentaries on the Laws of England.* Vol. 1. Oxford: Clarendon Press, 1765–69. Facsimile ed., Chicago: Univ. of Chicago Press, 1979.

Blake, Kathleen. *Pleasures of Benthamism: Victorian Literature, Utility, Political Economy.* Oxford: Oxford Univ. Press, 2009.

Boe, Ana de Freitas, and Abby Coykendall, eds. *Heteronormativity in Eighteenth-Century Literature and Culture.* Burlington: Ashgate, 2014.

Booth, Wayne. *The Rhetoric of Fiction.* 2nd ed. Chicago: Univ. of Chicago Press, 1983.

Boralevi, Lea Campos. *Bentham and the Oppressed.* Berlin: Walter de Gruyter, 1984.

Brunon-Ernst, Anne. *Utilitarian Biopolitics: Bentham, Foucault, and Modern Power.* London: Routledge, 2012.

Buffon, Georges Louis Leclerc, comte de. *The Natural History of Birds: Vol. I.* Trans. [Anon.], London: A. Strahan and T. Cadell, 1793.

Burns, J. H. "Happiness and Utility: Jeremy Bentham's Equation." *Utilitas* 17.1 (2005): 46–61.

Burton, Robert. *Anatomy of Melancholy.* Oxford: Henry Cripps, 1638.

Cameron, Kenneth Neill. "Shelley and the Reformers." *ELH* 12.1 (March 1945): 62–85.

Cardano, Girolamo. See Forrester.

Carey, Brycchan. *From Peace to Freedom: Quaker Rhetoric and the Birth of American Antislavery, 1657–1761.* New Haven: Yale Univ. Press, 2012.

Champs, Emmanuelle de. *Enlightenment and Utility: Bentham in French, Bentham in France.* Cambridge: Cambridge Univ. Press, 2015.

Clarke, Eric O. *Virtuous Vice: Homoeroticism and the Public Sphere.* Durham: Duke Univ. Press, 2000.

Collier, Jeremy. *A Short View of the Immorality, and Profaneness of the English Stage, Together With the Sence of Antiquity upon this Argument.* London: S. Keble, 1698.

Connell, Philip. *Romanticism, Economics, and the Question of "Culture."* Oxford: Oxford Univ. Press, 2001.

Crimmins, James E. "Bentham and Hobbes: An Issue of Influence." *Journal of the History of Ideas* 63.4 (Oct. 2002): 677–96.

———. *Secular Utilitarianism: Social Science and the Critique of Religion in the Thought of Jeremy Bentham.* Oxford: Oxford Univ. Press, 1990.

Crompton, Louis. *Byron and Greek Love: Homophobia in 19th-Century England.* 1985. Swaffham: The Gay Men's Press, 1998.

Delany, Samuel. *Times Square Red, Times Square Blue.* New York: New York Univ. Press, 1999.

Dickens, Charles. *Hard Times.* New York: Penguin, 2003.

Edelman, Lee. "Learning Nothing: *Bad Education.*" *differences* 28.1 (2017): 124–73.

———. *No Future: Queer Theory and the Death Drive.* Durham: Duke Univ. Press, 2004.

Epicurus. *The Essential Epicurus: Letters, Principal Doctrines, Vatican Sayings, and Fragments.* Trans. Eugene O'Connor. Amherst, NY: Prometheus Books, 1993.

Ferguson, Frances. "Envy Rising." *ELH* 69.4 (Winter 2002): 889–905.

———. "Not Kant, but Bentham: On Taste." *Critical Inquiry* 45 (Spring 2019): 577–600.

———. *Pornography, the Theory: What Utilitarianism Did to Action.* Chicago: Univ. of Chicago Press, 2004.

Fielding, Henry. *The History of Tom Jones, a Foundling.* Ed. Fredson Bowers. Oxford: Oxford Univ. Press, 1974.

Floyd, Kevin. *The Reification of Desire: Toward a Queer Marxism.* Minneapolis: Univ. of Minnesota Press, 2009.

Fone, Byrne. *Homophobia: A History.* New York: Picador, 2000.

Forrester, John M., ed. *The "De Subtilitate" of Girolamo Cardano.* 2 vols. Tempe: Arizona Center for Medieval and Renaissance Studies, 2013.

Foucault, Michel. *Discipline and Punish: The Birth of the Prison.* Trans. Alan Sheridan. New York: Vintage, 1977.

———. *The History of Sexuality.* Volume 1: *An Introduction.* Trans. Robert Hurley. New York: Pantheon Books, 1978.

Gabbard, D. Christopher. "From Idiot Beast to Idiot Sublime: Mental Disability in John Cleland's *Fanny Hill.*" *PMLA* 123.2 (March 2008): 375–89.

Goodchild, Philip. *Theology of Money.* Durham: Duke Univ. Press, 2009.

Habermas, Jürgen. *The Structural Transformation of the Public Sphere: An Inquiry into a Category of Bourgeois Society.* Trans. Thomas Burger. Cambridge, MA: MIT Press, 1989.

Haggerty, George E. *Queer Gothic.* Urbana: Univ. of Illinois Press, 2006.

Halperin, David M. "What Is Sex For?" *Critical Inquiry* 43 (Autumn 2016): 1–31.

Hamilton, Lawrence. *The Political Philosophy of Needs*. Cambridge: Cambridge Univ. Press, 2003.

Henderson, James P. "Beggars: Jeremy Bentham versus William Wordsworth." *History of Political Economy* 45.3 (2013): 415–42.

Hobbes, Thomas. *Leviathan*. Ed. Edwin Curley. Indianapolis: Hackett, 1994.

Howard, John. *The State of the Prisons in England and Wales, with Preliminary Observations, and an Account of Some Foreign Prisons*. Warrington: William Eyres, 1777.

Hume, David. *An Enquiry Concerning the Principles of Morals*. Ed. Tom L. Beauchamp. Oxford: Oxford Univ. Press, 1998.

———. *Political Essays*. Ed. Knud Haakonssen. Cambridge: Cambridge Univ. Press, 1994.

Immerwahr, John. "Hume's Revised Racism." *Journal of the History of Ideas* 53.3 (Sept. 1992): 481–86.

Johnson, Paul, and Robert M. Vanderbeck. *Law, Religion, and Homosexuality*. New York: Routledge, 2014.

[Johnson, Samuel]. *Taxation no Tyranny; an Answer to the Resolutions and Address of the American Congress*. London: T. Cadell, 1775.

Julius, Anthony, Malcolm Quinn, and Philip Schofield, eds. *Bentham and the Arts*. London: UCL Press, 2020.

Kant, Immanuel. "An Answer to the Question: What Is Enlightenment?" Trans. James Schmidt. In *What Is Enlightenment?: Eighteenth-Century Answers and Twentieth-Century Questions,* ed. James Schmidt. Berkeley: Univ. of California Press, 1996.

———. *Critique of Judgement*. Trans. James Creed Meredith. Oxford: Oxford Univ. Press, 2008.

Kavanagh, Declan. *Effeminate Years: Literature, Politics, and Aesthetics in Mid-Eighteenth-Century Britain*. Lewisburg: Bucknell Univ. Press, 2017.

Kelleher, Paul. *Making Love: Sentiment and Sexuality in Eighteenth-Century British Literature*. Lewisburg: Bucknell Univ. Press, 2015.

Kim, James. "'Good cursed, bouncing losses': Masculinity, Sentimental Irony, and Exuberance in *Tristram Shandy*." *The Eighteenth Century* 48.1 (Spring 2007): 3–24.

Klein, Ula Lukszo. "Eighteenth-Century Female Crossdressers and Their Beards." *Journal for Early Modern Cultural Studies* 16.4 (Fall 2016): 119–43.

Langbauer, Laurie. *Women and Romance: The Consolations of Gender in the English Novel*. Ithaca: Cornell Univ. Press, 1990.

Locke, John. *An Essay Concerning Human Understanding*. Ed. Roger Woolhouse. New York: Penguin, 1997.

———. *Two Treatises of Government*. Ed. Peter Laslett. Cambridge: Cambridge Univ. Press, 1960.

Mackie, Erin. "Welcome the Outlaw: Pirates, Maroons, and Caribbean Countercultures." *Cultural Critique* 59 (Winter 2005): 24–62.

Marx, Karl. *Capital*. Vol. 1. Trans. Ben Fowkes. New York: Penguin, 1992.

McKown, Delos. *Behold the Antichrist: Bentham on Religion*. Amherst, NY: Prometheus Books, 2004.

Mill, John Stuart. "Coleridge." In *Essays on Ethics, Religion and Society,* edited by J. M. Robson, 117–64. Toronto: Univ. of Toronto Press, 1969.

———. *Dissertations and Discussions: Political, Philosophical, and Historical*. Vol. 1. London: John W. Parker and Son, 1867. Rpt., New York: Cosimo, 2008.

Montaigne, Michel de. *Essays*. Trans. J. M. Cohen. New York: Penguin, 1993.

Myles, Eileen. "Comedy of Heirs: Catching a Glimpse of Heaven in the Confines of *Tristram Shandy*." *Bookforum* 27.2 (Summer 2020). Web. https://www.bookforum.com/print/2702/catching-a-glimpse-of-heaven-in-the-confines-of-tristram-shandy-24029.

Nietzsche, Friedrich. *Beyond Good and Evil: Prelude to a Philosophy of the Future*. Trans. Walter Kaufmann. New York: Vintage Books, 1966.

Norton, Rictor. *Mother Clap's Molly House: The Gay Subculture in England, 1700–1830*. London: Gay Men's Press, 1992.

Palter, Robert. "Hume and Prejudice." *Hume Studies* 21.1 (April 1995): 3–23.

Patapan, Haig, and Jeffrey Sikkenga. "Love and the Leviathan: Thomas Hobbes's Critique of Platonic Eros." *Political Theory* 36.6 (December 2008): 803–26.

Piersen, William Dillon. *Black Yankees: The Development of an Afro-American Subculture in Eighteenth-Century New England*. Amherst: Univ. of Massachusetts Press, 1988.

Plato. *Symposium*. Trans. Robin Waterfield. Oxford: Oxford Univ. Press, 2009.

Pontin, Ben. "Environmental Law-Making Public Opinion in Victorian Britain: The Cross-Currents of Bentham's and Coleridge's Ideas." *Oxford Journal of Legal Studies* 34.4 (2014): 759–90.

Popkin, Richard H. "Hume's Racism Reconsidered." In *The Third Force in Seventeenth-Century Thought*, 64–75. Brill's Studies in Intellectual History, vol. 22. Leiden: Brill, 1992.

Quinn, Malcolm. "Jeremy Bentham on Liberty of Taste." *History of European Ideas* 43.6 (2017): 614–27.

Rogers, Pat. *Grub Street: Studies in a Subculture*. London: Methuen, 1972.

Rosen, Frederick. "Bentham and Mill on Liberty and Justice." In *Lives, Liberties and the Public Good*, ed. G. Feaver and F. Rosen, 121–38. London: Palgrave Macmillan, 1987.

———. *Classical Utilitarianism from Hume to Mill*. Abingdon: Routledge, 2003.

Rosenthal, Laura. *Infamous Commerce: Prostitution in Eighteenth-Century Literature and Culture.* Ithaca: Cornell Univ. Press, 2006.

Schofield, Philip. "Political and Religious Radicalism in the Thought of Jeremy Bentham." *History of Political Thought* 20.2 (Summer 1999): 272–91.

———. *Utility and Democracy: The Political Thought of Jeremy Bentham.* Oxford: Oxford Univ. Press, 2006.

Schultz, Bart. *The Happiness Philosophers: The Lives and Works of the Great Utilitarians.* Princeton: Princeton Univ. Press, 2017.

Sedgwick, Eve Kosofsky. *Epistemology of the Closet.* Berkeley: Univ. of California Press, 1990.

Senelick, Laurence. "Mollies or Men of Mode? Sodomy and the Eighteenth-Century London Stage." *Journal of the History of Sexuality* 1.1 (1990): 33–67.

Shanafelt, Carrie. "Against Rights: Jeremy Bentham on Sexual Liberty and Legal Reform." *Lit: Literature Interpretation Theory* 31.3 (2020): 203–21.

———. "Jeremy Bentham and the Aesthetics of Sexual Difference." *The Eighteenth Century: Theory and Interpretation* 61.3 (2020): 335–52.

———. "On Teaching Gothic Fiction and Non-Empiricist Aesthetics." *CEA Forum* 43.2 (2014): 1–18.

———. "The Rhetoric of Consensus: Hume and Fielding on Moral Sentiment." In *David Hume: A Tercentenary Tribute,* ed. Stanley Tweyman, 85–106. Ann Arbor: Caravan books, 2013.

Sheldon, Rebekah. *The Child to Come: Life after the Human Catastrophe.* Minneapolis: Univ. of Minnesota Press, 2016.

Smith, Adam. *The Theory of Moral Sentiments.* Ed. Amartya Sen. New York: Penguin, 2010.

Soni, Vivasvan. *Mourning Happiness: Narrative and the Politics of Modernity.* Ithaca: Cornell Univ. Press, 2010.

The Statutes at Large, of England and of Great Britain: from Magna Carta to the Union of the Kingdoms of Great Britain and Ireland. Ed. John Raithby. London: G. Eyre and A. Strahan, 1811.

Sterne, Laurence. *The Life and Opinions of Tristram Shandy, Gentleman.* Oxford: Oxford Univ. Press, 2009.

Stockton, Katherine Bond. *God between Their Lips: Desire between Women in Irigaray, Brontë, and Eliot.* Stanford: Stanford Univ. Press, 1994.

———. *The Queer Child: Or, Growing Sideways in the Twentieth Century.* Durham: Duke Univ. Press, 2009.

Temple, Kathryn. *Loving Justice: Legal Emotions in William Blackstone's England.* New York: New York Univ. Press, 2019.

Traub, Valerie. *Thinking Sex with the Early Moderns.* Philadelphia: Univ. of Pennsylvania Press, 2016.

Trumbach, Randolph. "Sex, Gender, and Sexual Identity in Modern Culture: Male Sodomy and Female Prostitution in Enlightenment London." *Journal of the History of Sexuality* 2.2 (October 1991): 186–203.

Waldschmidt, Stefan. "Bentham, Pater, and the Aesthetics of Utilitarian Sex." *Nineteenth-Century Contexts* 38.5 (2016): 365–75.

Warner, Michael. *Letters of the Republic.* Cambridge, MA: Harvard Univ. Press, 1990.

INDEX

Agamben, Giorgio, 86

Analysis of the Influence of Natural Religion on the Temporal Happiness of Mankind, An (Bentham), 113–14

Aquinas, Thomas, 74

Arendt, Hannah, 86

Aristotle, 3, 73–74, 125

asceticism, 25, 34–35, 43, 46–47, 60, 62, 82, 110, 112–13, 115, 120–23

Beckford, William Thomas, 141–43, 148

Bentham, Jeremy: aesthetic theory, 25; on British penal law, 93–100, 162; on Christian doctrine, 107–12, 118–24; consequentialist critique of, 53; critique of based on consensus epistemology, 53–54; on the Declaration of Independence, 21–22, 86, 88; development of philosophical approach, 39–45, 82–84; efforts at reform and amelioration, 39–40, 56; on happiness and the disenfranchised, 35, 70–71; on humanity and the disenfranchised, 4–5, 16, 22, 26; *Introduction to the Principles of Morals and Legislation,* 5; on the issue of physical pleasure, 12–14; legal reform and sexual nonconformity, 90, 93, 100, 100–106; legal reform efforts in post-Revolutionary France, 101–3, 140; legal reform efforts in Spain, 103; liberal rights discourse, 85–89; literary reading and aspirations, 139–46, 163; misplaced critiques in philosophical discourse, 45–54; on the moralization of aesthetic variety, 63–69; personal religious beliefs,

112–18; plan for universal education, 30; prose style, 55, 130–31; on the "Religion of Jesus," 118–24; on reproductive and sexual freedom, 62; on reproductive futurity, 109–10; self-censorship by, 55–56; on sexual nonconformity, 14, 24–27, 44–45, 51, 59–61, 124–25; on slavery, 15–16; on the subjectivity of pleasure, 69–73, 77–78; utilitarian theory, 46–47, 61, 89–90, 167

Berkeley, George, on common sense, 2, 12, 77–78

Bieri, James, 153

Blackstone, William, 93, 95–96, 150

Blake, Kathleen, 30–31

Blake, William, 148–49

Boe, Ana de Freitas, 133

Booth, Wayne, on *Tom Jones,* 1, 161

Boralevi, Lea Campos, 14, 93; on Bentham and sexual nonconformity, 60, 62; on Bentham and the rights of the disenfranchised, 62

Brunon-Ernst, Anne, on critiques of Bentham, 32–33

Buffon, Georges Louis Leclerc, comte de, 165n15

Buggery Act (1533), 64, 98–99, 135, 168

Burney, Frances, 143

Burns, J. H., 90

Burton, Robert, 165n15

Butler, Joseph, 131

Byron, George Gordon, Lord, 148–49

Cameron, Kenneth Neill, 152

Cardano, Girolamo, 165n15

Champs, Emmanuelle de, 33; on the study of Bentham, 38

CPSIA information can be obtained
at www.ICGtesting.com
Printed in the USA
LVHW112034211022
731246LV00004B/253